Praise for *Brand Jesus*

"The hardest part about confr[...] idol when you see one, which [...] powerful idols are those most c[...] fortably swim in. In this remar[...] [...] compellingly readable book, Tyler Wigg Stevenson tears the mask off the god of consumerism at several very effective levels. He not only exposes its historical roots, its popular power and its imprisoning dominance, but also subjects it (and the culture that embodies it) to exceptionally sharp and creative biblical critique, through the lens of applied exegesis of texts from Romans. Even they have become so familiar in evangelical culture that they have been robbed of their power to challenge idolatry where it really lurks. This book will make you look at your world and at your Bible with different eyes, with realism and yet also with fresh hope and courage."

— **Christopher J. H. Wright,** author of *Mission of God*, and International Director, Langham Partnership International

"Have you ever felt uncomfortable about media reports referring to Christians more as a voting bloc or a marketing niche than as followers of Christ? Have you ever been slightly embarrassed by trinkets or bumper stickers that seemed to trivialize the centrality that the church or the Bible holds in your life? Ever wondered how we got to this point (and what we might do in response)? If so, Tyler Wigg Stevenson's *Brand Jesus* is for you. Thoroughly biblical, yet written with a firm grasp of today's culture, *Brand Jesus* should be on the reading list of all Christians more committed to the fullness of Christ than to the narrowness of how Christians are often defined (and sometimes define themselves) today."

— **David Jones,** President, John Stott Ministries

"With passion and uncommon insight, *Brand Jesus* exposes the death grip of consumerism, which pollutes our society and compromises our faith. Tyler Wigg Stevenson's biblically informed and theologically astute critique calls us back to the gospel and emboldens us to stand up to the culture of commodification. This is a welcome and timely book."

— **Randall Balmer,** Ann Whitney Olin Professor of American Religion at Barnard College, Columbia University, and author of *Thy Kingdom Come: How the Religious Right Distorts the Faith and Threatens America: An Evangelical's Lament*

"*Brand Jesus* is a wonderfully nuanced, thoughtful and compassionate epistle to the American Church that interrogates the unholy spirit of consumerism which threatens to eclipse the gospel. Yet, like the letter which Paul wrote to the Romans, the import of this subversive text stretches far beyond its original addressee. Within this book we are confronted with an argument that can speak to the whole church, helping to overturn the tables of our commodity driven religiosity."

— **Peter Rollins,** author of *How (Not) to Speak of God*

"One of the ongoing goals of Christ-followers should be applying the timeless truths of Scripture to the time-bound realities of our culture. In *Brand Jesus,* Tyler Wigg Stevenson identifies consumerism as the single dominant factor at play in North American culture, and unfortunately, within North American Christianity as well. Based on the biblical book of Romans, *Brand Jesus* helps contemporary Christians live faithfully within an irretrievably consumerist society. I for one want to submit my life to the challenge this book offers: the challenge of conforming our lives to Christ rather than culture."

— **Bruxy Cavey,** Teaching Pastor, The Meeting House, and author of *The End of Religion*

"Tyler Wigg Stevenson's skillful biblical exegesis and astute cultural observation delivers a critical message to the Christian church, exposing an insidious virus that drains authentic faith of its significance — namely consumerism wrapped in the name of Jesus."

— **Bruce D. Main,** author of *Spotting the Sacred* and President of UrbanPromise Ministries, Camden, New Jersey

⊕ **BRAND JESUS**

✛ BRAND JESUS

Christianity in a Consumerist Age

TYLER WIGG STEVENSON

SEABURY BOOKS
an imprint of
Church Publishing Incorporated, New York

Library of Congress Cataloging-in-Publication Data

Wigg Stevenson, Tyler.
  Christianity in a consumerist age / by Tyler Wigg Stevenson.
     p. cm.
  Includes bibliographical references and index.
  ISBN 978-1-59627-049-7 (pbk.)
  1. Bible. N.T. Romans – Criticism, interpretation, etc. 2. Consumption
(Economics) – Religious aspects – Christianity. 3. Materialism – Religious
aspects – Christianity. I. Title.
  BS2665.52.S74 2007
  261.0973 – dc22

                                   2007005321

Church Publishing Incorporated
445 Fifth Avenue
New York, NY 10016
www.churchpublishing.org

5 4 3 2 1

For Natalie Louise —
whose love for Christ's church
is but one of the numberless reasons
that I love her

Contents

Part IV
BRAND JESUS

Part V
FAST AND PRAY
Romans 12:1–2

Acknowledgments

I thank my God through Jesus Christ for all of you.
(Romans 1:8)

It seems strange that only two years have passed since I began this project, as it is difficult for me to believe that I could pack so much interpersonal indebtedness into such a short period of time.

In the late summer of 2004, my then-fiancée, Natalie, asked me what I'd like to do with the coming academic year. "I think I'd like to write a book," was my reply, and we wondered together how I might go about doing such a thing. Less than a week later I received an email out of nowhere from Jonathan Reiber, an acquaintance who had gone on to become an editor at Seabury Press, asking whether I might like to write a book for them. My first thanks are therefore due to Jonathan, who has long since become a valued friend and counselor. His invitation to write this book still seems nothing short of miraculous, as does his openness and patience with my ever-changing choice of topic. I am grateful to him and to all the staff at Seabury for their trust and willingness to support this project, especially Ken Arnold, the former publisher, and Lucas Smith, my editor.

Thanks here are also, therefore, due to Jonathan Granoff — in more ways than this my personal rainmaker — who referred Reiber to me in the first place.

While the book's inevitable shortcomings are, I assure you, my own, any praise it merits is due largely to those who have been incarnate help and comfort to me throughout its creation. I am especially indebted to the insights of friends and colleagues, which have helped mature my understanding of many of this book's themes. Of particular noteworthiness are: Luke Moorhead, for general theological counsel and conversation about Reconstructionism in particular; Professor Diana Swancutt, whose Greek exegesis seminar on Romans provided the textual background for this study; and Rachael Jungkeit for reading and commenting on the manuscript.

There are too many saints at Christian Tabernacle Baptist Church (Hamden, CT) to single out by name. Nevertheless, Shirley Moss, Joyce Blandon, and Pastor Keith King stand apart as pillars of support and friendship. And I am so thankful for my entire church family there, which serves as an exemplar of the faith.

I am deeply grateful for the encouragement of "Uncle John" Stott, whom I had the privilege of serving as Study Assistant from 2005 to 2006, while I wrote the first part of the manuscript. As the veteran author of forty-nine books and counting, his enthusiasm for my efforts as a first-time author meant a great deal. I also owe him a lifelong debt for the unselfconscious witness of his enduring commitment and pastoral love for the church. Moreover, it's entirely possible that my finishing this project was in part due to my shame at our comparative writing outputs — in 2006, at eighty-six, Dr. Stott had three manuscripts ready for publication!

Antepenultimate thanks are reserved for Michael Peppard. After already having given the generous gift of his time and biblical expertise in reading the manuscript, he then traveled to Nashville for a marathon editing session. The book's final form is due in no small part to his comments and insight. I find that the only thing for which I am more grateful than his contribution to the book is our lasting friendship.

I will never be able to thank my family enough for their support and encouragement. With the love I've received, it's a bit artificial to single anyone out, but I do want to thank my sister-in-law, Danielle Wigg, who had by far the most exuberantly affirming reaction of anyone upon hearing the news that the book had been accepted for publication. My sisters, Heather and Bethany, have been great cheerleaders throughout. The lifelong support of my grandparents, Valentine and Lillian Fedor, has gone a long way toward allowing me the time and space to complete the project. And I can never repay my debt of gratitude to my parents, John and Valerie Stevenson — especially my mother, who taught me to write.

Last, but absolutely not least, I thank my brilliant wife Natalie, from whom I steal all my best ideas and to whom this book is dedicated. She has encouraged me from the first glimmer of its possibility to follow a vocation as a writer, knowing full well that my doing so was likely to result in our testing the "for poorer" part of our wedding vows. From the day I conceived of writing *Brand Jesus,* through the editing of several draft manuscripts, to the typing of these final words, she has been my counselor, editor, and companion. Without her unflagging and selfless support, this book would not exist.

Introduction

To all in America who are loved by God and called to be saints . . .

In this predominantly Christian nation, it is easy to forget how daunting the Apostle Paul's message about Jesus Christ was, as Paul set about writing his epistle to the Romans.

In Romans, Paul writes to the center of the known world, the very heart of an empire. And he writes to convince the citizens there of a most improbable idea: namely, that all of human history turns around an otherwise unnoticed day twenty-five years earlier, when a peasant, a laborer from an ethnic and religious minority group, was executed by a backwater Roman governor in a distant corner of the empire. History turns thusly, he writes, because the peasant was the Son of God, and his death "demonstrates God's justice" in the present time.

If we weren't so used to hearing this story on Sundays, we might realize just how strange it really is.

The idea for this book began with just such a realization. In late 2003, while I was attending a conference, I heard an idea that has stuck with me ever since.

The presenter, Gordon Zerbe, was trying to show how radical Paul's message would have been to Roman ears. And so he posed to his listeners a scenario that went something like this: what would we think if someone wrote to a church in modern America — Silicon Valley or Manhattan, say — with the wild claim that the messiah had arrived sometime in the mid-seventies; that he had been an undocumented Filipino migrant worker who spoke about the inbreaking kingdom of God; that, while working in Guam, he had been brought in by local ecclesiastical authorities on trumped-up civil charges; that the local governor had caved in to their demands and executed him for treason; and that his life and death changed *everything* we thought we knew about God, the world, and ourselves.

For those unfamiliar with Paul's letter — commonly referred to by its audience, "Romans" — it is the longest of the epistles in the New Testament. Epistles were a type of letter meant for public reading and instruction, sent by early church leaders to various church communities throughout the Mediterranean. Of the New Testament epistles, Romans is arguably the most significant for Christian doctrine. It was likely written between AD 55 and 58, approximately 25 to 30 years after the death and resurrection of Jesus Christ.

Though Paul's missionary efforts made him the most important human figure in the spread of the gospel and establishment of churches in Gentile Europe, he did not establish the church in Rome, whose origins are unknown to us. So, though the Roman Christ-followers — Jew and Gentile alike — would certainly have known of Paul's reputation, his letter in part represents his effort to establish the credibility of his leadership: both in terms of religious instruction and in securing support for his anticipated missionary journey to Spain.

The improbability of this modern paraphrase, while not a perfect parallel, nevertheless reveals just how odd the Christian message would have sounded in ancient Rome. Like us, the Romans sat at the pinnacle of human achievement in their day. Their public spaces hummed with discussion of the most important ideas of their time — finance, philosophy, political theory, religion. And their government's decisions had world-shaking implications, given their unparalleled military might. In such a context, and without any of the cultural legitimacy that comes from two millennia of the institutional church, the gospel must have seemed more than a little bit crazy to many who heard it. How can the kingdom of Caesar know the kingdom of God? How can the ministers of the sword (Romans 13:4) know the foolishness of the cross?

No — *the gospel is foreign to the ears of empire.*

This was the epiphany I had about Paul's letter to the Romans, and it got me to thinking about contemporary America. We certainly don't act as though the gospel is foreign (especially not in my adopted hometown of Nashville). In fact, we do a fairly good job of integrating our daily lives in the world's only superpower with our individual and communal Christian identities. Unlike ancient Rome, the gospel doesn't seem strange in America. And that fact seems to me to be a symptom of something gone wrong.

Perhaps the gospel is in fact stranger than it appears. Perhaps there is something tellingly false about a gospel that we can so easily integrate into our contemporary American life. Perhaps the fact that we find the gospel to be so *sensible* means that American Christians have misunderstood what Paul was writing about to the Romans. In other words, perhaps our gospel isn't the gospel at all. And if our good news about Jesus isn't the real good news, then maybe we've got the wrong Jesus, too.

With this conviction — that the truth of Paul's message to the Romans is a much harder pill to swallow than we often make it out to be — I set out to have an extended conversation with our divine guide, the Holy Spirit, through the mouth of scripture.

My hope was to hear what specific message Paul's letter might have for the American church today, given the parallels between our historical context and that of imperial Rome. Given this similarity, might not the Spirit speak uniquely to our contemporary situation through the text of Romans — especially the introductory chapters, which address the Roman situation?

There is something in Romans that the American church needs to hear, even more than do those churches in nations that bear little or no resemblance to imperial Rome. This is not to say that Romans is meaningless to non-American churches: the Spirit moves as the Spirit wills, and speaks to the whole of Christ's church through the whole of God's scriptures. But we who live in the heart of a superpower have something particular to learn by reading Paul's letter to the superpower of his day — and striving to hear it with all its original radicalness.

Hence, *Brand Jesus.*

In Part I, I look at our historical setting to isolate and define consumerism as the dominant cultural pattern in our day. The historical survey in these initial chapters is not meant to be exhaustive. My hope is that the account of our culture in these chapters will be intuitively recognizable to the reader as a true description of who and where we are as a society.

I also hope that it provides enough of a basis for self-understanding so that we can profitably turn to the biblical text in Parts II and III. In these pages, we read Romans 1:18–32 and Romans 2:1–29, respectively, with an ear for what their message says to the contemporary America I describe in Part I. This section of Romans is Paul's attempt to show his audience why the lifestyles in which they have put their trust are insufficiently righteous — certainly a text with traction in our own time.

Part II considers our overall culture in the context of Paul's indictment of degenerate Gentile culture in Rome, particularly examining how the biblical text sheds light on the causes and effects of the consumerism that has come to dominate our national life.

Part III, following Paul's letter, has a more specific audience. We read Paul's address to Gentile moralists (2:1–4) as descriptive of contemporary complicity in the overall culture. And, looking at Paul's critique of Roman Jewish hypocrisy, we arrive at the main emphasis of the book: namely, how the Christian religious establishment has embraced (and helped create in the first place) the secular culture's consumerism.

The result of the church's doing so is the idolatry of Brand Jesus — the object of devotion for the Christianity of our consumerist age. We consider the rise of Brand Jesus in Part IV. This is where the rubber hits the road for the church. In considering the predominantly commercial and political (rather than theological) identity of the contemporary church, a number of practical examples are raised as manifestations of the church's consumerist theology.

Part V concludes the book by taking stock of the situation and suggesting how the church might proceed from this point. We take Romans 12:1–2 as our guiding light.

Despite the innumerable debts that this book has to other works and authors, I was surprised at the start of this project, and remain surprised at its conclusion, at the lack of availability of substantive, popular treatments of consumerism and faith.[1] Vincent Miller's profitable *Consuming Faith* (Continuum, 2003) is one noteworthy exception, but in the end I did not find a place to include it here: his focus on Roman Catholicism was substantially different from my evangelical

Protestant emphasis, and his scholarly disposition often seemed emotionally and ecclesiastically divorced from what I take to be a pressing spiritual reality. It will be valuable, however, to any readers wishing to pursue further the topics in these pages.

One can find a number of shorter pieces that refer to consumerism, but they tend to assume the fact and attributes of its wickedness without ever looking directly at what consumerism actually *is*. The prevailing attitude in such writings tends to be a distaste toward those who have a taste for "things." As I mention in the second chapter, this presumption usually leads to the writer's underestimation of consumerism's potency, pervasiveness, and effects.

My hope for this book is that it will be a contribution to this small library of relevant works. If this book is executed well enough, then I also hope it can serve as a wake-up call for the American church. We have completely failed to take into account how our communal life has invited consumerism into every facet and has made Brand Jesus the object of too much of our devotion. This is not a concern that we can regard with any dispassion; it is a dereliction of duty on the part of those who are ordained to witness about God's goodness in Christ Jesus.

As I see it, the appropriate response to the message of Romans in our present situation is to leave no corner of the American church untouched and unexamined as we seek to conform the whole of church life to the claims we make about God. At the same time, we will need to be mindful even of the character of our reformation efforts, and not confuse urgency with panic. Panic demonstrates a lack of conviction in God's enduring ordinance for the church. God will be faithful to God's promises. Let us be faithful to God.

By the power and sustenance of the Spirit, then, may all our service be to Jesus Christ our Lord through his church, and — as was, is now, and ever shall be — may every glory be to God.

μάρτυς γάρ μού ἐστιν ὁ θεός

Tyler Wigg Stevenson
Nashville, Tennessee
Advent 2006

Part I

PAST AND PRESENT

Chapter 1

Point-of-Purchase Devotion

There's a store downtown in the city where I live. Perhaps you've got one, too. It's a Christian store, and you might want to call it a bookstore. But as you walk up to the front door, and the sky is reflected from the floor-to-ceiling windows, all you can see is what's immediately inside the window displays. And that is a *lot* of Christian knick-knacks. Angel statuettes, fish-shaped paperweights, clocks with Edenic, pastoral scenes painted on them — the place has the works.

To step inside this store — or any like it — is to step into the world of Christian retail, and to gain a glimpse of the particular consumption patterns of some Christians today. Once you actually enter, you can see that some of this bookstore is indeed devoted to books, most of which are of the Christian self-help variety. The majority of the floor space is devoted to other goods, however: music, Christian-themed art, and accessories like clothing and jewelry. In the Christian retail industry, these are known as "Christ-honoring resources."

It's no surprise that such effort is made to selling this kind of gear. These days, after all, the stuff that we choose to buy says a lot about who we believe ourselves to be. We buy things that will let us "express ourselves." We "show our individuality" through our preferences as consumers; indeed, *we are what we like to buy.* I suspect that if you knew what kind of car I drive, brands of clothing I buy, type of jewelry (if any) I wear, music I listen to, and food I eat, you'd have a pretty good idea about who I am — or, at least, who I want to be.

In other words, the Christian bookstore is doing a significant trade in the everyday goods that all of us, Christian and non-Christian alike, use to tell the world who we are. At this store, however, such goods — and their consumption — are branded with religious significance. The store offers the trappings of a Christian lifestyle to anyone with the money to buy.

In recent years, the Christian market has meant big money. This is a new phenomenon. Until the end of the twentieth century, Christian retail stores were primarily independent, local ventures. They sold church supplies, religious-themed goods, and books that were little known outside church circles. The industry generated some crossover hits: Hal Lindsay's end-times romp, *The Late Great Planet Earth*, was one of the best-selling books of the 1970s. But mostly it was nickel-and-dime stuff.

That all changed in the 1990s. The success of some breakaway best-selling books — like the *Left Behind* series, *The Prayer of Jabez*, and *The Purpose-Driven Life* — is an indicator that the Christian lifestyle industry has arrived in force. Today a wide variety of guilds covers the spectrum of the Christian niche markets, the uncontested champion of which is the Christian retailers' group, the CBA. With well over two thousand member stores, the fifty-six-year-old association represents Christian retailers in an industry worth $7 billion in 2005.[1]

Seven billion dollars: no idle amount, and a figure that is even more striking when we realize that it comes from sales of relatively low-priced items: books, T-shirts, compact discs, popular art, and so on. Seven billion dollars is a lot of paperbacks and shirts, even when a few bestsellers are responsible for a disproportionate percentage of the revenue. What possible conclusions might we draw from the massive and increasing trend of specifically Christian consumption?

The easiest conclusion, assuming that buyers of Christian products are Christians themselves, is that there is a growing market — in other words, America has more Christians. But this is actually demonstrably false. Between 1990 and 2001, the percentage of Americans who self-identified as Christians declined.[*]

Another option is that sales of "Christ-honoring resources" indicates (or is causing) a nationwide improvement in the quality of our discipleship — that is, these goods are helping us to become better Christians. But this scenario fails the truth test, too. In Ron Sider's recent book, *The Scandal of the Evangelical Conscience*, he reveals that Christians are living just like their non-Christian neighbors by

---

[*]Precise numbers regarding the percentage of Christians are difficult to arrive at given the amendment of the official 1990 census population count, but the national percentage of self-identified Christians fell from 82 to 86 percent in 1990 to 75 to 76 percent in 2001. From the U.S. Census Bureau, "2006 Statistical Abstract," *www.census.gov/ compendia/statab/population*, items 11 and 69 (accessed October 4, 2006).

nearly every ethical standard. We'll look at this state of affairs in more detail later.

So, if we observe on the one hand that more Christian goods are being bought in America every year, and on the other that American Christians are neither increasing in percentage of the population nor demonstrating an improved overall quality of Christian witness, we are left to infer the rather sad conclusion that the growth in sales is due to the fact that Christians are simply buying more Christian things. "Christ-honoring resources" appear to "honor" Christ *simply by being purchased,* since no other demonstrable effects can be seen. In other words, they're a point-of-purchase devotional act.

The visceral response of many Christians who have an authentic personal passion for their faith will be that the diagnosis of this book cannot be correct. Maybe they've never set foot in a Christian "bookstore," and they think that the Christian gear — art, clothes, jewelry — is actually embarrassing. Or maybe they're Christian retail regulars, but it's a genuine part of their walk with Jesus. Both will say that their Christianity isn't consumerist at all. But this book actually isn't about Christian retail, however telling such trends may be (I explore them in depth in a later chapter).

No, this book is about consumerism: how it's come to dominate the way we live as a society and how American Christianity has happily bought right into the pattern of consumerist living by making God into a commodity.

The order of this age is that we are what we buy, and Christians evidently like to shop as much as any other group. We're just buying Brand Jesus.

Chapter 2

Buy to Be, Be to Buy

Consumerism makes an easy whipping boy. If you read the right periodicals or books, or listen to the right social commentators and pundits, you will doubtless have had your fill of breezily expressed, unsubstantiated claims about America's unhealthy love of material things. This is true whether the audience is secular or religious. It is, in fact, a truism that we live in a culture and age of consumption. When people make claims about our rampant consumerism, therefore, we aren't expected to evaluate them — we're just supposed to cluck in disapproving agreement. The woes of consumerism, it seems, don't need the support of data, since the information you need to render judgment is presumed to be all around: Have you *been* to a mall recently? Have you seen the teenagers?

I am not about to discount the claim that America, along with much of the West, is in the throes of consumerism. Nor would I contest that consumerism is indeed one of the more profound identifying characteristics of our culture. This entire book argues that our consumerist tendencies are real, profoundly negative, and increasingly significant to who we are — both to ourselves and as a culture in the world. The popular, knee-jerk reaction against consumerism, however, does far more harm than good, for two reasons.

First, such a reaction elicits in us rather self-delusional judgments. I have yet to meet more than a handful of serious critics of consumerism who genuinely live a life free of its taint. I certainly don't. Do you? I personally have never heard an anti-consumerist manifesto coming from the mouth of someone who wasn't completely surrounded by consumer goods — the fellow typing his anti-consumerism screed on his brushed-aluminum Macintosh at the local Starbucks, for instance. As such, our problem usually isn't with consumerism per se, but with *other* people's consumption. Most of the time, when I tsk-tsk at some example of conspicuous consumption, like something I just *know* that Jesus wouldn't drive — Humvees make easy targets, for example — I'm actually judging something I just happen not to like, rather than the consumption itself. Otherwise, why do I get so starry-eyed, rather than righteously huffy, over that classic Jaguar, with its dreadful gas mileage and Humvee-level price tag? Most of us are in no position to be casting stones as easily as we tend to do.

Second, and more significantly, when we respond unthinkingly against consumerism, we gloss over the magnitude of the very thing we're criticizing. I'm sure you can imagine a rant of the vices of consumerism — how we love things too much, how we're so materialistic, isn't advertising just awful, can you believe the retail Christmas displays went up before Thanksgiving this year, and so on — whether listed in the pages of your favorite magazine or coming from the lips of your favorite cranky aunt. But this amounts to an easy way of getting worked up without really saying much. The common element in such litanies is that consumerism is an evil that everybody knows about and agrees upon.

But why is it so bad?

Sure, America is full of people who want to buy a lot of things. But pause for a moment and ask yourself what's so wrong with that. Be honest: if you think about it, you probably buy a lot of things (this book, for example — tell your friends!) and you're a pretty decent person, right? What is it about being a consumer in a consumerist society that is so self-evidently wrong? In our public conversations, one can find a great deal of condemnation of consumerism and very little defense of it, but usually these condemnations are the starting points of arguments — the presuppositions — rather than the conclusions. Usually, the evil of consumerism is the conclusion we already know. It is taken for granted. And this is the real problem.

When we assume from the beginning that consumerism is bad, we fail to take it out into the light of day and really look at it. We fail to examine its true significance. We realize its negative impact only in superficial ways (i.e., it makes us so greedy — as though people have not been greedy in times and places that are utterly devoid of consumer goods) and ignore the far more profound implications of our consumerist culture and personal impulses.

Consumerism *is* bad. It is very, very bad, indeed. But it is no worse than humans are, and we are no worse than we have always been. If we are to deal genuinely with the problem of consumerism, we need to answer the question of how its evil influences our world and our lives.

This book is primarily intended for Christians, though I hope its observations might prove compelling to interested non-Christians as well. As such, it is an attempt to work through the theological implications of our consumerist ways. By theological, I mean: How does it really matter to God, and how does it matter for us in respect to God, that we are consumers? What does our consumerism mean for us as an American culture? And, because I am a Christian writing primarily for Christians, what does it mean for us as individual disciples of Christ, and collectively as his church, to contribute to and to be so profoundly influenced by such a culture?

But before we ask theological questions about the place where we're standing, we have to know where "here" is. And to understand where we're at, we first need to understand from whence we've come.

A Story about Stories

For most of human history, in most times and places, your identity — that is, who you are as a person in society — has been pretty well established for you before you were even born. Your people have done things in such-and-such a way for generations? You will do the same things in such-and-such a way. You were born in this town? You'll live and die in this town. Your family worships this god? You'll worship this god. Your family is upper, middle, or lower class? You'll be upper, middle, or lower class. Your father is a farmer, shoemaker, builder? You're going to be a farmer, shoemaker, builder. Your father owned this land? You'll own this land. You don't have a father? You probably won't be around for your own children. And that's just half the population. If you're born a girl, you're going to be a wife, mother, and likely, a widow, and you're going to hold on to the hope that life and a male-dominated society won't treat you as badly as they probably will.

Furthermore, all these givens will probably make sense to you. This is because what you understand as your identity is your place in a cultural story, bigger and older than you as an individual, which you inherit. This story — your *metanarrative* — is one that explains everything. It tells you where you've come from, who you are, and where you're going. It helps you make sense of the world into which you are born and it gives your life meaning — whether that meaning is good or not. It forms you as you grow and defines how you will live and die.

And, setting aside scenarios like the one depicted in *The Matrix,* a people's particular story is not simply a concoction that enslaves them without their knowing. It is deeply related to the reality of their situations. The inherited story is the essence of our identities; it is the essence of culture, of religion, of heritage, of roots. In other words, the stories we tell about ourselves are at the heart of all that we love and hold dear.

In twenty-first century America, however, we don't inherit such stories. Or, perhaps it is more precise to say that though we may inherit any number of cultural stories, in the United States, there is a bigger story — the American Dream — that trumps them all. The American Dream is the story that rejects other stories. As Americans, we inherit a story that says all inherited stories, no matter where you come from, pale in comparison to the power of freedom in this country.

Your people have done things in such-and-such a way? You invent a better way. Your father is a poor immigrant who doesn't speak English? You work hard in school, get a job in some company's mailroom, and someday you'll be the CEO. You're from a rural area? Make your life in the city. Your family is this religion, or no religion? Make sure the religion you finally pick, if you pick one, meets your spiritual needs. You're not white, or you're a woman (or both)? That doesn't matter, because we're all equals here.

Now, as we all realize, sometimes the American story doesn't match reality. If your family is poor, you are likelier to be poor, as are your children. Our equality is an ideal, not a fact, given that white men have an undeniable leg up in practically every undertaking. But whether or not the American story is actually true for most people, it is still our story, and it is the story we tell each other. Abe Lincoln was born in a log cabin, and look at what he did. Fatherless boys from Hope, Arkansas, do grow up to be president. The American story is that no matter what story you've inherited, only you can stop you from doing whatever you want with your life.

The price of that freedom is a certain rootlessness, a particular instability. It is a daunting ideal to live up to. If the story you are born into doesn't hold you in place, the burden is on you to make a story for yourself. And if you don't reach your dream, the story tells you, you have only yourself to blame — in other words, get cracking.

The Death of Big Stories

This situation is particular to America, but it hasn't always been the case to such an extreme degree. To understand the connection between the American lack of inherited stories and our topic, consumerism, we have to begin by looking at the twentieth century and the world wars.

It is difficult for those of us who did not live through the wars to comprehend how completely destructive they were to the world's inherited senses of order. Men died in previously unimaginable numbers. Horrors like the Holocaust gave us new standards for recognizing evil. Countries were wiped off the map and redrawn as if the earth was a chalkboard. A bomb was made that could and did destroy entire cities. And for the first time in human history, one event — World War II — enveloped the entire globe. This fact made the world an entity, a perceptibly singular thing, in a way it had never truly been before.

To appreciate the magnitude of the change, just imagine what it was like to have known the world before and after the wars. You start as a twenty-year-old in 1900, observing a collection of nations, many of which are still monarchies, vying for influence in their own large and small ways. Nothing heavier than air has ever moved through the heavens. In Detroit, horse-drawn carriages pass blithely over the future site of Henry Ford's factory. Those telephones — you've seen a few of them — are a hoot. The United States is at war with Spain, a country that you enthusiastically curse.

Now fast-forward to 1950, when you are seventy. Tens of millions of young men have died, and the world has been rendered unrecognizable to you. Cartographers' jobs have gotten simpler, since a geopolitical scene that was once a motley globe of puny nations now requires just three colors to map: the United States and NATO; the USSR and Warsaw Pact; and — well, anybody who's not in the first two camps is in the Third World by default. The United States and the Soviet Union fear each other so much that they are rapidly building arsenals sufficient to destroy each other and everything else in self-defense, if need be. You can now envision the destruction of the world, not by the wrath of God, but by ICBMs at the order of a mortal man. The world on fire — the whole world! — has become an imaginative possibility. And Spain, that fin de siècle American nemesis, has been reduced to a staging ground for the new global powers.

The point to all this is that in a mere half century, part of everyone's inherited story around the globe got severely disturbed. And many old stories about the unchanging natural order of things — the very paper, so to speak, on which people's stories had been written — started to make much less sense, or no sense at all. Both internationally and socially, the slate was wiped clean of stories, of identity, of order. Into this vacuum, free from old stories, stepped 1950s America, with all the gumption and innovation and sheer brashness that had always been characteristically American.

Of all the nations on earth, we were superbly equipped to operate in this world cast free from its moorings because we had never really cared too much about the moorings anyway. (The Soviets were similarly novel, being a twentieth-century phenomenon formed through a violent separation from imperial Russia.) So, after World War II, we did what we always did, reinventing ourselves to fit the situation. On the international scene, we emerged into the bilateral standoff of the Cold War. On the home front, we got to work rebuilding a squeaky clean domestic order. But this time was different, because the world was different. Because of the degree to which our inherited order had been destroyed, our reinvention was all the more complete. And this time was also different because we got very, very rich.

The 1950s saw a period of prosperity and growth on a scale and breadth unprecedented in American history. The flush of postwar development resulted in the interstate highway system and the housing boom that invented the suburb, creating the warp and woof of modern American society. Consumer goods flooded the market in completely new ways, as did the primary vehicle for their marketing: the television. Between 1950 and 1952, the percentage of American households with at least one television rocketed from 9 percent to 90 percent. America was tuned in.

We might argue whether the *Leave It to Beaver* vision of America that epitomizes the 1950s in popular recollection ever existed — a nuclear family with 2.5 children, living in a house with a white picket fence, an apple pie cooked by stay-at-home-Mom cooling on the sill, and a scotch and soda waiting for nine-to-five-Dad's evening return to domesticity. For many Americans, whether the poor, or the rural, or the nonwhite, this vision would never become any more tangible than Norman Rockwell's covers for the *Saturday Evening Post*.

Nevertheless, in the eyes of many who lived the 1950s, the above picture would become the quintessential image of what America was, supplanting all others. The America that preceded it, which was basically the Great Depression framed by two world wars and in which the United States was nothing like a world power, faded away in the gleam of the fifties. In talking with my grandmother, for example, it is clear that for her, the *truest* America will always be the increasingly prosperous Southern California of the 1950s in which she and my grandfather raised their children. The other Americas in which she has lived — rural town life in the Great Depression–era southern Illinois of her youth; wartime uncertainty in California as a teenage girl fresh off the bus from the Midwest; the turmoil of the 1960s and 1970s; the peculiar stability of the Reagan years; and her and my grandfather's retirement days in this increasingly unrecognizable information age — are judged against the halcyon fifties. The flaws and merits of other American decades are recognized by how well they conform to that whitewashed standard.

The "Good Old Days" of 1950s America, however, were actually a completely novel phenomenon. The 1950s way of life would have been unimaginable from any previous point in American history. In many ways, for an America emerging from the chaos of the first half of the century, the story of the 1950s was the first new story to be told. And this primacy helps to explain the decade's abiding potency. But it was a *new* story, and despite its continuing appeal, it lacked the sort of roots that come from cultural traditions and ways of living that are strengthened by generations adhering to them.

The old ways, where they had existed, were chiseled into stone, like the Ten Commandments on Moses' tablets. When the dust cleared from the first half of the twentieth century, however, we found ourselves with a blank slate where the old laws had once been carved. But we also found ourselves without a hammer and chisel, without the tools to create new permanence. In our attempt to imitate stories that previous generations had carved, we found that we could only write with chalk. And that which one generation only writes, another generation can smudge, alter, or erase altogether.

The revolts that began in the 1960s and spilled over into the 1970s were not uprisings against "old-fashioned" American values, because the values of the 1950s were not old in their fashioning at all. No, like the decades that followed, the 1950s was a novel thing. The rebellion of the sixties and seventies was, therefore, a rejection of the previous generation's story, rather than of eternal American truths. However, because the myth of the 1950s was the first postwar American story to be formed and then rejected, the opposition of later decades actually gave the 1950s the potency and timelessness of legend, as the bygone America that was truest to the country's foundational order.

The unity of the postwar recovery effort that characterized the fifties resulted in material prosperity, but it had not adequately accounted for diversity of identity. People who did not like their role in the story of the fifties, whether youth, women, or nonwhites, decided that it was not the story for them. Tellingly, they were able to make such a decision precisely because they were Americans, people for whom the main story will always be one where there is freedom to reject inherited stories. It was the peculiar American rootlessness of the 1960s rebels — a rather patriotic rootlessness, given that it stretched straight back to the Puritan forefathers — that relieved them of any inbuilt sense of obligation to conform to the story that had been written for them in the fifties.

The ideal of the fifties represented an attempt to write a unifying story that could make sense out of the vacuum and chaos left by the world wars. It was a good attempt, but one that had unavoidably shallow foundations. The revolution of the sixties and seventies represented the realization that, after the destruction of the world wars, there could be *no* new order with any real claim to endurance — let alone that of the 1950s. The sixties pushed against the fifties and the fifties fell like a tree in a gale. In the aftermath, the shallowness of the fifties' roots was revealed as having been unable to penetrate ground hardened by the fires of World War II. Even the inheritable stories that managed to survive the first half of the twentieth century — religion, most notably — were scorched by the world wars. So the sixties and seventies saw the growth of smaller plants — stories about race and gender and class, less ambitious than an unsupportable tree of towering national identity — grow in the thin topsoil that had accumulated over the scorched earth remaining from the first half of the century. In this social climate were born the much maligned and misunderstood phenomena that have loosely been characterized as postmodernism. As succinctly defined by one of its most famous philosophers, Jean-François Lyotard, postmodernism is "an incredulity

towards metanarratives." Simply put, in the second half of the twentieth century, many people stopped believing, not only in the power of
stories they had inherited, but in the power of inherited or inherit*able*
stories at all.

The rejection of the story of the 1950s therefore entailed the realization that, in the wake of the world wars, there would be no new
stories that would be strong enough to maintain a sufficiently durable
social order to pass between the generations. The American story —
which says you can shake off the bondage of your heritage — changed
from a statement of possibility to a mandate: your parents' generation
cannot define you.

This realization resulted in a crisis of personal meaning. Who are
we? From where do we come, and whence do we go? Why are we? The
various movements that characterized the age can be seen as efforts to
answer these questions, which people in cultures defined by inherited
stories never need to confront (at least, not to such a degree). We are
not a species cut out for meaninglessness. When there is no story or
storyteller to give meaning to us, we are left to make it for ourselves.

Thus was born the relatively modern ideal of *self-construction.*
Though not a new philosophical concept, until this point in history
there was never such a near-complete absence of inherited guidelines
to help us on our way. In the postwar era, the individual had increasingly unprecedented freedom, and therefore unprecedented challenge.
It was now up to the individual to answer for him- or herself the
question "Who am I?" — the culture was doing less and less of the
work.

The second circumstance that made the rebellion of the sixties
and seventies unique was the context of a social revolution set in the
massive prosperity, strong economic infrastructure, and abundance of
consumer goods produced by the fifties. Rebellion never takes place
in a vacuum, after all. This is why the fifties, which was born out
of a vacuum, was not rebellion but construction. But the discontent
of the sixties and seventies took place in the setting of an astonish-
ingly wealthy country. Certain sections of the sixties' rebellion, such
as the civil rights movement for African Americans and the rise of fem-
inism, were rooted in justifiable complaints at being excluded from the
growth in national wealth. But the general discontent of these decades
did not, by and large, emerge from widespread material deprivation. It
was not a demand for basic needs, not a social rebellion of serfs against

landowners, not an uprising of slaves against masters, but a rejection of one generation against the previous generation's conception of personal identity and meaning. And the rejection of the latter's stories by the former did not also come with any real rejection of the wealth that the 1950s had produced (if it had, we would live in a very different world).

The analysis of James Twitchell, a scholar of consumer culture and advertising, is worth quoting in full:

> In the older culture, aspirations to material comfort were sharply restricted by the limited capacity of the economy to produce. In the modern world, much greater material satisfactions lie within the range of even those of modest means. Hence a producer culture becomes a consumer culture, a hoarding culture becomes a surplus culture, a work culture becomes a therapeutic culture. And what you buy becomes more important than what you make.[1]

As it happened, consumer goods fit nicely in the open hands of Americans who, having been disinherited from any definitive sense of place in the world, were left grasping for anything tangible that could help them construct a sense of personal meaningfulness. Consumer goods ceased to be simply the things that we bought to eat, to cover our bodies from the elements, to shelter us, and to move us from place to place. And, while such goods had always served to delineate classes of people, in these decades, their ubiquity led to their becoming the very building blocks of our self-understanding as human beings.

Consumption Community

The linchpin to the above line of argument is the 1980s. If we had any doubts that consumer goods were increasingly the standard by which we understood our place in the world, the birth of the yuppie would undo them. Twitchell observes that the uniqueness of yuppies (young urban professionals) is "that they were the first consumption community . . . known *only* by their badges."[2] Although every identity group — Twitchell's "consumption community" — has distinguished itself from others by its dress, habits, music, and so on, these distinctives have always been secondary to the organizing principle of the group. For example, while there was a Maoist costume in the Chinese

Communist rebellion, being a Maoist was not first and foremost about one's outfit.

By contrast, the 1980s produced a group that was defined exclusively through its purchasing habits. As Twitchell points out, there was no iconic yuppie figure who embodied the heart and soul of the group because there *was* no heart and soul at the center of the yuppie identity — only a wallet. To become a yuppie, one did not have to assent to any yuppie creed or set of beliefs or commit to protecting and upholding the yuppie cause. One just had to buy the right things. And through those purchases, one gained admission to an identity, a place in the world, a way of life, a sense of things, and a social life filled with others who bought the right things, too.

In this sense, if the fifties planted the seed of American consumer culture, the yuppie was its first fruits. In the yuppie, we see the first identity based entirely on a pattern of consumption of goods. It was the first consumer *lifestyle.*

We use the word lifestyle so freely in contemporary speech — "so-and-so is living a such-and-such lifestyle" — that we've lost the remarkable sense of the term. It is a style, a fashion, of life: That is to say, it is an aspect of life dealing entirely with outward things, most especially consumer goods. There is nothing necessarily interior to a lifestyle in the sense that there is to being a practitioner of a religion, or an adherent of a political ideology. No, living a lifestyle revolves around appearances. This is not necessarily to dismiss the potency of lifestyles. They do not all depend entirely on what one buys, and can be highly conditional on what one does. But if you buy and do the right things, though you might not have the life, there is no one who can genuinely say of you that you are not truly living the lifestyle.

These lifestyles developed out of the vacuum of personal meaning that Americans faced. Because we had no inherited stories, we had to invent our own stories for ourselves. But the lack of external influences was not yet complete in the 1980s. Inherited stories lacked vitality in the latter part of the twentieth century, especially regarding American social order at home. This was not the case, however, on an international level, where the Cold War continued to threaten both rebels and the rebelled-against with undiscriminating annihilation. The iconic image of a hippie-planted daisy peacefully occupying a guardsman's rifle barrel was impossible to replicate with missile silos; there aren't that many flowers, let alone flower children, in the world.

As a result, to be alive in the 1980s meant living under the perpetual shadow of the Cold War. This put every lifestyle in context. You were a yuppie/punker/aging hippie/young Republican/dying discomaniac/tree hugger, and so on. Then, no matter how you understood your place in the world or what meaning you assigned to yourself, you were ultimately a yuppie/punker/aging hippie/young Republican/dying discomaniac/tree hugger, staring down the business end of a Soviet hydrogen bomb. There was no way to consume or rebel your way out from under the nuclear threat. The Cold War was the only powerful story we inherited from the postwar period. But as we know, it didn't last, and its demise cleared the way for the complete dominance of consumerism.

Consumerism Triumphant

Two seemingly unrelated events at the end of the eighties and the beginning of the nineties marked the full triumph of the consumerist age and provide us with the most immediate jumping-off point for where we are today.

The first was the fall of the Berlin Wall in late 1989. With the exceptionally rapid crumbling of the Soviet bloc and the fall of Communism in Eastern Europe, the global story that we knew ourselves to occupy changed dramatically. We are always defined by our limits — after all, the inherited stories that we rejected, as a culture, were all about knowing one's place in the world through limitation. And we had been limited, as Westerners and especially as Americans, by the bilateral power dynamic of the Cold War.

With the dissolution of a united Communist threat, however, America found itself as the world's only superpower, unchecked by any external force.* Without any check or balance to its international influence, it was, for all intents and purposes, free to act as it pleased. Unlimited abroad and unlimited at home for the first time in history, the freedom that had existed for decades on a domestic level was mirrored on a global level. Once the Soviet nemesis had vanished, there

---

*It should be noted that the perception of safety from nuclear attack was, by and large, a collective delusion, since the threat arguably got worse in the disrupted geopolitical balance after the Cold War's end.

was literally no worldly authority of substance that exerted any authority except America. The last vestige of any limitation had vanished in the West, leaving a void.

Into that gap rushed the aftermath of the second determinative event: Marlboro Friday, April 2, 1993. American consumer identity was lagging in early 1993, four years after the fall of the Berlin Wall. The brand consciousness that is at the heart of every lifestyle was suffering in the wake of the recession, and generic products were making inroads into branded companies' incomes. And, on that fateful Friday in the spring of 1993, Philip Morris announced that the price of a pack of Marlboro cigarettes would be reduced by 20 percent.

As journalist Naomi Klein records in her magisterial *No Logo,* "the pundits went nuts, announcing in frenzied unison that not only was Marlboro dead, all brand names were dead."[3] If the billion plus dollars that had been spent on Marlboro's ad campaigns could not sustain the brand from an attack by generic cigarettes, then it seemed that people did not care about brands enough to sustain them. This was a make-or-break moment for brand-name consumer goods, and for a time it looked as if they would break.

History has shown, however, that the companies that survived the brand-name crisis were actually the companies for which brand identity was everything. These consumer icons are global household names: Starbucks, Coke, Nike, Disney, Mercedes, and so on. They got to be this way, Klein notes, because "for these companies, the ostensible product was mere filler for the real production: the brand."[4] These companies took the pulse of consumer society and understood, quite explicitly, that people's self-understanding had become a thing to be purchased. After Marlboro Friday, Klein says, " 'Brands, not products!' became the rallying cry for a marketing renaissance led by a new breed of companies that saw themselves as 'meaning brokers' instead of product producers."[5]

This was, in spirit, no new realization. James Twitchell records that in a speech to a salesperson's convention in 1923, radio announcer Helen Cass urged the gathering to "sell [your customers] their dreams. . . . After all, people don't buy things to have things. They buy things to work for them. They buy hope — hope of what your merchandise will do for them. Sell them this hope and you won't have to worry about selling them goods."[6]

But Cass, however canny a salesperson, could not have foreseen an age in which our consumer habits told us who we were. The brand development of the late twentieth century is Cass's vision on methamphetamines: sell them *anything,* she might say at a Nike shareholders' meeting today, by scrawling the swoosh across it. Why? Because the customer who will not buy top-end basketball shoes simply to cover his feet *will* buy the image, the self-understanding, the identity that the swoosh conveys.

The triumph of consumerism is this very leap from making goods attractive through branding to selling the brand itself — in other words, selling consumer identity. Like it or not, in our society, *we are what we buy.* Savvy stores do not sell products, but self-image. The racks brimming with a dizzying variety of clothes do not offer a variety of *products* nearly as much as they offer varieties of potential *me's.* Given that we can buy our way into a lifestyle, each purchase — whether a house, car, clothing, food, accessory, music, and so on — represents an investment in our chosen identity, which we construct out of the amalgamated consumer goods that we each accumulate to such staggering degrees.

Throughout this chapter, we have seen a need for stories of personal meaning. When we do not inherit them, we have to construct them for ourselves. So it is worth mentioning that the full union of branding and consumer identity could never have occurred without a story to join the two. How did we really come to assign *so much meaning* to what we buy? After all, there are countless minor items with little to no relationship to our understandings of who we are — oddities like super glue and thumbtacks spring to mind — made by companies with brand identities that we think nothing about. Elmer's glue might bring to mind fond childhood memories of macaroni art, but our purchase of it doesn't have much to do with how we understand ourselves in the world.

To uncover the difference, ask yourself how many advertisements for Elmer's glue you have seen in your life. Now try to count the ads you saw for Nike or Lexus just last week. Building a brand identity strong enough to hang a lifestyle on requires a massive investment of money and creativity for advertising. The results are phenomena like the globally recognized Absolut Vodka bottle and Nike's iconic silhouette of a weightless Michael Jordan. Advertising has become our common story, communicating that which we hold dear. It *is* our culture, in many ways; any critic's supposed dichotomy between culture and advertising is hopelessly outdated, since the two are so intermingled through sponsorship, media, and money as to be inseparable. In the dominance of post–Cold War advertising, we at last found a shared story — one that had eluded us since the 1950s — that both orders our existence and allows for our individual self-creation.

Thus, "modern consumerism is ... not a replacement of religion," as Twitchell argues, "but a continuation, a secularizing, of a struggle for order."[7] Today, to be is to buy.

Chapter 3

A Digital Crown
for the Material Girl

The latter part of the twentieth century was tumultuous. Until the mid-nineties, however, we did not witness any truly shocking developments, any social phenomenon of sufficient novelty to equal or exceed its ultimate cause — that is, the world wars. As important as the development of consumerist identity is to our current situation, we must admit that it is not really a surprise, given historical events. Sometime in the century's final decade, however, all this changed. The end of the millennium saw a genuinely revolutionary event, the birth of a child that would exceed its parent. And such a tiny, stylish infant it was.

In the mid-1990s, a quiet revolution took place with the advent of the mobile phone. Our increasingly tech-savvy society took the development in stride and rapidly adapted. As we did so, we failed to notice the sweeping implications of the fact that the mobile phone became the first material object in history that was universally available while simultaneously being unique to each consumer. In a way that stands out as singular in the history of the human species, with the mobile phone, anyone can have a phone, but also *his or her unique phone, by virtue of its special digital identity.* And this fact augurs a shift in our perception of ourselves and of our place in history and the world. We are witnessing the digitization of much of our lives and, as a consequence, our identities; in this move, we can see the crowning glory of the consumerist ideal of self-creation.

The phone is a lens through which we can look at consumerism and the digital identity. We have seen how the quest for personal identity in the Cold War era led to a consumerist sense of personal meaning. Yet the mobile phone introduced a new level of control that one could exercise as a consumer. With the mobile phone, in one transaction we purchase both the physical object and the rights to a digital identity that no one else on earth can claim. The mobile phone made manufactured individuality a product available for purchase: one person, one number. This development stands head and shoulders above our ability to create ourselves by putting together, for example, a signature wardrobe. In previous versions of consumer identity, we have cobbled together brands to make a statement about ourselves. In the digital era, we really do gain a consumer identity that is genuinely unique, and it is here that we can see the seeds of serious theological implications for how we live our lives.

Of fundamental concern for us is the fact that though we may choose what we do with our lives, we do not choose the physical setting or characteristics of our humanity, of our God-givenness. This is the most substantive difference between physical and digital identities. Think about the passage of a life (not a lifestyle!) and how little of it we actually choose: in the beginning, we do not choose for our parents to meet and procreate. We do not choose the unique combination of DNA upon which our bodies and minds are built. We do not choose the hour, day, or year of our birth. We do not choose who raises us as children or where. Nor, for the most part, do we choose how we are treated in our youth. As adults, we do not choose our most basic physical features — though the rise in plastic surgery represents the desire to manipulate what we have been given in these areas. Though we can radically affect our health through our behavior, we do not finally choose how or whether to grow old. Finally, not having chosen our point of entry into time, space, and history, neither will any of us choose whether or not our bodies will one day die, and few of us choose beforehand when or how it will happen. These choices, among the most significant determiners of our lives, are not ours to make.

The sequence of the consumer's digital "life" and a large part of her consumer identity, however, run in a nearly perfect inverse parallel to the events of her physical existence. Unlike the relative choicelessness of the individual's God-given life, described above, not one aspect of her digital existence will be given to her. Both have a beginning; in her digital life, the consumer chooses the hour, day, and year. She does not choose her parents, but she picks from an array of companies eager to bring her into this world of ones and zeroes, who will give her her name; furthermore, with credit card in hand, she can change companies, or names, at virtually any moment. She chooses the unique calling plan (which, with photographic and textual transmission, along with Internet access, offers far more than voice communication) upon which her digital self will be built. Yet, unlike her DNA, she can change her calling plan with only a little difficulty and a little more money and, unlike her physical body, she chooses her digital shell from a dazzling array of phones, each sleeker than the last, and with still larger numbers of options for the customizable phone wallpaper and ring tones. (Ring tone sales nearly topped half a billion dollars in 2005, and it's a growth market.) Yes, the physical phones are simple fashion accessories, but as designers move toward increasingly more stylish options, what were once tools increasingly seem to be avatars, or incarnations, of our digital selves.

Second Life Now

Here is the absolute and categorical difference to which so little attention is paid and yet upon which so very much depends: there will never be an aspect of the consumer's digital identity that is not chosen and purchased via financial transaction. The same was never true of prior consumer identities. Strip away a yuppie's lifestyle trappings, which he has chosen and purchased, and beside the crumpled Lacoste golf shirt and Ralph Lauren khakis, you still have a human being with a family and history. Strip away the parts of digital identity that have been bought, and nothing remains. A human being has the mobile number, the e-mail, the chat room alias — but these identity markers are divorced from his or her flesh and blood in a way that no other consumer goods ever are. The result is a growing disconnect between our sense of the person we have bought ourselves to be (digital identity) and the person we have been created to be (flesh-and-blood identity).

This technological development marks a sea change in the way we think about ourselves. The cell phone is but one early example. The second wave of the move toward digital identities is in online communities like Second Life. Second Life is another world — there's no other way to describe it — that exists in the Internet. It is like a giant video game in which people move their characters (called "avatars") around a digital landscape.

But, unlike a game, Second Life does not move toward a purpose. It is just an alternate existence — a "second life," with commerce, entertainment, shopping, hanging out, and so on, but all online. Sub-scribers can make their online avatars look like anything they like and can acquire online money (in exchange for real American dollars) to buy digital designer clothing. They can buy "land" and develop it as they like; more invested clients (or corporations) can buy whole "is-lands" and shape the landscape to their pleasure. In its digital space, your avatar can do anything you can do in reality, plus a lot that you can't — like flying, or changing your appearance at will. It is unsurpris-ing that Second Life quickly developed adults-only sex clubs, where avatars can act out clients' fantasies.

For now, our interaction with Second Life is limited to sight and hearing. But as technology moves toward the point of electronically stimulating touch, smell, and taste, we can see that the goal of entities like Second life is the total replication and replacement of physical exis-tence. With this future capability, however, we should perhaps pause to think about the horizon toward which we have embarked. As we begin the blithe construction of digital identities upon our human ones, we can listen to the echoes of Babel in our ears and ask: To what extent is the creation qualified to be a creator?

Nor can this change be dismissed as a quirk of the online crowd. Traits of digital identity have already begun to define our economy and society with this new sense of self-mastery. Developments in man-ufacturing technology, for instance, have resulted in an astonishing capacity to personalize mass-produced goods. Less than a century has passed since the consumer could have a Ford Model T in any color he wanted, as long as it was black; now the car buyer can fully customize a car online. In a digital world, as levels of self-creation through con-sumption skyrocket, it's not enough control simply to buy the brands you like. Now we want the brands to cater to us as individuals. We want brand names customized.

Take, for example, Nike. Ever the cultural forerunner, in 2005, Nike began promoting the "iD" option on its Web site, which is a customiz-able version of a variety of Nike's traditional offerings: shoes, bags, watches, and golf balls. (Reebok and Adidas have followed suit with their own offerings.) The customer "produces" the product online, and then Nike makes it and ships it. Options are limited to the aesthetic, but they are manifold: With the women's Nike Shox Turb OZ iD, for example, the customer could decide on the base color of the shoe, as well as that of the accent, tip and heel, swoosh logo, shox supports, and laces. The result is 1,863,400 possible color combinations, most of which would clash hideously. Add to this the capacity to add a monogram or logo of one's choosing, and we suddenly find ourselves in a strange new world where the consumer can buy a mass-produced physical item that is actually unique.

On the Nike iD Web site, a series of menus shows the consumer the various customizable options in sport-specific footwear and equipment. In each, the consumer is greeted with sport-specific slogans that reinforce the foundational Nike iD message, which is basically that athletics *is* image, and vice versa. Notable slogans include: "My color combination hits as hard as I do" (football) and "It's always time to express myself" (timing). Given a second glance, the advertising for Nike iD is patently — and fascinatingly — nonsensical. The football player's color combination hits nothing like as hard as he does; hitting is not something color combinations even *do*. And why should the time-sensitive athlete be so concerned with the perpetual need to express him- or herself, anyway? Artists express; athletes train and compete. Shouldn't aesthetics be an extrinsic and needless component of athletic activity?

Fortunately, Nike solves the mystery for any uncomprehending consumers who thought that athletics was just about physical training. In the "Why Customize" section of the iD Web site, we are flatly solicited to take the bold next step toward complete brand-consumer hybridization: "The days of picking things directly off the shelves, or ordering off the menu as it appears, are over. NIKE iD was created to reflect your individuality. NikeiD.com + Your Personality = Customization." The message: Your increasingly demanding desire to find yourself in the act of consumption can find fulfillment here.

Now, items with a heavily aesthetic function have always been customized to the preferences of the consumer. But is there not a limit to such customization? What does it mean to want to customize so much?

A final absurd example: While reading a newspaper in 2004, I came across an advertisement for a Radio Shack emergency radio powered by an attached hand crank. Given the uncertainty of our terrorist-fighting age, one might suppose that such a radio could be a lifesaver in a time of disaster. One might therefore imagine that Radio Shack's promotion of the radio would rely entirely on the utilitarian features of the product, with perhaps some trading on consumers' fears. But one would be wrong. More than durability or the lack of need for an external power source, the biggest section of the advertisement was dedicated to pointing out the consumer's ability to choose between *five different color options.*

We should not dwell for too long on the meaning of one object, but it is worthy of note that the well-documented move toward customizable product *image,* rather than quality or utility, has become present even in the most utilitarian of material goods. The reason for this is that less and less of what we buy does not affect the consumer lifestyle — the self we have selected. The ideal of customization has spread even to areas of consumption in which our personalities and preferences need not be exercised. The digital age has taken consumer choice to an entirely new level, from the banal (the green emergency radio complementing the canned beans in the hall closet) to the profound (our digital identities, which, since they are created by choice and only by choice, represent the cutting edge of the exercise of this ideal).

In our world, people are not people before they are consumers. In the mind of the market and in the minds of advertising executives — and even in their own minds — they are people perhaps *because* they are consumers. We were not this way sixty or even thirty years ago. Then, our status as consumer might have justifiably been claimed as merely one among many social roles that we played. But such is not true of most people today. In writing the above text, I used "individual" and "consumer" interchangeably without even thinking about it, as if they meant the same thing. I didn't even notice that I was doing it while I was typing. The way we talk tells us a great deal about the way we think, and if we talk as if being a person is the same thing as being a consumer, we have a rather unsettling situation on our hands.

The Context of Consumerism

There must remain a great deal more to all of us than our ability to purchase the lifestyle of our choice. We do have human relationships and cares and commitments that are only tangentially related to things that are bought and sold. We have to say that no matter what we do, we can never become simple walking mannequins, our only sense of self coming from the accessories with which we adorn ourselves. No matter how many platinum cards one carries, at the heart of every consumer is a human being. If we equate the two in our daily speech, that reflects a laziness of language. Our doing so can tell us important things about how we think about ourselves, but we cannot completely substitute our given humanity with a purchased identity.

At the beginning of this section, we asked what it means for us to live in this consumerist society that everyone is so worked up about. We have answered that question: *To live in a consumerist world means that who we understand ourselves to be is deeply and significantly related to what we buy/consume.* And this is true to a much greater extent than we'd like to imagine. In the act of consumption, we purchase our very sense of selves. This is where we find ourselves in early twenty-first century America, and indeed the West-dominated global economy. Because we lack strong inherited stories, we are left with the burden of constructing our own sense of meaning and place in the world. By and large, we have done so with the tools that lay closest at hand — consumer goods. And with the digital age, the ideal of self-creation through consumption has gained a new potency, given that technologically enabled, digital forms of identity are the most complete "selves" that can we can gain through purchases, without having anything given to us.

This situation is serious, but I hope we can also avoid the pitfalls of some of consumerism's more rabid critics. Much of what I've described above will be distasteful to many readers — for my part, I'm certainly not happy about the fact that I am what I buy. But we also need to be realistic. Most of us are probably pretty decent people who are just doing our best in the situations we find ourselves in, even when doing our best means doing things that aren't so great. McDonald's or Nike advertising executives, to take a conventional target, aren't the demons that anti-globalization activists would have them be; they leave work and go home to kiss their kids goodnight. The issues we're talking about involve real people, in all their fragile, flawed, sinful realities.

Furthermore, if it's an anxious time in which to live, well — such is life. There are probably very few, if any, ages in Western history that weren't frightening to live in. We don't have to trivialize the crisis of meaningfulness that we're in to realize that it's a bit of a luxury, as far as worries go, compared with the crisis of, say, having our village wiped out by Cossacks. Put in that context, we might start to think that maybe getting an undue pleasure from the brand of fleece we buy isn't such a bad deal. But then we think about the near-slave labor that probably produced it, and we come back to reality. Evil never goes away. It just assumes a form proper to the age. We simply have to take consumerism on balance as a major issue for our time.

That said, there are profound ethical, political, and — most significantly — spiritual implications of the issues we are talking about. The rest of the book will deal with these. Christian readers will be wondering how all of the above relates to the promised theological investigation into consumerism. I hope that the remaining chapters, which examine our situation in the light of scripture, will be satisfactory in that regard. But before we could look at the theological understanding of where we are, we first needed to understand, in broad strokes, where that is.

Up to this point, we've focused primarily on the ideal of self-creation that's present in consumerist society, looking at advertising, marketing, and brand identity. What we haven't yet examined is the spot where the rubber hits the road: the point of purchase that stands between us and all the lifestyles that stand ready for us to buy. We live in a world where we gain our very selves — not just things — by opening our wallets. In Part II, we'll look at the very scary implications this has for our lives.

Part II

AMERICA

Romans 1:18–32

Chapter 4

American Idols

As Americans, we inherit empire. Not every nation in the world's history is a stand-alone global power; we are. So was Rome. And through the words of scripture, the Holy Spirit speaks to us out of that peculiar similarity we have to the imperial Romans. It speaks to us across the lines that we imagine divide us. It speaks to us on the left and on the right, in our megachurches and house gatherings, in our SUVs and our hybrids alike. It speaks to us because wherever we understand ourselves to be in this culture of ours, we are in a culture like Rome's, with similar sins.

Paul's letter to the Romans has a great deal to tell us about the source and consequence of our particular culture, which is, in sum, that those who ignore the Creator God, trusting instead in creation, will suffer certain consequences. This sin might well be the peculiar sin of great civilizations, which must be uniquely tempted to rely upon their own considerable worldly power.

Because Romans is such a go-to section of scripture for Christians, many will find it difficult to break out of the usual way of reading the book, which is both universalized and individualistic. That is, in one popular reading, the first few chapters are usually read as proof of universal human fallenness, with an emphasis on each individual's need for salvation. I'm not saying that this interpretation isn't true. But for our purposes in understanding the spiritual similarity between ourselves and ancient Rome, we must instead read Paul's words as being simultaneously *communal* and *specific* — which is also a true reading.

Take, as an example, Romans 1:23: "[T]hey exchanged the glory of the immortal God for images ... like mortal man and birds and animals and reptiles." It is certainly not the case that each Roman took up with four kinds of idols. We cannot read Paul's words and pretend that they will apply equally to each and every person — he is talking about the decay of a group. This interpretation does not come naturally for those of us who emphasize the need for personal conversion and have a corresponding method of reading scripture. Yet it is important that we revitalize what is a truly biblical concern with entire cultures — the nations, or families of the earth — instead of only focusing on individuals. What is compelling in Romans is not the fact that it will indict each of us individually, but that it indicts our culture communally.

Moreover, while the condemnation is on a culture-wide level, Romans does not condemn all cultures equally. There may be a universal message in the text. But there is also a specific word for cultures like ours, which bear such a strong similarity to imperial Rome.

> The wrath of God is being revealed from heaven against all the godlessness and wickedness of men who suppress the truth by their wickedness, since what may be known about God is plain to them, because God has made it plain to them. For since the creation of the world God's invisible qualities — his eternal power and divine nature — have been clearly seen, being understood from what has been made, so that men are without excuse. For although they knew God, they neither glorified him as God nor gave thanks to him, but their thinking became futile and their foolish hearts were darkened. Although they claimed to be wise, they became fools and exchanged the glory of the immortal God for images made to look like mortal man and birds and animals and reptiles. (Romans 1:18–23)

Keeping the above guidelines for reading in mind, Paul's indictment of Roman Gentile culture is actually fairly simple. It boils down to this: God's wrath is continually being revealed against the godlessness and wickedness of the culture, and this state of affairs has come about because the Romans refused to glorify God as God and to give God thanks for their lives.

Now, a Roman Gentile of the time would probably have offered what we can admit is, on the face of it, a pretty reasonable response: "How is it that we can be held guilty for not glorifying the Jews' God, or giving him thanks," the Roman would say, "when he hasn't revealed himself to us? We weren't at Sinai, we didn't receive the covenant." Paul's anticipation of this response in verses 19–20 brings us to the crux of Rome's guilt:

> . . . what *may be known about God is plain* to them, because *God has made it plain to them.* For since the creation of the world God's invisible qualities, his eternal power and divine nature, have been clearly seen, being understood from what has been made, so that men are without excuse.

Later in Paul's letter, he will point out that the Romans cannot be morally culpable for failing to obey the Torah, which they of course never received, as the Jews did. One can't be expected to derive the Ten Commandments through the contemplation of a daisy. In the meantime, however, the Romans have failed to give due recognition to the Lord of the Jews, who was known to Rome as the Creator of the world. By observing the shape that the Creator's hand left upon creation — light and dark; the earth, sky, and sea; plants, animals, and humankind — the Romans could and should have deduced at least the power and divinity behind the world. To put a finer point on it, they should have recognized themselves, fundamentally, as *created beings.* And with this deduction, they should have known enough about God — his invisibility, power, timelessness, and nature as a Creator — to "glorify" and "give thanks" to God, as verse 21 indicates.

. . . neither glorified him as God . . .

By the simple act of living in and observing creation, Paul says, the Romans should have figured out that there is something bigger than they were, and that that something has certain attributes of divinity. Yet this very observation and theological deduction is the very thing the Romans failed to do.

There are parallels between the Roman refusal to glorify God and the consumerist ideal of self-creation. As we explored in the last chapter, the heart of consumerism is the sense that we can make ourselves, create ourselves, by what we buy. We imagine that who and what we are is fundamentally in our own power to shape. What that belief does to our bloated sense of self-worth is bad enough. But far worse is what the belief that we are our own creation does to our sense of God: If we are our own creation, then it is only reasonable that we are not anybody else's. Whether or not one consciously disbelieves in a creator, when we define ourselves along consumerist lines, we act as though we are our own creators and as if there were no creator outside of ourselves. If there were a creator and we were the work of another's hand, then our creator, and our createdness, would surely count! The creator would matter. The existence of a creator — even if we thought, like early deists, simply in terms of a "divine watchmaker" who wound up the universe and then let it tick away — would shatter the notion that we belong to ourselves. A creator, simply by being there, denies us the complete creative control over ourselves that we demand as consumers.

We hate things we haven't decided for ourselves. Consider our culture's (justifiable and welcome) concern with discrimination on grounds of gender, race, age, sexual orientation, and the like. While it is good and right that we should expunge all legal means of such discrimination, it's certainly telling that our horror at discrimination is rooted in the conviction that nothing we have not chosen for our-selves — like our race — should be held against us. If one wants to claim these "created" attributes and celebrate them, fine. There are a variety of consumer-based ways to turn one's gender or race into a de-finitive lifestyle, which are then seen as good because we have chosen them. But heaven forbid that anything about us should *matter* if we have not chosen it to matter, let alone to the point where it impinges upon our completely free exercise of will. Our culture has a deep-seated mistrust of any reality that is foisted upon us. And if, as a people, we therefore mistrust createdness itself, our attitude toward the Creator must be one of rejection, denial, and even resentment at the one who would infringe on our perceived right to unrestrained self-control. To act in a consumerist fashion and to accept the values that accompany such behavior is to act as if there were no creator with final rights over us. This is exactly what Paul tells the Romans they have done.

The consumerist life demands that we live the same, double-sided lie that the Romans lived and deny the createdness that testifies to a Creator. Consumerism is itself the refusal to recognize, even in the most basic of ways, the God who created us. Thus, we act just as the Romans did, refusing to "glorify him as God." God is due glorification by God's creation; to fail to do so is a falsehood. And the very vitality of consumerism depends on our willingness to ignore this falsehood, "to suppress the truth," on a day-to-day basis.

Since consumerism's version of reality is a closed loop of consumer-choice-consumption, it has no place in it for a reality that precedes or lies outside of this loop. No matter our advances in technology, our consumerist preferences cannot finally master and determine the cycle of life and death, our bodies and minds — nor anything that lies outside of our conscious control. A look at the lie — that we have control over ourselves — reveals the truth. We are created, there *is* a Creator (however mysterious), and our imagined ability to create ourselves along patterns of consumption is an illusion.

...nor gave thanks to him

For each of our sakes, I hope that most of us, regardless of religion, have at one time felt a pure, raw gratitude: the sort where we are thankful for some good thing, but have no one to thank for it. This kind of gratitude, which for Christians can only be directed to God, is akin to being inverted, turned inside out. We direct our energy and passion not to ourselves but to the One who has blessed us. Such thanksgiving, which is directed entirely outwards, is the polar opposite of all narcissism and selfishness.

As consumers, however, ingratitude is endemic to our very beings. Indeed, gratitude and thanksgiving are attitudes that cannot survive in the hostile consumerist climate. This is because there is nothing to be grateful for in consumerism, and no one to be grateful to. The things we consume in order to create a lifestyle — goods, services, experiences — are surrounded with a sense of entitlement, not thanksgiving. This is the way we think about property. To buy something, whether a product or a service, is to have rights over it, including the ability to dispose of it as we wish.

Consumerism: nothing to feel grateful for and no one to feel gratitude toward. But the problem goes even deeper than a thankless commercial society. It goes even deeper because, as we've seen, at the heart of consumerism is the fact that we are buying and selling ourselves. Our image, our identity, who we are in respect to others, how others view us, and how we view ourselves — in a consumerist society, all of this is up for sale in the products and services that we choose. This means that *we become the products.*

If we apply the attitude toward products that we have just explored, this should be a chilling statement. A product isn't something you're grateful for. You don't give anyone thanks for it. And you're free to dispose of it however you want to. Take care of it? It's yours to take care of. Abuse it? It's yours to abuse. Destroy it? It's yours to destroy. You own it. You are free — think about this: *free* — to do as you like with it.

Except "it" is you. You are both the owner and the product, the master and the slave, in a totally closed loop that shuts the door on any gratitude. After all, when it comes to your sense of consumer identity, which is to say your dominant identity, nobody — especially not God — has given you a blessed thing.

Can we really have any doubt about our resemblance to the Romans? How is it that for the latter part of the twentieth century we have read Romans week in and week out in our churches and Bible studies and private devotions and not seen our own faces staring back at us?

Chapter 5

Since the Creation of the World: Genesis 3

I mentioned in the last chapter that, contrary to many interpretations, we were not going to read Romans 1:18–32 as an account of human-kind's fall from grace, such as is recorded in Genesis 3. Paul does write to his Roman audience about the fall, but he does so later in the letter (see 5:12 and following). The fact that he gets to it eventually is even more evidence that this is not what he is talking about in Romans 1; instead, in that section of Paul's letter, he is interested in the fall of Roman culture.

At the same time, there is nothing new under the sun — even sin, at which we imagine ourselves to be so creative. Our sin looks like the Roman sin and the Roman sin looks like the first sin. We are interested in the particularity of the matter, but it is also instructive to see how we're all just performing variations on the same theme.

In Genesis 3, we read how the serpent urges Eve to eat the fruit from the Tree of the Knowledge of Good and Evil, though God has said, "When you eat of it you shall surely die." The serpent exhorts her: "You will not surely die. . . . For God knows that when you eat of it your eyes will be opened, and you will be like God, knowing good and evil." We lack the space here to do a thorough interpretation of this passage. But look at it in its broad strokes. First, the serpent makes God out to be a liar, denying what God has said about death as the consequence of eating. Second, the serpent distorts the truth of the situation. Yes, God knows that humans will become "like God" in knowing both good and evil, where to this point they had only known the good. What the serpent doesn't add is that humankind cannot have knowledge of evil and live, as God can. We are, as a species, unqualified to be judges between the two. For humans to know evil is for humans to choose evil and, in that choosing, to die. If you doubt this, consider whether the evils of our shared history, or even of the twentieth century alone, do not confirm our incapacity as judges of the moral universe.

The link between this passage and the Romans and our own consumerist condition lies in Adam and Eve's desire to stand on their own two feet, as it were. They want what theologians call "aseity," which is the quality of total autonomy, of not being determined by any other being. Of course, only God has this "being in oneself" or self-sufficiency, because God alone is not dependent on another being for existence. Conversely, all other beings are dependent on God.

When the first humans take the fruit, which is both attractive and "desirable for gaining wisdom," they are rejecting the condition of their existence, which is an existence that is entirely sustained on the basis of God's gifts alone. In taking the fruit, they are taking something for themselves, the illusion of aseity that they think will let them exist out from under God's rule. In other words, they are taking *themselves* as their own possessions. They want to stop relying on God's gifts alone, desiring the freedom of the transaction that we explored in an earlier chapter. They establish who and what they are based on something taken by their own efforts, for which they do not feel grateful to anyone. Thus, they become (literally) the first consumers when what they take in does not simply sustain their lives, but gives them meaning through the exercise of choice.

See them as they are, desiring to stand alone, apart from God, judges in their own right. And their doing so is fundamentally self-deceiving. It is a lie. Though they are making a stand, as it were, trying to act as independent beings, nothing about them is independent. The sin is in their attempt to gain autonomy, not in their success in doing so — for as humans, we simply cannot attain the aseity of being "like God" that consumerism, like the serpent, pretends to have on offer.

The situation that those first humans imagine as a great defiant stand of self-reliance is actually entirely of God. The only thing they bring to it is the sin. Imagine it: The eyes that gaze on the tree, the sound waves of the serpent's speech, the air through which they travel, and the ears upon which the sibilant words fall — all are made and sustained by God. The hand that takes the fruit and even the strength of limb that goes into the taking, likewise. The teeth that chew the fruit are God's. God sets the ground beneath them while they eat and God holds the sky overhead, and God creates the air that feeds their

God-made lungs as they breathe in around God-shaped mouthfuls of that God-grown food. The sun in the sky that day burns because of God and its warmth on their faces as they allow sin into the world is God's gracious, life-sustaining touch as they irrevocably reject him. Everything is the gift of God. So when they seek freedom from the divine gifts, they are actually seeking after destruction, nonexistence.

The first humans' sin was thanklessness to God; this was also the sin of the Roman pagans, according to Paul; this is likewise our sin as consumerists, carried out day after day after day. We can see that the problem common to all three situations is that we have falsely situated ourselves in relation to God. The first humans had, perhaps, the least excuse. They knew God with an intimacy that no other mortal has ever experienced. And yet, from the pervasiveness of sin, we can only assume that any of us would have been equally liable to act similarly. As the inheritors of that first sin, however, the choice that the first humans had is now denied to us. Its result is ingrained.

Chapter 6

Darkened Hearts

...their thinking became futile and their foolish hearts were darkened

When we moved into one of our first apartments, my wife and I inherited a coffee mug from the previous occupant. It was a nice enough mug, glazed pottery, despite the fact that it had a hairline crack down the side. Still, it held liquid and I don't know if either of us even registered the fact that it had a fracture. We thought nothing of it until one day I noticed that the bottom of the mug was wet with coffee. The area around the crack was wet, too, and brown with the coffee that had seeped through it.

I threw the mug away. I might simply have wiped away the coffee, which was really just a few drops, and kept on using it that day. It would have been fine. But one day, probably sooner than I expected, the whole thing would have broken in two and spilled its contents everywhere. With regular use, that mug had been falling apart, slowly but surely, since the day when some sharp impact had resulted in that seemingly negligible hairline fracture.

Humankind is rather like that mug, that clay vessel, and the first sin rather like the unseen impact that caused the hairline fracture. By itself, that first impact doesn't destroy us right away. We're not shattered, after all, we're just cracked. But it's not simply a matter of cracked versus shattered, flawed versus destroyed. The critical thing is that we're not whole. And over time, with any activity whatsoever in each of us, that seemingly insignificant hairline fracture gets worse and worse and worse. The decay is often imperceptible to us, a slow erosion with each use. But the original crack will turn into a seeping or even destroying leak. This happens with individuals and societies alike.

40

Paul's letter describes an erosive process like this happening in the minds and hearts of the Romans as a direct result of their turning from God. As inheritors of imperfect vessels, they were never going to know God with the wholeness that the first humans originally had. But in their rejection of the God they might have known, they encouraged the erosive process of sin, and what was once a crack — that, though it made them not whole, was still small — turned into a full-fledged break. As a people, by committing their own replication of the first sin, they subjected themselves to its full decaying power.

At this point, you may understandably be wondering about the fairness of the whole situation. How, after all, can we be blamed? We've inherited cracked mugs and there's nothing we can do to mend them properly, so it hardly seems right that we'd be judged for the problem.

But that very question — how can I be blamed for something I didn't personally instigate? — is quintessentially individual-focused thinking. The Bible, by contrast, is overflowing with images of group culpability and identity, wherein the families of the nations are judged. It's no good to think in terms of each of us being right and wrong: Romans 1 is all about who we are together, as a people.

Remember what Paul is telling us in this very account of Romans 1: "Look, folks, your reasoning is flawed. You can't trust your own judgment. You can't trust your ability to discern right from wrong. You're living amidst the clutter of thousands upon thousands of years of inherited sin: no wonder your view is obscured." The very basis on which we evaluate a situation fair or unfair, right or wrong, is corrupt. To grasp the spiritual truth communicated in Romans requires a huge sidestep out of our usual mind-sets.

Imagine for a moment a judicial system where a judge takes a bribe. You'd rightly say that her being on the take means that she is incapable of giving a true verdict. Yet this incapacity to render justice doesn't prevent her from judging, all the same, and her unjust judgments form unjust precedents. Then imagine generations of judges, each of them deciding to take bribes as well, and each of them making their own corrupt judgments based on and adding to a system of legal precedents generated by their corrupted forebears.

Now, even if some remarkable judge came along one day and decided not to accept bribes in exchange for judgments, how could she possibly bring justice out of an irreparably corrupt system of legal precedents? The whole structure in which she seeks to judge is flawed. It hardly matters whether this unavoidable corruption is fair or unfair to her as an individual, it simply *is*. The initial corruption was the crack; all subsequent corruptions represent the decay, with each generation further and further distanced from an ability to make sound judgments. We are interconnected to generations past and future.

As a people, we have access to knowledge of God as Creator. This knowledge does not have the intimacy of the original humans' knowledge, nor the privilege of the specific revelation to Abraham's line, nor the intimate face-to-face quality that Christ's disciples enjoyed. Nor, for that matter, is it salvific. But as a group, we could acknowledge God as Creator. Yet we have denied that knowledge, refused to give God glory, and replicated — in our own fashion — the ingratitude and autonomy of the original sin. As a result, our society has positioned itself improperly toward God.

By God's good grace, individuals and groups within the culture may reject this positioning — let us hope so! — and seek out the salvation that is restored communion with God. But the redemption of people within the culture does not mean the redemption of the culture as a whole. Our moral reasoning has eroded; having misunderstood our priorities from the beginning, as it were, there is nothing naturally occurring in us that gives us an accurate perception of our degenerate position. We lack the ability to understand how far we have fallen, no matter how intelligent and righteous we imagine ourselves to be. It takes an alien voice — in this case, the Spirit of God speaking through scripture — to show us.

...they became fools and exchanged the glory of the immortal God

This alien voice of the Spirit, exhaling through the mouth of scripture, tells us that the symptom and evidence of our condition — we who so resemble the Romans receiving Paul's original indictment — is idolatry. They "exchanged the glory of the immortal God," which is to say the invisible Creator, "for images made to look like" the Creator's creation. Instead of perceiving the hand of the invisible Creator in the visible creation, we fixated on what was visible and at hand: idols.

It is important to point out that idolatry is not the first step here. Before we made idols, we turned from the invisible qualities of God and, having turned our hearts from those things that could not be seen with the eyes, we found ourselves unable to find them again. But that inability to find didn't do away with our longing for something greater than ourselves. And so we swap the dimly remembered glory of the immortal God for images of created things: "mortal man and birds and animals and reptiles."

This list of idols had a highly specific context in pagan Rome, where statues of gods and goddesses from the empire's territories sat in their own shrines. Paul certainly would have been thinking of the animal-headed Egyptian gods, among others, which had earned such popularity as mystery cults in the empire's capital.

There is no easy contemporary analogue to this situation in the West. So, to understand this scripture in light of our situation, we need to look at the principle behind the condemnation of idolatry; namely, it represents the fallacy of giving to God's works the glory due to God, of ascribing transcendent qualities to nontranscendent things, of imagining that there is power in powerless objects. The luck that some believe a rabbit's foot brings, for example, is a construction of their minds rather than any metaphysical potency inherent in some poor creature's severed limb. The act of idolatry is therefore the symptom of our having rejected God as we offer devotion to that which does not deserve it.

With this diagnosis of the principle against idolatry, the analogue to our own time becomes clear. Our self-creation via consumption is patent idolatry because it puts transcendent meaning into utterly nontranscendent things. Consumerist behavior demonstrates a relationship between creation and creation — the consumer and the consumed — instead of the Creator and creation. We find that we have given objects a power to create and shape us that is not naturally theirs. In a consumerist society, the fact that we are changed by the objects of our consumption — the clothes, goods, and services that make up various lifestyles — is not actually due to the objects' power. Rather, the change transpires from our shared participation in a cultural illusion.

The proof of this is that no Western lifestyle — marked and formed by all its accoutrements and accessories, and lived with such conviction and potency in its own setting — can be transplanted into an utterly foreign culture. Out of its native context, a lifestyle's symbolic power simply vanishes. Take polar opposites — a yuppie and a punk — from their New York street corner and plop them into the middle of the African bush. Instead of eminently recognizable and *meaningful* figures, we now simply find a guy clad in unfortunate pastels and a teen wearing a lot of inexplicable zippers and spikes. Consumer selves cease to exist outside of the system, perpetuated by everyone, which give them their meaning. That's because there is no heart at their heart. There is only a void playing dress up.

Like prayers offered to idols, we offer the resource of our devotion to the consumer selves that are utterly of our own making. These consumer lifestyles are the never-finished goals of our own quest for meaningfulness, order, and location in the world, but they lack any integral ability to grant us what we ask from them. That we ourselves believe the meaning we ascribe to them is not surprising.

But we *know* that we are not gods. We invest material things with undue qualities, but we do not venerate our lifestyles with the same veneration that the ancient Romans venerated their idols. The parallels are remarkable, but they are not complete. "Idolatry" is more than an inflammatory word that Christian writers can use to describe whatever contemporary phenomenon they think is getting a little too much attention. It is even more than the ascription of transcendent qualities to nontranscendent things. It is also the devotion to and worship of those things that are the work of our own hands. And, while we are certainly invested in our lifestyles, it would be a stretch to claim that as a culture we worship them. It is perhaps a bit unbelievable to say that we regard our retail-bought selves as gods; shallowness isn't idolatry.

The two-fold character of idolatry is (1) a powerless object (2) that is revered as a god. We have the object — the consumer self. But what is the god? That is, what is the power behind the powerless object to which we offer our devotion? What is the power that keeps us collectively enthralled to these idols that are so patently and evidently meaningless, in and of themselves? What is the spiritual potency that binds together the collective delusion that holds the consumerist society together?

Chapter 7

Two Masters

All of our self-created selves are *bought*.

This common denominator lies underneath the surface of the varied lifestyles that otherwise seem to have nothing in common and may seem completely opposite. In fact, we probably pride ourselves on our uniqueness, on the difference between who we are and the way "they" are. Part of the self-image of our erstwhile yuppie and punk, sitting disconsolately somewhere in the Kalahari, is the conviction that each is *unlike* the other. And yet to become who they are — yuppie and punk — each has used exactly the same means: financial transaction. Their identities are different, but not their means of obtaining them. Money has changed hands. Whatever we decide to be in a consumerist society, our being it is dependent upon having the necessary funds. If who we are is up for sale, then one cannot be if one cannot shop! And one cannot shop unless one has access to wealth.

Wealth is the secret beneficiary behind every transaction, the god overseeing consumerist society who is satisfied by the offering of our financial resources toward our own self-creation. I refer here not to abstract ideas — like poverty, riches, and so on — nor to actual money, but to a real spiritual agent at work in the world. When we buy something to satisfy consumerist impulses, we pay for the item — but more significantly, we pay homage to the force of wealth that is at work. Each consumerist purchase is a prayer offered up to wealth, whether intended or not. When we believe ourselves to be made new by that which we buy, we say, in effect, "You, O Wealth, you are the one who creates me. You shape me, you make me who I am. You establish me on the earth. You lift me up in the world, and set my place amongst the esteem of others." And this is serious business, because it flies in the face of one of the New Testament's most striking teachings.

The parallel that Jesus establishes in Luke is remarkable for the starkness of the choice he presents. There is simply no avoiding its either/or nature: "No servant can serve two masters. Either he will hate the one and love the other, or he will be devoted to the one and despise the other. You cannot serve both God and *mammon*" (Luke 16:13).*

Now, the English translation of *mammon* is "wealth" or "money," and this is the direction that most popular translations tend to go. The problem with doing so is that *mammon* is an Aramaic word, while the rest of Luke's gospel is written in sophisticated Greek. When Luke wrote down the teachings of Christ, he translated Jesus' words from their original Aramaic into the common Greek that was the lingua franca of the Roman Empire. So, when Luke leaves one of Jesus' words in Aramaic, it means that Christ is saying something essentially untranslatable. This is the case, for example, with "amen," which was Hebrew for "truly," but which was used so specifically that Greek speakers adopted it to close prayers. If Jesus simply meant "money/cash/assets/riches" when he said *mammon*, there are a number of Greek words that Luke could have used, but he didn't. Luke kept the Aramaic *mammon.* The connotation when Jesus talks about *mammon*, therefore, is that of a proper noun. It is not a generic concept that can be translated between different languages; no, Mammon is the name of a force in opposition to God.

Notice the contrast between this and the way Jesus talks about human government. He doesn't say in the gospels that you can't serve both God and Caesar. No, he says the opposite: we are supposed to give to Caesar what is Caesar's — in fact, the money that is due to Caesar — and we are to give God what is God's. This isn't to say that governments can't become idols for humans. The twentieth century is filled with horrific examples of this. But this doesn't have to be the case. Following Jesus doesn't entail declaring war against human government and the social order it brings.

The same does not appear to be true with Mammon. Here the word has almost a demonic connotation — at least a spiritual connotation —

---

*The same parallel appears in the Sermon on the Mount (Matthew 6:24), but the context in Matthew appears to be counsel against anxiety regarding physical well being. In Luke, the message is explicitly concerned with the consequences of devotion to the spiritual force, *mammon.*

that sets it up as an alternative to God in a way that Caesar doesn't have to be. Mammon and God are mutually exclusive masters.

For Jesus to isolate Mammon like this, and to such a degree, gives Mammon the force of a veritable super-idol. If Mammon and God cannot be served simultaneously, then Mammon must be an idol above all other things that can become idolatrous for us. For, while it would be true to say we cannot serve both God and an idol, note that "an idol" is not an independent entity. "Idol" describes something defined by our improper devotion to it. A statue is a statue; only when people start worshipping it does it become an idol. Its idol-ness comes from its devotees, rather than anything inherent to it. Like all objects, it *can* become an alternative to God. But Mammon — it is, itself, *necessarily* idolatrous.

To consider what this will mean for our Romans reading, we need to reflect on how Mammon, in Jesus' usage, connects to what we've already said about original sin: namely, that effort of human beings to take for themselves an existence that God hadn't given to them. Rejecting God's gift, they tried to claim autonomy for themselves. But — and here's where Mammon comes in — Mammon is what they got.

Mammon, as Jesus uses it here, is another name for the spiritual goal to which the original humans aspired in their first sin. The sinfulness comes from their disobedience to God. But why are they disobeying? What's the motive? They wanted to claim something that could be their own: not as a gift, because everything they had was a gift. No, they wanted something free and clear, something they could possess, hang on to, say, "I have rights toward this." In the first sin, they tried to be owners rather than the stewards that God had made them to be. *They tried to become wealthy.* They were willing to trade stewardship of all God's gifts — in which they owned nothing — for ownership of the one thing, knowledge of good and evil. And ownership depends on a concept of wealth, Mammon, to rule it. The first humans, in seeking to own themselves, gave birth to the one who would rule over them.

As we've seen, their sin was a lie. The things they claimed as possessions — as wealth — were in fact the gifts of God. Everything is a gift, even what we pretend is our property. The truth of our original existence as God intended it, where everything was a gift from God and everything was ours, can't be denied. It's still the case. The reason Jesus poses God and Mammon in such a stark contrast is because what's really at stake when choosing between them is: (1) God, and the existence that God gave us in the beginning, and to which God wants us reconciled; or (2) Mammon, who rules over and perpetuates the existence we've chosen for ourselves in the fall. The second is the existence to which human beings are committed and in which we continue to invest ourselves. That existence is the one overseen by the spiritual power of Mammon, which says: mine and not thine, thine and not mine.

This is why the illusion of selfhood offered by consumerism is so pervasive despite its fragility (i.e., the fact that consumerism so obviously lacks the capacity to give us what we want it to, but our entire culture has come to place its trust in it). *We're not believing in consumerism per se, but in the whole sinful order of the fallen world, to which we sold ourselves into bondage.* And that order is powerful, indeed.

That existence is one in which we call some of creation worthy and some of creation worthless — though God created all things good. So, when serving wealth, you know what's worth getting. You know what sort of business to run. You know what sort of things you want to acquire and have dominion over, and you know what is worthless. And the people who acquire the right sorts of things are wealthy, and the people who don't, aren't.

The Pharisees, Luke says, loved money. They loved it spiritually; they loved the system that left some people with the worthwhile things and others without. They didn't get it! The Pharisees heard "Mammon" as though Jesus was talking literally about the contents of their purses. But what they didn't realize was that love of actual money was merely a symptom of serving Mammon — that is, serving the lord of the original sin, and serving the world that we made for ourselves through it.

Mammon embodies original opposition to God and God's wishes for us. That is why Paul writes in 1 Timothy 6 that the root of all evil is the love of money. I know that many Christians reading this will say that they do love God and they don't love money. But in our culture, regardless of what we say with our mouths, the way that many of us live expresses most of all a love of money. We speak about our love of God, but we live out our love of Mammon. We live it out to the degree that it is the rare, rare Christian person or Christian community that authentically loves God over its love of money. And as long as we continue to love money, we have the root of evil in our midst, and that means everything we do is corruptible.

Chapter 8

Mammon Worship
Hits the Mall

Though the Romans thought they were wise, they were actually fools, because they exchanged the glory of the immortal God for images made to look like humans, animals, birds, and reptiles. The problem, of course, wasn't what the idol looked like but the fact that it wasn't God, and yet they worshipped it. They acted as if the idol had the power to give them their place in the world — even though it was powerless to *do* anything.

Fast-forward to contemporary times. Taking the examples given here in Romans, a modern reading might be, "They exchanged the glory of the immortal God for images made to look like [insert consumer identity here]." Like the Romans, our problem isn't which image we go for, but that we go for images at all. We may not bow down in temples to do so, but we still exchange the glory of the immortal God for images that we purchase. And, just as the spiritual reality for the Romans was that they were worshipping idols, the spiritual reality for our society is that it worships Mammon with almost everything it does.

The ancient Roman system of worship, criticized by Paul, actually makes a rather good analogy to our modern consumer economy. The Roman cycle of festivals and holy days followed the calendar, with some fixed on certain dates and others rotating with the seasons. A key part of life as a good Roman citizen was to honor these days properly. This usually meant going out in public to a particular temple or the site of a religious festival and making an offering of some value. The public nature of these offerings was crucial to the social identity they created. "Conspicuous consumption," we might call it nowadays.

Do we not have a similar calendrical cycle in modern America? Saturday offers the weekly shopping day; semi-regular sales surround fixed holidays like Valentine's Day, Mothers' Day, and so on; the seasonal aisle at the supermarket rotates with the calendar. Of course, all of the shopping days culminate in the High Holy Day of our consumerist calendar: the day after Thanksgiving, known in the retail industry as "Black Friday." This Friday, as the harbinger of Christmas gluttony, is the pivotal point of the consumer year. Toward which Friday should the Christian lifecycle be oriented? Black Friday or Good Friday? That's easy. But which Friday sees the most fervent participation from Christians and non-Christians alike?[1]

You'd be justified to ask why we ought to call consumerism worship. Sure, it's probably not good. But worship? The problem is that while consumption doesn't necessarily start out as worship, in three short steps, that's what it becomes. The first step is that in consuming, you get what you pay for. Let's not deny the fact that idolatry has its lures. Though idols might be powerless to act, the power our imaginations give to them is substantial indeed. Picture it: You're out at the mall, you pop into the gleaming new Niketown, and you remember that you need a new pair of socks. The pair on the rack in front of you contains just two ounces of cotton. The socks don't cost anything like $12 to make, and there's certainly nothing integral to them that's worth even a fraction of that. They're not structurally any different from the ten-pack of generic pairs you could get for the same price at the Wal-Mart over on Frontage Road. Both were probably made in a foreign land by workers making pennies an hour.

But you do get what you pay for. And what you pay for with these Nike socks, like no other socks in the world, is that magical swoosh. When you participate in the consumerist economy, you get a little bit of that Nike magic, that Nike lifestyle. Others see you and know who you are and what you're about — you connoisseur of sport, you — and you know the same about them. Groups of people who buy the same things can recognize one another as fellows. Thus, we succumb to the lure of belonging, of community, even when no real community exists.

The problems arise in the second step. In receiving that lifestyle, you become obligated to it. You've given some of your resources, your hard-earned money, to buy those socks and the lifestyle that comes with them. Now you have to live into it. Having spent good money on that swoosh, you're obligated to maintain the meaning you've given it.

And that's when what started out — harmlessly enough, we might add — as an effort to replace a pair of holey socks moves irreversibly toward step three: worship. Being obligated to your lifestyle, you soon become enthralled. Socks alone won't do it. But you're not going to stop at socks. You become enslaved to the reality that you've bought into. You become dependent on the swoosh to tell you who you are. If, all the sudden, you couldn't afford the swoosh, it wouldn't be any meaningless loss. You would be one who had the swoosh once, but no longer. One whose bargain-basement socks say nothing (good) about the person you wish to be. You are dependent upon retail grace.

So much of who we are is built upon our worship of wealth. It's impossible for someone whose life is fundamentally built around the cycle of acquisition and expenditure of wealth to deny that her life is subject to Mammon, because the vast majority of her day is taken up with dedication to it. The Romans couldn't spend all day at the sacrificial festival to this or that idol and then claim in the evening that they were devotees of the one Lord. Likewise, Christians and non-Christians alike cannot go about acquiring wealth so that we can consume goods that determine who we are, and then turn around and assert that that isn't what we're fundamentally about. We subject ourselves to this spiritual force.

I'm not arguing against buying and selling or commerce. The vision God gives of Eden and the new creation is one where we have enough, where we have the plenty of God's gifts. This isn't an impoverished or ascetic existence, but an abundant one. It's important to distinguish between an economic argument and a theological one. The theological point is that there are ways we behave with our money that radically transcend the simple act of living in a material world. We have to buy and sell to live in this world — no question about it. But when our spending (almost unavoidably) takes on a transcendent value, and who we are becomes about how much and what we own, that's consumerism — distinguishable from the simple consumption in which we must engage in order to live.

Looking ahead to Romans 1:25, we see that this subjection is to "exchange the truth of God for a lie." In our case, this is the lie of Mammon, of wealth: that some things are worthy and others are not. And believing this lie, and living this lie, we do ourselves actual spiritual harm, as the rest of our Romans passage shows.

Chapter 9

Hypersexuality

Therefore God gave them over in the sinful desires of their hearts to sexual impurity for the degrading of their bodies with one another. They exchanged the truth of God for a lie, and worshipped and served created things rather than the Creator — who is for ever praised. Amen. Because of this, God gave them over to shameful lusts. Even their women exchanged natural relations for unnatural ones. In the same way the men also abandoned natural relations with women and were inflamed with lust for one another. Men committed indecent acts with other men. . . .

(Romans 1:24–27a)

Romans 1:24 begins to introduce the effects of the spiritual degradation described in the preceding verses. The culture that forsook the Creator for the creation now faces the consequences of its actions. And they are profound. Minds made for the contemplation of God turn away from the divine, choosing the material instead. They imagine transcendence to be where it is not. Consequently, they are left with an understanding of reality that is completely skewed. Having rejected the transcendent, all they have left are their bodies. This results, as Paul says, in their being given over to "the sinful desires of their hearts to sexual impurity for the degrading of their bodies with one another."

If you are up to speed on the contemporary debates about same-sex partnership, marriage, ordination, and church inclusion of gay men and lesbians, you will doubtless recognize this passage straightaway. (If you are not up to speed, count yourself lucky to have somehow sidestepped the only seldom-veiled vitriol.) Romans 1:24–27 is far and away the most substantive text employed today in Christian considerations of same-sex issues, given that the Old Testament prescriptions against same-sex sexual activity are buried among other Levitical laws that no Christian follows anyway, and that the other New Testament references to male-male sexual activity are limited to single-word terms, the precise meaning of which is debatable. So opponents in the battle invariably stake out Romans 1:24–27 as a dueling ground, either claiming it for the final word on the subject or dismissing it as culturally antiquated and irrelevant.

I cede the field to the duelists and their squabble: I am completely uninterested in talking about homosexuality in this discussion. For our purposes in looking at Romans 1 and consumerism, I contend that this passage has nothing to do with homosexuality as any modern person understands the term. The passage is not relevant to Christian talk about gay men and lesbians because the same-sex sexual activity it describes is not "homosexual" in any sense that we understand the word.

While examining this passage, however, we can't and shouldn't avoid the issue of homosexuality altogether, because the reasons *why* these verses aren't actually about it shows us what they *are* about, instead. This is undeniably a text about sexuality, but it is not about homosexuality per se. Instead, in our day this passage speaks most clearly against our *hyper*sexual and increasingly fetishistic society.

We saw in the previous passages the degeneration of a people's spiritual nature. The effect of this, Paul says, is that the next aspect to fall is their passions. And it is the passions — by which Paul meant enslaving psycho-physical desires, rather than the positive joie de vivre with which we associate the term with today — that are at the heart of this passage. Having given transcendent glory to nontranscendent things, the Romans completely lost their ability to *feel* properly about material things. The longing for the divine that is inbuilt in all of us was deprived of its proper outlet and became focused instead on the creation that they substituted for the divine.

The resulting passions are unnatural, Paul says, and for many readers this is where the discussion stops: Men desiring men and women desiring women is unnatural; the Bible says it; end of story. Getting to the truth, however, depends on our reading past the meaning that we expect to find and looking instead at what the text actually says.[1] What the NIV translates as "unnatural" is the Greek *para physin*, which literally means, "over/in excess of nature."

There's no question that Paul's use of "in excess of nature" was intended as a condemnation, contrary to what some interpreters have claimed. It is clearly a bad thing to have passions that are in excess of nature. But what Paul describes here is patently not what is going on in any contemporary understanding of homosexuality as an orientation.

Forgive a gross oversimplification and imagine that the popular understanding of sexual attraction — regardless of one's position on the morality of it — is more or less analogous to an arrow that points at one gender or the other. In popular perception, the basic question of hetero versus homo is which direction the arrow points. Or, to be slightly more nuanced, some people understand sexual attraction as existing somewhere on a continuum between totally same sex and totally other sex. While allowing for the complexity of people's sexual lives, this understanding still locates people in relation to one side or the other. In both of these popular modern understandings, the important attribute is that there are basically two options (whether or not one believes both to be equally moral possibilities).

It is a truism to point out that such conceptions would have been completely foreign to Paul. For Paul, the question was not which direction one's arrow pointed; indeed, the idea that one might prefer the sexual company of one's own gender to the exclusion of the other would have struck him as incomprehensible. For Paul, the question of sexuality concerned how much passion one had. Instead of depicting human sexuality as an arrow, the best metaphor would be a cup. The cup, by nature, can hold a certain amount. Fill it with more than it can hold — in excess of the cup's nature — and it will overflow. This is precisely what Paul saw going on with Roman sexuality. Because the Romans were disoriented to God, they lost their ability to understand the natural order and thus their created limits. They were therefore filled with passions to overflowing. They brimmed over with lust. What were understood to be natural outlets for their passions — husbands for wives and wives for husbands — ceased to satisfy the hyper-natural lusts that consumed them. They needed stranger, more difficult objects in order to meet their sexual desires. And in pagan Rome, this meant seeking partners of the same sex.

Untruthful and ugly stereotypes of homosexual men and women portray them as excessively lustful. But certainly not even those who promulgate such stereotypes would argue that gay men and lesbians desire partners of the same sex *because* the opposite sex failed to satisfy some all-consuming lust. Surely, no one who is homosexual or who knows anyone who is homosexual would say that homosexuality is based on the quantity of one's sexual desire, rather than its direction. And because none of us would say such a thing, none of us can claim with integrity that what Paul is condemning in Romans 1:24–27 is the phenomenon understood by contemporary society as homosexuality.

Now, to be honest, I don't think Paul would have been open to the gay and lesbian movement. Neither, however, would Paul — as a sexual ascetic — have been very happy about the generally celebratory culture of sex that exists in contemporary churches, in which church leaders seem to be falling all over themselves to show that married Christians can have just as much bedroom fun as nonbelievers, if not more.

But Paul is even more of a stranger to our time than we are to his, and what he would or wouldn't have thought about any given contemporary topic, aside from being impossible to know, is also largely irrelevant: It isn't our speculations about opinions that Paul may or may not have held that are authoritative for the church, but those of his writings that God sovereignly maintained in holy scripture. Our task is to deal with what he wrote and what the Spirit is saying through it, to us, today. And if Romans 1:24–27 is not about homosexuality in the modern sense, what is it about? What does it have to say to us?

The contemporary analogue to the situation Paul describes is "fetishization," that is, degrees of lust that cannot be sated by "normal" practices but require extraordinary activity — fetishes — to achieve satisfaction. I use fetishization here not to describe an abnormal fixation on an object or practice, but rather in the more general sense of a hyper-abundant lust that demands exceptional stimulation.

As Romans 1 instructs, once God is replaced with an idol, one's priorities — one's whole sense of the order of the universe — become corrupted. The spiritual disorientation results in a moral disorientation, since the forsaken capacity to order right and wrong correctly is at the heart of an ability to make moral decisions. And the first indication of this moral disorientation is what we do with our bodies, especially in terms of sexual passion. We begin to see that the undue focus on the self, which is a constitutive aspect of idolatry, leads to an undue focus on self-gratification. This is the hypersexualization that Paul rightly condemns as unnatural/*para physin* in our passage.

The worst is yet to come, however. In Paul's description of the Roman situation, the foundational problem is their refusal to glorify

God or to give God thanks. Everything that follows from this action is built on everything that precedes it, and there is no improvement. So, when a hypersexualized culture indulges its lust through fetishization — which meant same-sex activity for the Romans and means something else entirely for us, as we see below — it only intensifies the hunger that it sought to sate. Contrary to Oscar Wilde's famous quote about temptation, craving can never be satisfied by its indulgence.

Given that this is the case, it seems we would need no convincing that the horizon for sexual titillation in Western culture is expanding at exponential rates. There is no concrete way to measure such a claim, and some polling evidence points toward an increasing sexual conservatism among American young people. But even if these polls are accurate, the anecdotal evidence supports the claim that such conservatism has not been reflected in public life, especially in advertising, cinema, television, and music. That which passed for outrageously sexual in the 1950s — Elvis's gyrating pelvis, for example — would not warrant notice today. If it did attract any attention, it would be an ironic observation of how silly and innocent it seems.

Our culture itself is undergoing hypersexualization and fetishization. The situation described by Giles Morris, writing in *Esquire* magazine about his personal addiction to Internet pornography, could be writ large onto our eros-infatuated society as a whole:

> [If] you've got the slightest kink, the vast amount of perversion out there on the net will bloat it out of all proportion. Prior to my love affair with the internet, I had only the most passing curiosity about S&M. A few months later I was logging onto sites about being paddled raw by a governess clad from head to toe in black rubber. Pretty soon the kick you get from the vanilla stuff wears off and you need something harder.[2]

The evidence of a hypersexual, fetishistic culture is the desensitization that makes it harder and harder to feel anything at all. Take, as anecdotal proof of where we've arrived as a culture, the Janet Jackson Super Bowl incident. The public outcry that followed Jackson's "wardrobe malfunction" was utterly telling about the nation's sexual disposition. On the one hand, there was the unsurprising liberal backlash that, caring nothing about the episode, complained about people getting worked up about public indecency instead of [insert liberal issue here] — as if the former mattered not at all, and as if people cannot be concerned about multiple issues at once.

On the other hand, we witnessed an astounding level of outrage from those whose complaint was a nanosecond of bare breast on prime time TV. It seemed this scandal had traumatized children whose purity had, until that mammary glance, been unsullied by the media-saturated society in which we live.

These seemingly opposite responses did not reveal, as it might seem, a nation divided between the liberated (or degenerate) and the righteous (or uptight), as the two sides would alternately claim. Instead, it revealed a nation so hypersexualized that it didn't bat an eye about the context of the whole episode, which was ritualized sexual violence accompanied by a sexually explicit song. The left was silently oblivious to this, and I wonder: Would there have been a peep of protest from the right about Justin Timberlake's ripping at Jackson's breast in his closing line ("I'm gonna have you nekkid by the end of this song") if her costume had stayed on?

It seems not — nobody cared about that. A choreographed sexual assault by a (white) man on a (black) woman was utterly passé. The violence and lasciviousness of the halftime show that producers had designed to titillate did not even get a nod. Instead, all we got was a public chorus of kvetching from the right about the cosmic importance of protecting the American public from a flash of nudity, followed by the drearily predictable condescension from the left.

The trenches dug on the left and right are meaningless, because what we imagine to be a battlefield is actually a courtroom, where the fact that we are fighting over such specific instances of nudity is convicting evidence that on the charge of cultural sexual degeneration, we have earned our guilty verdict. When all that remains to skirmish over is the acceptability of a few square inches of skin, we have offered total cultural surrender to hypersexuality.

It doesn't matter who wins. Either the conservatives will hang on forever and seek Pharisaic solace in the imagined righteousness of keeping women's chests, at least, from public view, or we will go the way of Europe and cease to care. These are not substantially different outcomes. The war has already been fought and won by lust. We know this because, as a group, we appear to require ever more unnatural/ *para physin* levels of stimulation to pique our interest in anything, regardless of medium.

An example that may well stand for the whole of the normalcy we occupy is Fox's *Fear Factor,* a popular show that, though nobody accuses it of setting unattainable standards of good taste, is not usually cited for moral depravity, either. Indeed, this show — in which contestants compete at a variety of tasks that are alternately disgusting or terrifying or both — occupies a happy slot for family viewing. And in that slot, it routinely offers up the unique (and uncommented on) combination of sex, humiliation, violence, and incest that represents the new frontier of what it takes to turn America on.

Description without analysis should be sufficient to illustrate the point. One particularly instructive instance was the episode of "Family Fear Factor," first aired in May 2004, in which parent-child teams competed against one another. In the episode, viewers enjoyed the "Family of Roaches" stunt, wherein a quasi-pubescent son was seated and locked in a Plexiglas box with an open top, after which several gallons of giant Madagascar hissing cockroaches were poured over him. His mother — a woman in her early thirties who, like most of Fear Factor's female contestants, wore a bikini over her swimsuit-model figure — then had to get on her knees and plunge her face into her son's lap, where the mass of cockroaches hissed and scuttled. After burying her face in the swarm and filling her mouth with insects — she was prohibited from using her hands — she ran across the room to spit the bugs out onto a set of scales. Then she returned to her son, who never stopped shouting for her to hurry, for more bugs. (She was hindered in doing so because the huge mouthfuls she took meant that most of the bugs crawled out from her lips and fell across her toned body onto the floor.) After several trips, the overflowing scale, weighted down with the saliva-coated cockroaches, released a door and revealed three sets of keys, which she delivered to her son and which he used to unlock and free himself.

Was this horrifying? Yes. Do such instances cross our vision every day, their perversion unnoticed? Most likely. Did the viewing audience have eyes to see? Maybe not. Did the mother and son realize what they were performing for the cameras? Hopefully not. Can we really pretend that "natural" sexuality — whatever it might be — is enough to satisfy the American viewing public any more?

No.

In a sexually unchained culture, audiences entertained by the likes of *Fear Factor* require increasingly excessive transgressions in order to satisfy lusts that are desensitized through overuse. When popular stimulation combines shame, violence, and sex, what hope do any of us have for moderation?

We cannot underestimate the significance of the fact that our idolatry is here linked to erotic, sexual perversion. So let's bring this back to consumerism: How does Mammon worship fit into this whole social picture? The whole, broken scenario begins with our disconnect from God. As a response, we fail to see ourselves as God-*given*, and the resulting disregard for ourselves and others is manifested by sexual fetishization. But as we will see, turning back to Romans, this is only the beginning of the profound ethical consequences caused by our Mammon worship.

Chapter 10

Every Kind of Wickedness

> . . . and received in themselves the due penalty for their perversion.
>
> (Romans 1:27b)

Though our cultural situation corresponds so naturally to Paul's Rome, with our increasingly fetishistic cultural desires, Paul's closing words in verse 27 pose an interpretive problem. We have to wonder what it might be that we would "receive in ourselves as the due penalty for our perversion."*

This is not an easy question, because the historical details that explain this rather puzzling phrase, "received in themselves the due penalty," are so alien to our own context. To understand what Paul meant, we have to understand how the Romans saw men and women. To be a man or woman was not so much something that one simply *was* in ancient Rome. It was something that one *did* with one's sexual behavior.

To be human meant existing on a sliding scale, with men (aggressive and, sexually, penetrating) on one end and women (passive and sexually penetrated) on the other. A biological male who was passive and allowed himself to be penetrated by another man could, therefore, actually *become* a woman in the eyes of others — this transformation to the "lesser sex" being the "due penalty" that was "received in [himself] . . . for [his] perversion." He would not, as some conservatives

---

*For starters, we have to reject the mostly abominable interpretations that modern commentators read into this verse, such as the theory that HIV/AIDS is the "penalty" for our day. On the one hand, we have already cut off the possibility of such a reading by showing that the sin for our day is not homosexuality, but rather hypersexuality. On the other, we should wonder about a supposed divine penalty against American homosexuality that would take such a devastating toll on African children. It is unbiblical to imagine that God would, prior to the final judgment of all creation, punish one group in particular through a plague of worldwide scope.

today view gay men, be a man who did things he shouldn't but who nevertheless remained a man. No, if passive and penetrated in Paul's Rome, a biological male could cease to be a man and become a woman.

The same was not true of men who penetrated other men, which was a normal and relatively accepted practice in Rome. Nor was it true of women. Notice that this business of "due penalty" in the Romans text applies only to men. That is because women, whose female physiology did not allow them to be penetrators, could not undergo the opposite transformation and become men by acting aggressively. Female same-sex behavior was aberrant, according to Roman protocol, but women weren't in danger of switching genders by engaging in it.

We can see that no easy analogue exists today for "received in themselves the due penalty for their perversion," given the cultural gap between the words' original context and ours today. Nevertheless, we suppose that the Spirit continues to speak to us even through alien words. So how do we make sense of this? Even though the context of gender and marriage and sexuality that this teaching originally addressed has vanished, what contours of truth reside in these words that the Spirit can quicken for us in our day?

The enduring principle in this passage might be the simple fact that what we do with our bodies has an actual effect on us. A man's sexual activity cannot turn his biological maleness into femaleness, but on a social level, it is indisputable — however much we might disagree now — that such actions made men into women in Roman eyes. Our actions do change who we are.

In a rather counterintuitive sense, this is a deeply countercultural message to consumerist ears. In a consumerist society, the myth is that we can put on and take off identities at will without any effect (for ill or good) on the mannequin underneath. If you want to be one person for a time, your doing so shouldn't inhibit your free ability to change your mind and become someone else later. Put differently, according to the rules of consumerism, no consumption now should ever stand in the way of your freedom to consume differently in the future.

But this is a myth, not the truth. Sure, you can trade consumer identities at will. But the person who buys, wears, and discards these masks is affected by them. You can't simply leave it all behind. Like a drug that stays in the nervous system, the traces of our actions remain with us. If we view our lives as an unfolding story, then we might understand this fact by the illustration that no matter who we choose to be at the moment, we are also always the person we once were. Indeed, such an understanding is central to the grand Christian narrative, in which once we were merely sinners, but now we are sinners saved by grace.

Let's look at an example pertinent to our hypersexual situation: the booming, multibillion-dollar business that is pornography. Consuming pornography, for instance, does not simply mean that one accrues moral guilt on some heavenly tally that can be wiped away with the right prayer. No, it makes one's mind more carnal, and when disseminated, it makes our cultural mind more carnal. It actually changes who one is and we are.

Applying a biblical standard to our situation would mean trying to make coherent sense of the following: (1) If certain social practices derive from the moral degradation inherent to idolatry, and (2) if one of these social practices is hyper-natural sexuality and fetishization, and (3) if participation in this social practice has an *actual* effect on our society — the due penalty we receive in ourselves for our perversion — then what is the effect, the penalty?

Simply put, the result of our current cycle of lust consuming lust is a completely eroticized society. We are damning ourselves — straight, gay, married, single, whatever — to an all-consuming carnality.

What Paul tells us here is that we have lost the necessary equipment to evaluate what is and isn't natural. That's a scary thought — that we no more have a natural ability to discern right and wrong than we do to discern UV or infrared light — because the one thing we all feel very sure about is our capacity to judge. But our judgment has been corrupted by our misunderstanding about our place in relation to the God who created us. When we made ourselves the work of our own hands and worshipped Mammon — the deification of our original sin — by bowing down to that image, we lost any claim we might have to a reliable sense of the natural order of creation. The God we turned from has given us "over to shameful lusts," where our "thinking becomes futile" and our "hearts are darkened." Our moral reason is suspect, lacking trustworthiness, because as a culture we find ourselves several steps descended from idolatry. It is as if we descended a cliff by jumping from ledge to ledge and now find that our hands lack sufficient strength to haul us back up the slope that gravity so readily helped us to descend. As members of a consumer society, we simply lack the ability to discern right from wrong, natural from unnatural, because our minds are eroticized.

Karl Barth, arguably the most influential Protestant theologian of the twentieth century, comments on the confusion described in Romans 1:26–27 in his magisterial *Epistle to the Romans.* The confusion between human and God that is inherent to idolatry generates more and more confusion, Barth writes, until

> what cannot be avoided or escaped from becomes confused with some necessity of nature, and this is in very truth a demonic caricature of the necessity of God....What is at first merely open to suspicion moves inexorably on to what is positively absurd. Everything then becomes Libido: life becomes totally erotic. When the frontier between God and man, the last inexorable barrier and obstacle, is not closed, the barrier between what is normal and what is perverse is opened.[1]

This is the situation we find ourselves in today. And small surprise that, being in it, we are ill equipped to recognize it for what it is, even though examples are riddled through our daily news. We may not have gotten worse as a species, but the consumerist excesses of the digital age have certainly honed our capacity and willingness to do more harm.

> Furthermore, since they did not think it worthwhile to retain the knowledge of God, he gave them over to a depraved mind, to do what ought not to be done. They have become filled with every kind of wickedness, evil, greed and depravity. They are full of envy, murder, strife, deceit and malice. They are gossips, slanderers, God-haters, insolent, arrogant and boastful; they invent ways of doing evil; they disobey their parents; they are senseless, faithless, heartless, ruthless. (Romans 1:28–30)

Paul concludes his invective against Roman pagans with a list of vice so far-reaching that there is very little point in examining each of the twenty-one evils he lists. Do we need distinct examples of "wickedness" and "evil" in twenty-first-century America? No. What we are meant to take from this is a classic definition of total depravity:

Not that we are all as wicked as we could possibly be (we are not), but that every part of ourselves is subject to sin. There is no bastion of righteousness naturally occurring in us that can keep us from stumbling.

As I mention above, my purpose is not to demonstrate why the world is so much worse now than it has ever been, but rather how our evil is manifest. This is important because it should never be taken for granted — especially by consumerism's critics — that the consumption characterizing our age is a self-evident evil. As James Twitchell observes, what is all that bad about having things? It's not for nothing, he says, that we call them "goods." The question is not whether Twitchell's claim about our day and age is correct (it is), but whether there is anything wrong with a situation in which such a claim is true. He says no; he is wrong.

The answer to Twitchell, I suggest, is the way in which we live out our consumerism. He is perfectly correct that there is nothing wrong with abundance, and there is certainly a lot to commend it. If the only argument that can be employed against it is a pinch-mouthed, Puritan glare, then consumers should indeed consume guiltlessly. But such is thankfully not the case. In Twitchell's otherwise clear-sighted accolade to consumer culture, he neglects to engage the fact that its fruit is a profoundly unethical life — a life that, to his credit, I think he would condemn if he took a hard look at it. Given that our consumerism is Mammon idolatry, we should see a movement paralleling the trajectory of Romans 1:18–32, leading directly into the rather wholesale sinfulness described by the chapter's final verses.

My point with the following list of examples is definitively not to fire a fusillade of bullet-point vice that will decimate any lingering hope left in the reader. There is good in our society; too bad it is not usually newsworthy. No, the point is to show how the untrammeled values of a consumerist (i.e., idolatrous) society are particularly manifest in ethical decay. But in our contemporary world, the age-old vices of lust, rage, and pride take on a particularly consumerist expression.

Privacy, Pseudonymity, Pornography

Consider a recent article in the *New York Times* commenting on the growth of mobile phones, with their increasing capacity for downloading quality color images and video, as vehicles for pornography. The reporters observe in passing that pornography has historically helped to drive the popularity of new technologies, such as VCRs, DVD players, and so on. However, they fail to draw explicit connections between this fact and their quote from Robert Entner, a market analyst, regarding the characteristics that make mobile phones optimal pornographic technology: "[The mobile phone] has every component that has proven conducive to the consumption of adult entertainment — privacy, easy access, and, on top of it, mobility."[2]

Entner's statement is, on one level, a no-brainer. What he means by "easy access" is the fact that the consumer does not have to make himself known in order to access pornography. A digital buffer stands between the act of his purchase and anyone recognizing him. The theological significance of Entner's statement is fascinating, since "privacy, easy access . . . and mobility" add up to anonymity. Digital technology offers a level of namelessness hitherto unknown by humanity.

Or — considered in a different way — because we are always physical bodies with given names, this mobile phone technology is so conducive to pornography because it offers a significant level of disconnection between our given existences and our digital actions. In this way, it is actually *pseudo*nymity: The user has a digital name, but the relationship between the name and the actual person is weak, invisible, and intangible, taking the form of service contracts and billing statements that link a flesh-and-blood individual to his identity as a mobile phone (and pornography) consumer.

Another *Times* article brings the catastrophe of this pseudonymity into clarity. In this story, *Times* reporter Kurt Eichenwald uncovers the account of Justin Berry, who, at age fourteen, began selling pornographic videos of himself over the Internet with his home computer and webcam. Justin's story is a tragic one, though ultimately redemptive. For our purposes, what is so disturbing is the article's repeated confirmation that the technology that allows such artificial construction of identity is directly connected with an explosion in pedophiles' access to child pornography.[3]

Justin's story is a story for our time precisely because of the dehumanizing effects of technology. Commentators frequently point out such effects; this is nothing new. But the discussion about technology's dehumanizing consequences often misses the point. After all, the Internet and other forms of instant communication have immense power to humanize us to each other, as well. When the Internet community instantaneously links us to victims of natural disaster halfway around the world, as it did during the tsunami of 2004, and then enables relief organization and charitable giving in hitherto unprecedented ways and scale, we do not lament technology's isolating effect. No, then we celebrate its ability to turn strangers into neighbors.

So why and how does technology dehumanize? It dehumanizes us when it allows the untrammeled exercise of those impulses that we have identified as quintessentially consumerist. It dehumanizes us when it facilitates our urges to make ourselves in an image of our choosing. Technology has always done this — that is what technology *is* — from the moment when our ancestors figured out how to strap a sharp stone to a stick and the saber-tooth's fangs became just a little less determinative of their existence. But we have reached new levels when our technology permits the construction of an entire alternate universe, like Second Life, which is layered on top of our flesh and blood and in which we can live free from real consequence.

Richtel and Marriott's article implies that child pornography is booming on the Internet because the medium has removed the critical barrier of social shame: "The distribution of child pornography in America was a smallish trade, relegated to back rooms and corners where even the proprietors of X-rated bookstores refused to loiter." This is true, but not for the reasons the authors believe. Theologically speaking, shame is significant not as a social phenomenon affecting individuals' actions, but as the internal realization of an external moral reality that presses in on our immoral lives. When shame is taken from us, we live in a make-believe world of dreamy nightmare.

In the case of child porn, technology's elimination of shame means that, because there is no pressing reminder that their desires are wrong, consumers can inhabit a world where they are free to make themselves along the lines of their desires. As the article reports of previously isolated pedophiles, "The Internet has created a virtual community where they can readily communicate and reinforce their feelings. . . . Indeed, the messages they send among themselves provide not only self-justification, but also often blame minors with Webcam sites for offering temptation." These pedophiles have made a world so isolated from the real that it completely inverts the truth.

"That's my heart. In the game."

The possibilities of such an inversion — where the digital becomes the real — are not going unnoticed. Neither, however, do all find them to be unwelcome. In particular, the American military is seizing the opportunity created by a generation of young men who have grown up playing war in the hyper-reality of video games. In today's play-time scenarios, combatants make war in increasingly realistic virtual environments, using weapons that are the spitting image of real soldiers' tools. When they shoot enemies, their opponents die bloody deaths with all the digital realism at the game programmers' considerable disposal. In a remarkable investigation by *Washington Post* reporter Jose Antonio Vargas, the head of the technology division at the Marine training ground at Quantico is quoted as remarking that the consequence of such play is that today's young soldiers "probably feel less inhibited, down in their primal level, pointing their weapons at somebody," which "provides a better foundation for us to work with."[4]

We should pause to acknowledge that the murderous impulses of our humanity have always taken form in the games we play. In the last twenty years, however, they have leaped across the threshold of digital reality and sprinted forward without a backward glance. Gone are the days of playground cops and robbers in which an index finger and a cocked thumb made for a Colt .45, and one's adversary had to *agree* — often after much shrill argument — that one had indeed managed to shoot him with one's imaginary, bloodless bullet. However unsavory such games may seem to some, consider that for the entirety of human history — until now — the consequences of pretend violence were constrained to the invisible territory of the imagination.

The same is not true today, where the violence in the mind is enacted on the television screen. As a result, when boys weaned on violent video games grow into soldiers at war, there seems to be a shocking inability to distinguish between the real and the pixilated. One young veteran, an avid gamer, recounts his first combat situation to the *Post's* Vargas:

> You just try to block it out, see what you need to do, fire what you need to fire. Think to yourself, this is a game, just do it, just do it . . . of course, it's not a game. The feel of the actual weapon was more of an adrenaline rush than the feel of the controller. But you're practically doing the same thing: trying to kill the other

person. The goal is the same. That's the similarity. The goal is
to survive.[5]

There are similarities and differences between real and virtual combat. But the startling fact is that the soldier locates the difference in
the *greater adrenalin rush* offered by a real gun over a video game con-
troller. In contrast, the soldier finds the goals of games and war similar:
to "kill the other person" and "to survive."

Shockingly, the place in which there is an absolute, categorical difference between the digital antics on the one hand, and flesh-and-blood
fighting on the other — one deals with mortality, the other does not —
is precisely the area in which the young veteran failed to distinguish
between his video game and soldiering activities. There is no "continue" feature for the opponents he shot in the war; there would have
been none for him if he had been killed. Despite this, he describes
what he was asked to do in Iraq as "practically . . . the same thing" as
the "shooter" games he plays for fun with his friends while gathered
around the television and game console (and, indeed, that he played
even while off duty in Iraq).

How this relates to consumerism, of course, is in the comfort level
that young soldiers (who are also young shoppers) have while occupying an unreal reality. Vargas quotes author Evan Wright, who spent
time with the Marine First Recon Battalion in Iraq, as saying that many
of the young soldiers were "on more intimate terms with the culture
of video games, reality TV shows and Internet porn than with their
own families."[6] Their experiences in the game world have left them
fundamentally dislocated from the real world. It is not that reality is
their foundation and the make-believe world of TV/games/Web a place
that they visit. No, what has emerged is a layered existence that blends
reality and hyper-reality.

A man who makes himself a killer in the digital world over which
he is a demigod is far more capable, ethically speaking, of bringing the
violence of war-based video games like "Halo" or "SOCOM" into the
land where bodies are actually broken and blood is actually shed. This
is not to say that the two worlds are equal. As author Wright reports,
"a lot of them discovered levels of innocence that they probably didn't
think they had." When they were faced with the flesh-and-blood results
of their actions, Wright "saw guys break down. The violence in games
hadn't prepared them for this." While it is a relief to know that the

real world can (and should) trump the digital one, as evidenced by the capacity for human regret shown by the soldiers, such remorse may be a Pyrrhic victory. For each who is saved, another may be lost entirely.

Consider the alarming double significance of one returned veteran's words as he was interviewed by Vargas while playing the first-person shooter "SOCOM 3: US Navy Seals" in his bedroom. In the game, which is lauded for the realism of its action, the on-screen soldier's heartbeat is audible while the character is preparing to get a "steady shot." "Can you hear the heartbeat?" the veteran asked Vargas. "That's my heart. In the game." If given the chance, the soldier would certainly protest that he knows — indeed, that there *is* — a difference between his real-life and digital heart. But his account of his own battlefield actions, corroborated by the independent stories of his brothers-in-arms and fellow gamers, tells a different story: It tells of two worlds with porous and poorly guarded borders, where the ease of on-screen killing offers a smooth transition into killing others easily.

Some within the military, especially those charged with training young soldiers, see the potential in this generation of homegrown soldiers. Take the comment of retired Marine Col. Gary W. Anderson, former chief of staff of the Marine Corps Warfighting Lab: "Remember the days of the old Sparta, when everything they did was toward war? In many ways, the soldiers of this video game generation have replicated that, and that's something to think about."[7]

But *what* are we to think? The modern military must perform the unenviable, though arguably necessary (from a worldly point of view), task of turning civilians into men and women ready, willing, and able to kill. I am not going to engage the morality of war here. Regardless of our point of view on war, however, should not all of us be alarmed to live in a culture that is making drill sergeants' jobs easier?

Murder Most Casual

The problem, of course, is that not every American boy (and, less frequently, girl) in the "video game generation" will join the military and go to war, where fatalities on the other side are, after all, rather the point. To extend Col. Anderson's metaphor, we may be growing a new generation of Spartans, but only a small percentage of them are being shipped overseas to kill the neo-Athenians. The vast majority of those who "feel less inhibited" at "a primal level" about pointing a gun at someone and firing are remaining here at home, in a country with more guns than adults. And a lack of inhibition against killing another person becomes especially alarming when it meets the hopelessness that is endemic to the poor in consumerist societies.

In the first chapter, we touched briefly on the effects that consumerism has on the poor. In a world where one's reality must be purchased, those without money are condemned to be nothing. Those who cannot buy a lifestyle have but one default option, and that is to take it — often violently.

An indicator of the situation is the sharp rise in the past half decade of "flash-point" killings: homicides, usually committed by youth or young adults living in poverty, which result from seemingly inconsequential arguments. A *Washington Post* article on the rise of flash-point murders in the Washington, D.C., area — which, in 2005, for the first time exceeded murders over drugs — offers a litany of tragically banal homicides. We read of deaths resulting from rage over a too-casual dismissal; an unwanted attempt to shake hands; a request for more polite behavior; a foul in a game of pick-up basketball; an argument over a dog, over laundry soap.[8]

The *Post* article says that those intimately acquainted with such crimes' perpetration, investigation, and prosecution all cite the "toxic combination" of gun proliferation, a culture that "celebrates violence," and "a pathological need on the part of some young men for respect."[9] The last is foremost in importance: the hair-trigger fury in a generation of poor men and women that arises over perceived disrespect.

For those with eyes to see, this concern with respect and the rise in such murders should not be surprising. Indeed, in a generation that came of age in the brand-named, post-Marlboro Friday era, the respect of others is all you've got — is all you *are* — if you don't have the money to buy a lifestyle.

Consider the characteristics of the very particular social situation occupied by the American poor today. First, the overriding message of popular culture, to which the poor are not immune, is that to be somebody is to buy something — services, goods, and so on. Second, since in theory anyone can buy, there is a particular desperation to contemporary poverty that would not have existed in the era of serf, peasant, or slave, when one's "somebodyness" was understood as resulting from unchangeable factors outside one's control, such as social class or birth status. In those days, one's status was a given; today, nothing is. Third, despite the hopefulness created by the first two characteristics, the very poor live in a reality from which they know escape is virtually impossible. They are thus impotently responsible for being nobodies in an age of somebodies. Is it any wonder that people who grow up in such a situation, who realize that the world will never recognize them in any other way, have developed a "pathological" demand for respect in the most minor arenas of life?*

This poverty of selfhood answers the disbelieving, heart-wrenching question asked by the parent of a flash-point murder victim — "You kill someone for nothing?" Yes, life is that cheap, life is that worthless, life is indeed nothing. Because the murderer's life is, theologically speaking, nothing to him, how could we expect that the life of another would matter? The idolatrous lie of consumerism, that we are ourselves to make, is bad enough when it is told to one who has the resources at least to try. But when it is told to those who have nothing, their only recourse is to become thieves, claiming respect, recognition, and selfhood itself at gunpoint.

"The only thing you have when you're involved in that lifestyle is respect," said DeJuan Conaway, who reformed himself after a year in jail for attempted murder (he hadn't liked the way someone had looked at him on the basketball court). "If you don't have respect, people will try to rob you. Your friends are watching you. They'll say, 'You let that guy disrespect you?' Then your friends," seeing that you allow yourself to be disrespected, "might disrespect you. Or if you're with a female, she may not want anything to do with you."[10]

The robbery Conaway refers to is as symbolic as it is material. Yes, he may have meant people stealing money or possessions, but what he proceeds to describe is a theft of self. Let yourself be disrespected, Conaway says, and your friends might take your respect. Your girlfriend might leave you. In a consumerist society, you are what you have; when you *have* nothing without respect, you *are* nothing without respect. It is no small wonder, then, that the person disrespecting you is nothing to you, or that it is nothing, in such a situation, to kill him in your rage. Paradoxically, the murderer benefits. In the act of killing, a murderer can gain the full attention that the law, at least, is willing to give to a life otherwise unrecognized, unremarkable, and undistinguished.

---

*I am not seeking to justify flash-point murders on the basis of their social-theological situation but seeking to explain them. Understanding and absolution need not go hand in hand.

Chapter 11

Our Better Judgment

> Although they know God's righteous decree that those who do such things deserve death, they not only continue to do these very things but also approve of those who practice them.
>
> (Romans 1:32)

We are all ethically compromised by our culture's consumerism. Some of us have sufficient material resources to pay and thus play the prolonged, idolatrous game. But no one is shielded from the consequences of his or her actions. The poor face physical death, and the poor and rich alike are trailed by the spiritual death that comes with the imagination that we are our own creations.

Interestingly enough, despite the evidence that stalks us through the pages of our daily newspaper, we don't seem to believe that *we* are actually consumeristic. Twitchell points out that, despite our living in the country with the highest per capita consumer debt and the greatest number of mass-produced goods, "in repeated Gallup polls, when respondents are asked to choose what is really important [in life] . . . 'having nice things' comes in dead *last*."[1] Never mind our spending such a considerable portion of our time, money, and effort in the effort to acquire them. We think our priorities are straight: no surprise that we don't recognize the ethical consequences of their distortion as such when we see them.

"They know God's righteous decree that those who do such things deserve death," Paul wrote, and he was on to something here. No matter what we say, we do know that there's something wrong with the situation. What emerges from this collision — our suppressed sense of wrongness crashing headlong into our conviction that we're not so bad — is the widespread belief that our consumerism is an affliction, not a sin.

72

Consumerism results from those wicked marketers, we think, those Madison Avenue men who make us want what we shouldn't, and wouldn't want at all, were it not for their nefarious influence. Twitchell again: "Today everything is oppression and we are all victims. . . . Left alone, we would never desire things (ugh!). They have made us materialistic. But for them we would be spiritual."[2] When our consumerism manifests itself, we imagine ourselves to be its victims. Hence, the Gallup responders — sitting in suburban family homes twice the size of a typical family home fifty years ago but nevertheless so cluttered that the three-car garage is used for storage instead of cars — can say with all deluded earnestness that nice things aren't that important to them.

This is a load of malarkey. If we are going to make the world, and ourselves, in our own image, we should at least have the courage to own up to the project. (That we do not, however, is unsurprising. What is an idol, after all, but the projection of our own agency onto an external symbol?) As Twitchell writes, "We have not been led into this world . . . against our better judgment. For many of us, especially when young, consumerism *is* our better judgment."[3] Consumption is not "*doing* something to us that we are not covertly responsible for. We are not victims" of it.[4]

We should be grateful for scholars like Twitchell, who can point out the (commendable) democratizing impulse at work in a global economy. But Professor Twitchell is more correct than he knows, since the judgment of his analysis — namely, that consumerism is our better judgment — extends also to the evils of consumerism, such as those listed above, which he does not engage.

We cannot project our consumerism, and the sin that emerges from it, onto any external source. Mammon may own us, but we brokered the sale, closed the deal. We have brought the situation on ourselves. And so we stand in solidarity with the ancient Roman audience of Paul in this final, terrible way: "They not only continue to do these very things but also approve of those who practice them."

We know that our deeds deserve death. Admit it. We know this because we cannot read of an explosion in child pornography, ready-made warriors, and flash-point urban killers without realizing that these things — which are just examples, three grains of sand on a beach — deserve condemnation. And yet, reading these examples, do we realize that no one of us is respectable enough to be holier-than-thou? By our actions, we are each *thou* to each other, consuming and complicit in thousands of little ways. Wealth does not buy innocence from the sins of consumer society, only the illusion of it. We are each and all culpable together.

Just like the Romans.

Part III

CHURCH

Romans 2:1–29

Chapter 12

Sins of the Body

> Therefore you have no excuse, whoever you are, when you judge others; for in passing judgment on another you condemn yourself, because you, the judge, are doing the very same things. You say, "We know that God's judgment on those who do such things is in accordance with truth." Do you imagine, whoever you are, that when you judge those who do such things and yet do them yourself, you will escape the judgment of God? Or do you despise the riches of his kindness and forbearance and patience? Do you not realize that God's kindness is meant to lead you to repentance? But by your hard and impenitent heart you are storing up wrath for yourself on the day of wrath, when God's righteous judgment will be revealed. (Romans 2:1–5, NRSV)

If there is anyone, ancient or modern, who makes it through Romans 1 with conscience intact, chapter 2 quickly disabuses him or her of any claims to innocence. In fact, the blistering scathe of 1:18–32 becomes all the more intense when we realize that Paul is in fact just getting warmed up. As bad as Roman pop culture was, far worse was the moral and spiritual hypocrisy of those who imagined themselves as above or outside it (Gentile elites and Roman Jews in 2:1–16 and 2:17–29, respectively). It is these hypocrites to whom he turns in 2:1–3:4.

In 2:1, Paul moves from speaking in the third person ("they") to the second ("you") and addresses an imaginary opponent or interlocutor: "Therefore you have no excuse, whoever you are, when you judge others...." This hypothetical opponent has heard the condemnation of 1:18–32 and come away feeling self-righteous about the misdeeds of those "others." He or she seems to agree with Paul in the substance of the attack thus far, and concurs about the general wickedness of society, as this person is one who "pass[es] judgment on someone else."

This imaginary listener whom Paul addresses is often referred to by biblical interpreters as "the judge," due to his or her judgmentalism.

The ethnic identity of the judge is up for debate. Many contemporary scholars read 2:1 in light of 2:17 and read the judge as the morally superior — though finally hypocritical — Roman Jew, who would have condemned the excesses of Gentile society. However, for our reading, we will follow the convincing conclusion of the substantial minority of interpreters, both ancient and modern, who have understood the judge in a far more general sense: likely a moralizing Gentile who considered him- or herself better than the elements of Roman society described in 1:18–32. In this reading, Paul speaks of the depraved Roman Gentiles in chapter 1 (members of whom are not among the congregation to which he writes), turns to Gentile moralists in chapter 2, and then concludes his attack on religious identity politics by criticizing the Roman Jews in 2:17 and following.*

Following this reading, imagine the scene on the day Paul's letter arrived in Rome. At this point in history, "Christianity" barely exists, and Gentile and Jewish followers of Jesus Christ are trying to figure out their connection to historical Judaism. Their congregations are comprised of Jews and Gentiles alike, with a considerable amount of tension between the two groups. Perhaps the congregations are even segregated along Jew-Gentile lines. But as the letter is read aloud, every head is nodding at the description of the wickedness of pagan culture in 1:18–32. The entire assembly can feel a bit good about itself by comparison to *those people,* at least!

Then, as Paul turns to the imaginary judge — "you have no excuse, you who pass judgment on someone else . . . because you do the same things" — he catches out those Gentile elements in the group. Were they perhaps relying on the vestiges of some other moral code? Of the Stoicism or other philosophy that they had practiced prior to encountering the gospel? Had they brought assumptions about philosophical righteousness into their Christian lives? They are snared in their own self-satisfaction, they and those Gentile moralists they know. Their complicity — or even active participation — in the very misdeeds that they judge has undermined them.

---

*For readers interested in the textual merits of this move, I have posted a defense on my Web site, www.glassdarkly.net.

Then, just as the faces of the Gentiles have begun to fall in recognition of what is being said and the Jews of the congregation begin relaxing into their seats — this Paul, after all, is a Jew like them, a Pharisee by training! — Paul switches to the hypocrisy of the Roman Jew's smugness in verse 17. Perhaps the sins of the Gentiles are not theirs to claim, but neither is the righteousness of perfect observance. As the letter proceeds, Paul's repeated claim of God's impartiality is reflected in the downcast visages of those who have trusted in human distinctions. It is also there in the spark of radical hope — perhaps just a glimmer in their eyes — that this impartial God has freely offered a righteousness that is for all.

In this historically informed (though minority) interpretation, we read Romans as more than a simple opposition of gospel versus Judaism. Instead, Paul is understood to make a much more all-encompassing "triangular comparison" of gospel versus Judaism *and* gospel versus Gentile moralism.* If 1:18–32 painted a complete picture of Gentile morality, then why would Paul acknowledge in 2:14 the possibility of Gentiles doing "by nature things required by the law"? No, 1:18–32 must be only a partial description, accounting for the dark side of Gentile culture, which is complemented by the potent force of Gentile moral philosophy. Such a reading, which acknowledges the (finally inadequate) striving for righteousness that some Gentiles practiced, is consonant with Paul's message of the insufficiency of both Jew and Gentile identities, and leads to the gospel claim of justification through the faith that is alien and God-given to Jew and Gentile alike.

You Are Doing the Same Things

Reading Romans this way, we must reject a simplistic outlook that would lead us to pretend that all of secular society cares nothing for righteousness. We cannot reasonably dismiss the non-Christian world, whole cloth, as a hotbed of wickedness. Only when we recognize the authentic secular concern for morality can we also argue for its final inadequacy in terms of personal virtue and social redemption. The secular quest for righteousness is genuine in desire but deficient in potency, that is, the mere hope for an ethical, humanist world lacks the

---

*I am grateful to Diana Swancutt, associate professor of New Testament at Yale Divinity School, for this point.

power to overcome the human depravity that will always undermine the goal. Because we are who we are, such secular quests will always result in the hypocrisy described by Paul in 2:1–4, with those who set themselves up as judges becoming complicit in the same vices they condemn.

This phenomenon of hypocritical judgment is certainly happening in our time and place, though it is not necessarily apparent from a surface view of culture. Take, for example, the litany of particularly consumerist sins explored in the last chapter: the explosion of pornography online, including child molestation; virtual realities and the consequent devaluing of human life; murder over seeming trifles. Yet, like the Gentile moralist of Paul's day, most readers would not see themselves in this account. "I'm no pedophile," each of us would understandably exclaim. "I'm no pornographer, no murderer!"

The same deniability was doubtlessly on the lips of Paul's Gentile audience, as well. After all, what are the odds that even one of Paul's hearers would have lived up to the hyperbolic description of idolatry and wickedness that he offers in 1:28–32? When Christians work themselves into rabid fits over the depravity of humankind, non-Christians walk away, shaking their heads at a description of reality that fails to recognize the complexity of their own lived experience. The Romans knew then, as we know today, that, as John Stott inimitably puts it, "not all human beings are crooks, blackguards, thieves, adulterers, and murderers."[1] And yet too often I hear willfully ignorant Christian denunciations of "the secular world" — I trust that many readers will have similar experiences — as if secularity and "the world" were simple concepts, or as if every non-Christian practiced rampant and unmitigated wickedness. The truth of the matter is much more complex, and we do nobody any favors by simplifying it. There are those — religious and not — who hold high moral standards.

What interests us, then, is the way in which Romans 2:1–4 denies the credibility of any secular claims of innocence regarding consumerism's sins — and we must remember that when we speak of consumerism in this way, we are speaking not simply of a cultural trend, but of a theological reality, the culture-defining idolatry that traps everyone who lives in it, to a greater or lesser extent. Though there are any number of twenty-first-century "judges," the finger falls upon us all as readily as it did upon the Gentile moralists of Paul's day: "You, therefore, have no excuse, you who pass judgment on someone else, for at whatever point you judge the other, you are condemning yourself, because you who pass judgment do the same things."

But we have already seen that Paul's words cannot be simplistically applied to our current context. Most people are neither pedophiles nor murderers. And yet the concept of shared culture — that is, of being part of the same group — with which Paul is working makes the claim that, as the moralist Gentiles did "the same things" as the depraved Gentiles, so the moralist Americans of our day do "the same things" as those depraved Americans (the "criminals") whom we condemn. So what can "the same things" possibly mean, if not the most specific misdeeds of the culture?

For our understanding of "same things," we need to look to the common social project that we are all engaged in, judged and judges alike, namely, the idolatry of consumerism. This is true from the stratospherically wealthy down to the desperately poor, for whom consumerism is little more than a hope to which they might aspire. By this I mean that to live in American society in the twenty-first century means that one must understand oneself as a fundamentally commercial being, no matter whether one likes this fact or not. This is manifest in varying degrees, of course. Shrilly hyperbolic denunciation does no more good here than it would have done in Rome. Nevertheless, while consumerism is an ideology in which some participate more vigorously than others, it is also unavoidably the very context in which all of us — even its opponents — understand our existence. And by our participation in it, we "do the same things."

To demonstrate this with some concrete — though hypothetical and admittedly overdrawn — examples, consider four people occupying four very different stations in life: the millionaire venture capitalist whose daredevil edge lies in his new cigarette racing boat; the middle-class manager who buys at Macy's but aspires to Nordstrom's; the laborer bragging to her friends about her new flat screen plasma TV (bought on credit); and the young thug who kills for a verbal slight. The determinative difference between them is fundamentally one of resources. They have different amounts of money, and thus freedom and agency, to create and express themselves. But they are each fundamentally engaged in the same consumerist project. Each is a consumer. Each, in actions that seem so outwardly different from one another, craves resources to acquire status, lifestyle, *self*.

"Wait just a minute!" you may justifiably protest. "It's all well and good to name four distinctly commercial identities and label them as consumerist. But that's not how my life looks. I don't shop that much, I don't really care about brands. I'm fairly content with where and who I am. So you can't lump me in with those people who are so explicitly consumerist."

I am sympathetic with this protest; I'm inclined to make it about myself. But in the protest itself, the hypocrisy of the judgment is exposed. We are not talking so much about consumerist deeds as we are talking about consumerist existence. And for those of us living in contemporary America, there is no more chance of our opting out of consumerism than there was the possibility for a Roman Gentile in Paul's day to opt out of pagan society. It is the very fabric of our daily lives.

To understand fully our captivity to consumerism, contrast your family's life with that of a hypothetical American household from a hundred years ago. In that nonconsumerist society, the labor of most people would have been dedicated to the production of food, clothing, and shelter. Today, however, we labor to acquire the money that will let us buy those goods from someone else. We have shifted from a society of production to a society of consumption.

There's nothing necessarily wrong with this move. It has resulted in a quality of life and material comfort, accessible today even to the lower classes, which would have been unimaginable for kings in earlier times. But in this system, where the financial resources of most people exceed (to varying degrees) the baseline necessary to maintain their lives, we must do something with the surplus capital. And the disposal of that resource is the exercise of determining our identity through consumption. We consume in order to live — well and good. But the considerable amount we consume beyond that establishes our place in society, our identity, our very beings. And, as described in Part II, this project of consuming identity is the start of Mammon idolatry. We are not all equal adherents to the cult of Mammon. It has its share of zealots as well as those nominal members who attend the church of Mammon, so to speak, only at Christmas and special holidays! But we are all in the same net.

The above description undoubtedly feels claustrophobic to anyone who hopes that there is still some patch of noncommercial, nonconsumerist ground left on which to stand. And yet consumerism, like the tar baby of fable, only traps us the more securely for all we punch and kick at it. This depressing truth becomes most apparent when we consider the actions of those who, for good or ill, have made anti-consumerism their lives. Of particular poignancy are the culture jammers — anti-corporate activists who subvert advertising — interviewed by Naomi Klein in her book, *No Logo*. Klein's depiction of their efforts begins approvingly and hopefully; by the end of the book, however, both Klein and her interviewees evince a dawning, horrified recognition that even anti-marketing rhetoric can and will be marketed. As Klein writes, "It turns out that culture jamming — with its combination of hip-hop attitude, punk anti-authoritarianism and a well of visual gimmicks — has great sales potential."[2]

Examples of resulting activist despair abound. The (in)famous consumer advocate Ralph Nader, for example, was approached by the super-hip ad agency Wieden & Kennedy, which offered him $25,000 to appear in a Nike ad. He was to hold a pair of shoes and say, "Another shameless attempt by Nike to sell shoes."[3]

Klein, who writes of Wieden & Kennedy's exploits with a sort of awed gall at their sheer chutzpah, reports that they have made a business out of "hunting down and reselling the edge" to market anti-corporate anger as *a brand identity itself.* "Masters at pitting the individual against various incarnations of mass-market bogeymen, Wieden & Kennedy sold cars to people who hated car ads, shoes to people who loathed image . . . and, most of all, ads to people who were 'not a target market.' "[4]

We live in a society where anti-consumerism has itself become a consumable product that defines (even in part) a target demographic. People whose entire lives consist of conscious resistance to the consumerist system are finding their experiences packaged, marketed, and sold back to them as a commodified anti-consumerist identity. So how can the rest of us expect that we've somehow escaped being hemmed in by the same forces? Regardless of whether we carry out the humdrum of our day-in-day-out in conscious recognition of its consumerist foundation, we have to conclude that the space of our very existence is commercialized.

This is demonstrably the case because there is simply no way to fight back. Slogans of resistance like "dolphin-safe," "certified organic," "recycled," and even *No Logo* have become logos that define a particular type of liberal, socially conscious and concerned consumer.[5] For the activists, it has become increasingly evident that there is nothing they have, no pure essence, that cannot and will not be claimed by the system they oppose. The quintessential example of this truth is demonstrated in the little-known history of the bubbly manifesto, "I shop, therefore I am." This slogan is evident on countless suburban auto bumpers, T-shirts, and — most recently — on shopping bags as the theme of an ad campaign from a British department store, Selfridge's. What has become a declaration of gleeful peroxide spunkiness, however, was first adapted from Descartes' famous aphorism by artist Barbara Kruger (see her 1987 screen print *Untitled*), whose work tried to attack the excesses of consumerism. In less than twenty years, the system that Kruger assailed has demonstrated once again that it is the best judo practitioner in the world. It will take any force directed against it — even Kruger's excoriating slogan — and turn it to its own advantage.

Even if one were to try to produce, rather than consume — say, by growing a majority of one's own food, or by weaving and sewing cloth for one's own clothes — these actions would be extraordinary *because* they represent such a dramatic stand against the consumerist status quo. Hardly anybody takes such a stand, but those who do wind up dedicating a massive amount of personal resources toward establishing themselves in opposition to consumerism. That is, the handful of rebels who do manage to opt out are the exception who prove the rule of consumerism. Consumerism is not an option for our lives, it is the given.

With this rather grim fact, we return to our Romans text with the realization that in our day, the "same things" done by both judge and judged are the actions, conscious and unconscious, that constitute an existence in which we understand ourselves in light of what and how we consume.

The fullest implications of this are incomprehensible unless we can think outside our modern, individualist presuppositions. For Paul and the Romans, the culpability and complicity of the group underlie each individual's life. Even the righteous Roman was still a Roman, and her Christian righteousness did not totally remove her from the misdeeds of the pagan culture in which she lived. The consumerism and individualism — the two go hand in hand — of our own age, however, lead us to balk, outraged, at the very notion that we could be some-how accountable for sins of our culture that we have not perpetuated ourselves.

Our politically polarized society is a symptom of this condition. Take, as an example, the anti-Bush bumper stickers that proclaimed, "He's not MY president!" Presumably, the rationale for this disclaimer is that the drivers of those cars had cast their vote for another candidate, and thus did not wish for President Bush to represent them.

Irrespective of one's politics, however, such a proclamation is pat-ently false. Are you an American citizen? Then the president is *your* president. It doesn't matter whether you like him or voted for him — the president, unlike all the other choices we make as consumers, is not guaranteed to please or reinforce our sense of self.

What we are seeing in this voter rage is the essence of consumerist frustration, namely, the refusal to cede any portion of one's identity to a commodity that doesn't reflect one's personal choice. The sheer disbelieving outrage of Democrats' bumper stickers demonstrates the pervasiveness of consumerist ideals. In their conception, President Bush is an alien invader, an imposition on their Americanness that they didn't ask for and therefore won't accept. "Don't blame me," an-other bumper sticker reads, "I voted for the other guy!" The underlying conviction here is that it is the *substance* of one's vote that matters, rather than the *shared activity* of voting that is the singularly uniting responsibility of all Americans.

(Furthermore, because voting always entails the risk of loss in a way that transaction/consumption does not, it is actually an action of resistance in a consumerist society. Though there is a relationship be-tween political and commercial identities, they are not the same, and the ideal of the common good — as opposed to that of the individual — is certainly more natural to politics than it is to commerce.)

But the entire biblical canon paints a picture of communal respon-sibility that flatly contradicts our understanding of a purely individual responsibility. The Bible tells us that we can share in the punishment for actions that we have not personally willed. Christ himself refers to a "wicked and adulterous generation" (Matthew 12:39ff.), referring to the degradation of a people living in a certain period of time, and contrasts it with "the people of Nineveh," who repented at Jonah's prophecy. Even more strikingly, he denounces entire cities for failing to repent *as a body* (cf. Matthew 11:20ff.). And innocents — from Noah's generation, to Exodus-era Canaan, to exilic Israel, to the Bethlehem of Jesus' birth — have consistently paid the price for deeds in which they had no hand.

This is not to say that individuals are unimportant; to the contrary, they are critical. On the one hand, they can be lifted "like brands from the blaze," as in the cases of Noah and Lot. On the other, the righteousness of a few can postpone judgment over the many, as demonstrated through Abraham's remarkable argument with God in Genesis 18; the preservative principle of a faithful remnant is then seen again and again throughout salvation history. But the individualism endemic to a consumerist economy has led us to dismiss the communal and to imagine sin and guilt as a purely individual phenomenon. And this is an entirely artificial resolution to the dynamic tension between individual and group guilt that is maintained in the Bible.

Among the numerous ills that accompany consumerism, therefore, one of the most noteworthy is the wholly inadequate understanding of sin — especially in terms of its scope — that attends it. It is this individualistic understanding of sin that leads us to misunderstand the message in these first chapters of Romans, especially as regards the complicity of the judge. The doers of the "same things" are not, themselves, all pedophiles and murderers and explicit idolaters. Nevertheless, the Bible names us hypocritical judges who "do the same things," simply because we live so enthusiastically in the same culture that gives rise to such evils.

I should point out here that the takeaway message from a realization of community guilt ought to be its inevitability rather than any mentality of cultural secessionism or ghettoization. We should not now be filling propane tanks and readying the canned goods for a flight to the hills. Every human group, no matter its religious makeup, is a society in the world, and if Paul were speaking to us today, he would doubtless be emphatic about the inability of any group to live in a way generative of righteousness. The righteousness worthy of God, Romans claims, is not the province of any human — whether Jew, Gentile, or Christian. So, the appropriate response to the communal guilt we bear should *not* be to wage a culture war that will beat society into righteousness — a currently popular project that we will discuss further — but, rather, to live in the midst of it as a witness to alien righteousness.

The point, brothers and sisters, is that no matter how inoffensive we imagine ourselves personally to be, this inoffensiveness is not the righteousness of God. We get up to sin in the morning, we go about sin during our days, and we lie down on a bed of sin at night. We sin without consciously willing to do so, or by consciously willing not to do what we ought, because the architecture of our lives is built over and out of iniquity.

The theologian Karl Rahner succinctly illustrated this point by describing the seemingly innocuous act of buying a banana. How did the fruit get to your grocery store? How was it shipped? Farmed? Were the workers responsible for its journey from tree to table treated fairly and in a way honoring to God? Was the harvest of the land for the good of many? Do you have an assurance that the fruit in your shopping cart has not caused grief and human suffering at any stage? Of course not.

And if this is true of something as small as a piece of fruit, think about the unavoidable, iniquity-saturated infrastructure in which we live our lives. If this age, under the heavy hand of the "prince of this world," were not so bent toward wickedness, then why would it be so difficult to live a righteous life? *The pervasiveness of evil means that our own merits can never attain to the righteousness that is pleasing to God.* There is blood on all our hands. But our consumerist's understanding of sin, limited as it is to the petty misdeeds with which most of us fill the unhappy banality of our lives, is wholly inadequate to the task of understanding the world in which we live.

If we jump ahead in Romans to Paul's citation of Psalm 14 — "there is no one righteous, not even one" — we will understand it far better by going beyond the oft-quoted sound bite of the first verse and reading that "they have *together* become worthless" (Romans 3:10–12). "All have sinned and fall short of the glory of God" — *all*, not *each*. The point is not that each one of us is the worst sinner in the world (which one will often hear in conversion testimonies), since we are patently not, any more than most of us are above average in physical attractiveness! The point is, rather, that we have collectively gone astray to the point that there are no exceptions. Neither Jews nor Gentiles as groups, nor any individuals within them, can pretend to righteousness.

This is why the grace of God is so remarkable! Grace is not merely that God would forgive and be reconciled to some individual who, aside from an occasional cross word to her neighbor, never harms a living soul. No, grace is that God would forgive and be reconciled to a *people* — *Homo sapiens* — who, conscious deeds notwithstanding, live their days in and days out in societies so steeped in wickedness and suffering that to live is to sin.

In the course of writing this book, I've had numerous random encounters with people in which it somehow emerges that I'm working on a manuscript. When pressed, I talk about the project a bit, describing it as a reflection on consumerism and its effect on the American church. I've been struck by the nearly universal reaction of satisfaction that I get in response to this description. Oh, the church needs that, people will say. Isn't it awful? Christians are so materialistic these days.

At first, I found such responses gratifying. These people clearly shared my sentiments; maybe there would be an audience for this thing, after all. But I've become increasingly aware of how out of place such a response is. Satisfaction at a book on consumerism presumes that it is a work of judgment on someone else — those materialistic people who need just such a message. And this is precisely what Paul excoriates the judge for imagining: that the judgment he or she levels is not equally applicable to him or herself. I have realized that I am that judge. Whenever I feel good about the condemnation I'm leveling, I myself am the glaring omission in my target audience. The consumerist idolatry that grips our country is horrible. But I'm right in the middle of it. It doesn't grip *them*, whoever they might be. It grips *me*. It grips *us*.

The judgment comes home, as it were. Though I've done things I regret, I'm not a pedophile, I'm not a pornographer, I'm not a murderer. But if I start supposing myself to be virtuous because the sins I've actively willed (through what I've done and left undone) are relatively minor, then I ignore that infrastructure, that architecture of wickedness on which my imagined virtue is built. The relatively venial sins that make up my daily output of iniquity are such because I'm insulated from the worst the world has to offer.

And I'm insulated from the mortal sins, if I'm honest about the situation, by the relatively unimaginable wealth that I possess by being middle class in twenty-first-century America. However much I might feel pressed by bills, I am among the richest humans ever to walk the earth by virtue of the society I live in. In my cocoon of money, I lead such an elite existence, no matter how everyday and typical it might seem to me, that I really never need to have a face-to-face meeting with evil. I can imagine that the world is a basically hospitable place, that people are basically good, and that it is the norm for life, rather than the exception, to live healthy, happy, and long. Now, this isn't the way the world is. But it's easily the way I could imagine it if I accepted the terms of tenancy offered by the gated community, this pseudo-Eden, that is our consumerist culture.

We are complicit in so much more than is immediately obvious. For starters, my existence as a white American, however much I may renounce any conscious racism, is irretrievably and irredeemably based on the heritage of national sins that are chattel slavery and racial segregation. I am better off in terms of the world *because* Christian brothers and sisters who are the descendents of slaves are worse off. It is not that these different states of well-being are two independent facts. No, there is a connection. True, it is neither simple nor one-sided. The power of social forces does not render us either victor or victim to the point of being absolved from our personal responsibility before God. Moreover, not all white people are better off; not all black people are worse off. There is more at play than meets the eye. But how often do we realize sin at all beyond the individual?

How can my senses be so dull? How can I pick up that banana and not *know*, not somehow sense the strings of sin that I tug with it? Secretly, I think I am good, but I only think this because I have such a shallow understanding of evil. And I have cultivated such a shallow understanding because only very rarely does manifest evil manage to penetrate the protective shell of the wealthy society that surrounds me. Only in such an environment can I imagine that my faith — by which I mean trust in the providence of God — is robust. Tell me what tiny corner of my life depends on God for its security, exactly, when for the rest I can trust in my health insurance, 401k, a good police force and fire department, and the favorable position of being middle class, Christian, American, straight, white, male, educated, and married?

As I write, I can imagine the "angry man" conservative commentators, lampooning me for asking straight white men to apologize for who they are. This is not what I am doing. Nor am I saying that one category is the oppressor, relieving all other categories of their moral responsibilities as human beings before their God. The point is that no one's life is a clean slate; as the Bible tells us, we are complicit in sins that we have not personally willed. Living in a fallen world is like walking on a floor covered in mud. Our feet are going to get dirty whether we want them to or not. Our feet will get dirty, in fact, even if we stand still.*

Now we have begun to understand the judge's dilemma, which is the totality of depravity. The difference between the judged and the self-appointed judge is not one of righteousness, but the ability to imagine one's own innocence and separation from a world wracked with suffering. Our imagining this to be the case, however, does not make it so. Those of us who actively will only venial sins are able to do so only because we tacitly accept others sinning mortally on our behalf. Like the biblical kings whose superstition led them to bury their children alive under the foundations of their fortresses, there is blood beneath every stone of our towers.

For he will repay according to each one's deeds: to those who by patiently doing good seek for glory and honor and immortality, he will give eternal life; while for those who are self-seeking and who obey not the truth but wickedness, there will be wrath and fury. There will be anguish and distress for everyone who does evil, the Jew first and also the Greek, but glory and honor and peace for everyone who does good, the Jew first and also the Greek. For God shows no partiality. All who have sinned apart from the law will also perish apart from the law, and all who have sinned under the law will be judged by the law. For it is not the hearers of the law who are righteous in God's sight, but the doers of the law who will be justified. When Gentiles, who do not possess the law,

---

*Some will justifiably ask how I can understand sin in such a way and still believe in the sinlessness of Christ, since I have essentially said that living and sinning go hand in hand. Answering this question in depth would require considerably more space than I have here and represent a serious deviation from the thrust of my argument. I would start, though, by looking at what it means for Paul to claim that Christ became a curse for us (Gal 3:13). This becoming happened on the cross, of course, but we cannot understand the cross unrelated to the incarnation. If this becoming a curse on the cross is the perfection granted through obedience unto suffering (Heb 5:8–9), then the work of the cross (Christ's death) must be understood as the perfection of what Christ was about in the incarnation (Christ's life), that is, he chose to be surrounded by iniquity. He chose to eat amidst it and speak in its language and care for those so bound by it that they could not even conceive of what freedom might be like. There *is* a difference between life in sinful culture and actively willing sin, but while Christ managed to do the former and not the latter, we invariably fail. In our lives, we have collapsed the theoretical distinction between living and sinning, and as such, our active sin reinforces the environment that gave it birth. The sinlessness of Christ means, in addition to his personal righteousness, that he gave no aid, comfort, or sustenance to the climate of sin in which he became incarnate.

do instinctively what the law requires, these though not having the law, are a law to themselves. They show that what the law requires is written on their hearts, to which their own conscience also bears witness; and their conflicting thoughts will accuse or perhaps excuse them on the day when, according to my gospel, God, through Jesus Christ, will judge the secret thoughts of all. (Romans 2:6–16, NRSV)

We've spent a considerable space exploring the nature and scope of the judge's guilt. By contrast, we will only skim the consequences of this guilt, as described in 2:6–16. While there is a particular value to understanding our contemporary selves in relationship to the judge in 2:1–4, the fate that awaited the judge is no different from that which awaits us. We should read and understand 2:6–16, but there is nothing in it to translate, so to speak, that is specific to our day. When Paul speaks in the second person to the judge, we have to work to understand how that message applies to us. When he speaks in the third person about judges, though, we needn't struggle to understand ourselves in light of his words.

As Paul warned, those who "by persistence in doing good seek glory, honor and immortality" will be given eternal life; those "who are self-seeking and who reject the truth and follow evil" will see wrath and anger. In the meantime, the fact that judgment hasn't come down upon all our heads is not an indication of God's favor, but of God's mercy. We're living on borrowed time, as it were, which is the riches of God's kindness, tolerance, and patience, meant to lead us "toward repentance."

Paul's point here is not that one can earn the favor of God by doing good; even if it were, I hope that the above exploration of complicity would convince us that the bondage of sin cripples any attempt we might make at attaining righteousness through our own effort. In fact, as Paul writes, when Gentiles "do by nature things required by the law," their very capacity for goodness brings along with it a conviction of guilt. It's not that they can do nothing right, because they can. We all have it in us to show kindness, love, and compassion. But the fact that we can do such things indicts our lives for what is essentially a comprehensive failure to live up to what we ought to be.

So, Paul's point in drawing this distinction between life and wrath is not an imperative (go, do good), but rather the indicative statement of 2:11: "God does not show favoritism." As we've discussed, Paul's concern is to show the Roman Jews and Gentiles that neither group enjoys the favor of God sufficient for salvation.

Toward this end, he demonstrated the guilt of the Gentiles rather conclusively by 2:16, and now moves on to the climax of his argument, namely, the unenviable task of convincing the chosen people that there is no identity group upon which God smiles.

Given that we live in a culture obsessed with identity and its self-expression through consumption, Paul's is a pertinent message for our day. But if it is pertinent to the worst excesses of our consumerist society, and if it is all the more pertinent to the hypocritical judges who presume to stand over it, then it will have no mercy whatsoever in convicting those who act as if their religious identity grants them the benevolence of the Lord. So we arrive, at last, at the titular subject of this book.

Chapter 13

You That Boast

> But if you call yourself a Jew and rely on the law and boast of
> your relation to God and know his will and determine what is
> best because you are instructed in the law, and if you are sure
> that you are a guide to the blind, a light to those who are in
> darkness, a corrector of the foolish, a teacher of children, having
> in the law the embodiment of knowledge and truth, you, then,
> that teach others, will you not teach yourself? While you preach
> against stealing, do you steal? You that forbid adultery, do you
> commit adultery? You that abhor idols, do you rob temples? You
> that boast in the law, do you dishonor God by breaking the law?
> For, as it is written, "The name of God is blasphemed among the
> Gentiles because of you." (Romans 2:17–24, NRSV)

In Romans 2:17–24, Paul launches into his worst condemnation
yet: those who claim religious privilege based on identity, but whose
hypocrisy leads to the defamation of the God they claim to follow.

For Christians reading these verses of Romans, there should be a
chill at the base of our spines. Paul's finger is pointed straight at us. We
are the only group to whom Romans 2:17–24 could be addressed in
twenty-first-century America. Millions of those who call themselves
Christians demonstrate the precise spiritual attitude — lifestyle, not
life — condemned by Paul in verses 17–24. That they would live their
religion in this way is no great surprise, however, given the Christian
culture and church of our day.

The indictment ought not to be leveled at individuals so much
as at the church and its leaders, for whom a combination of well-
intentioned evangelistic zeal and declining treasuries has led us to
bend over backwards in the attempt to meet the consumer demands
of a comfort-driven age. We have turned the lifelong activity of faith

into the commodity of belief. And in the marketplaces of our churches, from the humble roadside stands to the gleaming "Christian lifestyle center" shopping malls, we hock our product: that best-selling, inexpensive, factory-made, lifestyle-enhancing, identity-defining, eternal-life-giving, easy-to-use, soul-stain remover — Brand Jesus.

This is quite a charge to make. So let's turn to the Bible and see if the evidence supports it.

We know from Paul's first words that whomever he's addressing in 2:17 is in trouble. Notice that he doesn't say, "You who *are* a Jew." No, he says, "You who call yourself a Jew." In Paul's eyes, you were a Jew, a rightful bearer of that privileged name given to the followers of the one true God, if you had faith in God (we'll explore this further, below). But to "call yourself a Jew" — well, this was, in contemporary terms, to claim Jewish identity or lifestyle by wearing the trappings, minus the interior commitment.

Lifestyle. As we've looked at the term above, a lifestyle isn't generated from within. It isn't based at all on what comes out of us. No, it's the appearance or style that our lives have from without — this style being, in fact, the primary commodity in a consumerist society. One's lifestyle is one's identity, perceivable by others, based on external markers.

So, what are the markers of this Roman Jewish lifestyle with which Paul is so unimpressed? First, that it relies (literally: "rests") on the law. Notice that this doesn't mean that the person is obeying that law. Paul has anticipated what it means to rely or rest on the law in 2:13, when he distinguishes between the passive "hearers of the law" and those who actually do what it requires. The Roman who calls himself a Jew, Paul is saying, celebrates the fact that the law was given to the Jews, that he is a hearer of it (in the dual sense of being a descendent of the original "hearers of the law" at Sinai, and also one who would listen to the Torah recitation at synagogue). But he doesn't bother to carry out its commandments. "You who call yourself a Jew and rest on the law . . . " — but the law is supposed to be a place of action, not rest!

Second, the one living this lifestyle "boasts in [his] relationship to God" (literally: boasts in God). The Roman who calls himself a Jew claims the privilege that comes with being set apart by God as a recipient of the law, a "hearer" of it, but ignores the responsibility that comes with the name. Thus, the "boast in God" for this self-proclaimed Jew is an assumption of God's particular favor based exclusively on one's identity.

Third and fourth, the self-proclaimed Roman Jew claims to know the will of God and thus is able determine what is best, based on his instruction in the law. At stake here is a presumptuous judgment. The person lives a lifestyle of authority, as if he had access to both God's eternal purposes and the ethics of daily living. He carries himself as a man of stature who is sure of his place before God and — thus — before all other people. It is this conviction of authority that, even more than the personal blessedness that comes from "resting on the law" and "boasting in God," leads the self-proclaimed Jew to imagine himself as a "guide to the blind, light to those who are in darkness, corrector of the foolish, and a teacher of children" (2:19–20a). He imagines that the law is a divine possession, "the embodiment of knowledge and truth," which is given to him in order to set him above others (2:20b).

Before we move on, notice the seductive similarity between lifestyle and real life. Every marker that Paul mentions would be true of the "true Jew" who is defined by faith (see 2:29): a recipient of the law, in a privileged relationship with God, having intimate knowledge of God's will, and one who is able to discern what is best. As 2:19–20 describes, the Roman who actually is a Jew would indeed be a guide, a light, a corrector, and a teacher. Such a one would be, as promised by God to Abraham, a blessing to the entire world. But in the Roman who "calls [oneself] a Jew," these properly interior attributes are evident only in terms of their outward appearances, hollow facades decorating a lifestyle of assumed spiritual privilege. Religion has become the commodity that creates identity, and it is all the more tragic because it bears the form of righteousness.

Blasphemed Because of You

As I read Paul's letter to the Romans and think about the American church, I wish to God that the shoe didn't fit us so well. I wish that the soles didn't seem custom cut for our feet, that the leather didn't seem broken in at exactly the right spot. I wish for some slippage in the heel or cramping in the toes or something — anything! — that we could point to and say that this scripture probably belongs to someone else. Unfortunately, the message of Romans 2:17–24 fits our contemporary context as if made to order.

It requires alarmingly little translation to slip ourselves straight into these verses. It's as if we've already walked miles in them. The only difference between Paul's description then and much of American Christianity now is "the law" on which the self-proclaimed Jew is meant to rest. But it isn't a stretch to figure out what the law is for us. The law, after all, was the gift that set apart the Jewish people. It was the gift of God's righteousness that distinguished them from the Gentiles. It was a gift of such magnitude that one could not properly claim to have received it if one did not live a life of grateful obedience in response. Receiving the gift of the law, in fact, couldn't occur in a single instant; no, receiving the gift was a process that began the first time one submitted in faithful obedience and that continued to one's last breath. Of course, the self-proclaimed Jews whom Paul criticizes didn't see it that way. They had the law as a commodity given and now possessed. They could rely on it.

For American Christians, can the analogue to the law be anything but Jesus Christ? But Jesus isn't the law, you say, and those were the Jews — the situation for Christians is totally different. True enough on the first count: Jesus isn't the law. But if our situation is totally different, why do we treat Jesus as the self-proclaiming Roman Jews in 2:17–24 treated the law? Why do we act just like the Roman whom Paul accuses of "calling himself" a Jew? Jesus Christ, a gift that sets us apart, a gift of righteousness, a gift that takes a lifetime to live into but which we imagine we have received in a moment. By substituting only a few words, observe how neatly we find our account in scripture:

> But you, if you call yourself a Christian and rest upon Jesus Christ and boast in [your relationship to] God and know his will and determine what is best because you are instructed in Jesus Christ, and if you are sure that you are a guide to the blind, a light to those who are in darkness, a corrector of the foolish, a teacher of children, having in Jesus Christ the embodiment of knowledge and truth. . . .

Yes, we might say. Yes, that is the case! I call myself a Christian, I do rest on Jesus Christ, and he has given me my relationship with God, and I do know God's will, and I can determine what is best, through the gift of discernment. Christ is the embodiment of knowledge and truth, and I have him!

But so thought the Roman Jews in their day. And the tragedy was not that they claimed false truths, but that their behavior made a mockery of their glorious truth. The true Jew should have lived up to 2:17–20 just as the true Christian should live up to the above paraphrase. But, like the self-proclaimed Roman Jew who misunderstood the nature of the gift of the law, there are millions of self-proclaimed Christians who have misunderstood the nature of the gift that is Jesus Christ. And, like Paul's self-proclaimed Jew, these self-proclaimed Christians have adopted a Christian lifestyle, claiming by virtue of this identity all of the privilege and knowledge and status before God that is the gift to one who bears the Lord's name. But this lifestyle comes from without and is manifested without the interior change that represents the authentically Christian life.

Two questions immediately spring to mind. First, aside from a neat scriptural parallel, what is the basis for such an accusation? And second, if this is indeed the case, why has such a thing happened?

The first question is tragically easy to answer, and we will get to the second in the next section. In 2005, Ron Sider published an exposé of American Christian life titled *The Scandal of the Evangelical Conscience.* Its pages excoriate American Christians for failing to live lives that are significantly more righteous than those of their secular neighbors. American Christians failed, in fact, on every count that Sider investigated. In the conclusion to his first chapter, "The Depth of the Scandal," Sider writes:

> To say there is a crisis of disobedience in the evangelical world today is to dangerously understate the problem. Born-again Christians divorce at about the same rate as everyone else. Self-centered materialism is seducing evangelicals and rapidly destroying our earlier, slightly more generous giving. . . . Born-again Christians justify and engage in sexual promiscuity (both premarital sex and adultery) at astonishing rates. Racism* and perhaps physical abuse of wives seem to be worse in evangelical circles than elsewhere. This is scandalous behavior for people

---

*One of the weaknesses in an otherwise excellent book is the tacit assumption that evangelical Christians are white. This assumption is demonstrated by the fact that the standard used as a "good measure of racism" is whether one would object to having black neighbors. Allowing, even theoretically, for the fact that some black Americans might object to having black neighbors, this question surely presumes either a white audience or that racism only means anti-black sentiment.

who *claim to be born-again* by the Holy Spirit and *to enjoy the very presence of the Risen Lord* in their lives. . . . Perhaps it is not surprising either that *non-Christians have a very negative view of evangelicals* . . . 44 percent [of non-Christians] have a positive view of Christian clergy. Just 32 percent have a positive view of born-again Christians. And a mere 22 percent have a positive view of evangelicals.[1]

I quote Sider at such length because his description of American born-again Christians and evangelicals (which I have italicized for emphasis) shows a startling parallel to our Romans text. First, look at the sentence beginning, "This is scandalous behavior. . . . " Notice how the attributes of the hypocritical Christian — "claim to be born-again" and "to enjoy the very presence of the Risen Lord" — echo those of Paul's self-proclaimed Jew: "rely on the law" and "boast in [their relationship to] God." Indeed, virtually no work is needed to align modern Christians with the notion of "boasting in [their relationship to] God," since a much-touted personal relationship with Christ is the hallmark of every form of popular evangelical spirituality, bar none.

There is no need to map the extensive connections between the fruits of Sider's research and our Romans text. It is sufficient to point out that, just as Paul alleged of Roman Jews, it appears to be the case that there is a yawning gulf between the public face of religious moralism and the private behavior of the American church today. Indeed, we may be even worse than the Romans. Whereas Paul found it sufficient to level five rhetorical questions in 2:21–23 as charges against the self-proclaimed Jew, Sider has uncovered far more ammunition for American evangelicals. One could imagine what Paul might write today "to all God's beloved in America, who are called to be saints" after reading Ron Sider:

> You, then, that teach others that there are no racial divisions in Christ, will you not teach yourself to welcome a neighbor with a different color skin? While you preach against domestic violence, do you beat your wife? You that forbid adultery, do you commit adultery? [This charge, evidently, needs no updating.] You that abhor divorce, do you rob your spouse of a mate? You that boast in Jesus Christ, do you dishonor God by disobeying Christ's commands? For, as it is written, "The name of God is blasphemed among the nations because of you" (2:21–24, updated).

In the last verse, we come to the crux of the matter. Romans 2:24, citing Ezekiel 36:20, is perhaps the most devastating allegation in the Bible. There is nothing — nothing! — that we should fear more than this: that the name of God would be blasphemed among the nations because of us.

But this has come to pass. Recall Sider's closing sentences. In a country that is at least 75 percent Christian, just 44 percent of non-Christians think highly of Christian clergy, and that number is cut in half when it applies to opinion about evangelicals as a whole. True, this is an indicator of opinion about people. But if our fellow citizens think so poorly of us, what must they think of the God whose name and Spirit we claim, on whom we claim to stake our salvation and the basis for our assessment of the world? A clear theme throughout the prophetic books of the Old Testament is that the behavior of the God's people affects the regard of unbelievers for the Lord (see, for example, Ezekiel 20). Given the manifest hypocrisy that we demonstrate — which matches, if it does not indeed exceed, that of Paul's self-proclaimed Roman Jews — how can we imagine that our actions have not brought the name of God itself into disrepute? Like the one whom the author of Hebrews describes as falling away after tasting "the heavenly gift," are we not susceptible to the charge that "on [our] own [we] are crucifying again the Son of God and are holding him up to contempt"?

The significance of the fact that this might be true of American Christians exceeds the bounds of rhetoric to convey. We have caused people to spit at the name of God. If this is the case, then there is little to do but sit in horrified silence for a time at the sheer magnitude of our iniquity.

Circumcision indeed is of value if you obey the law; but if you break the law, your circumcision has become uncircumcision. So, if those who are uncircumcised keep the requirements of the law, will not their uncircumcision be regarded as circumcision? Then those who are physically uncircumcised but keep the law will condemn you that have the written code and circumcision but break the law. For a person is not a Jew who is one outwardly, nor is true circumcision something external and physical. Rather, a person is a Jew who is one inwardly, and real circumcision is a matter of the heart — it is spiritual and not literal. Such a person receives praise not from others but from God.

(Romans 2:25–29, NRSV)

We return now to the second question posed above, namely, why are so many self-proclaimed Christians buying into the religious lifestyle, image, and identity, but not making the radical spiritual-ethical commitment of discipleship? How is it that there is so much Christian hypocrisy?

This is no idle matter. As Christians, we make, as Sider writes, "proud claims to miraculous transformation."[2] Later in Romans, Paul writes compellingly about dying to sin and the alien righteousness that is from God in Jesus Christ. If this is ours to inherit, then where have things gone wrong? Are the promises of God through scripture invalid? Has the power of God vanished? Or are we today somehow constitutionally different from those first-century believers who experienced the miraculous transformation about which Sider writes? No, none of these can be the case. If any of these questions were answerable in the affirmative, our faith would be in vain.

So we are left with only one option for finding the break in the wire, so to speak. If we have not seen the sanctification that is given to people who are in Christ, then a good many self-proclaimed Christians are actually *not in Christ.* If they were, they would see sanctification. As they do not, they are not. And given that sanctification is an internal matter, we cannot even limit this assessment to those whose ethical failings Sider reports. No one knows the heart but God. And only the abundance of our hypocrisy tells us that something is very, very wrong in the heart of American Christianity.

These self-proclaimed Christians do not necessarily know that they have a problem. The vast majority of us probably go through our days with a great sense of self-assurance about our salvation and eternal destiny. We probably pray to Jesus and read the Bible. We will in fact claim, as pollster George Barna found true of 40 percent of all adult Americans in 2005, to be born-again Christians: that is, those who have "made a personal commitment to Jesus Christ that is still important in their lives today" and who "believe that when they die they will go to heaven because they have confessed their sins and accepted Jesus Christ as their savior."[3]

Focus on this for a moment. Forty percent of Americans describe themselves in ways identifiable with born-again Christians. Forty percent of Americans claim to be bound for heaven because they have (1) confessed their sins, and (2) accepted Jesus Christ as their savior—an acceptance, or commitment, that remains important to them. And yet this 40 percent lives in ways that are statistically indistinguishable from the 60 percent who make no such claims of God's favor.

The startling question is, then, is Jesus Christ actually the one whom many self-proclaimed Christians have accepted? Or, as seems to be the case, have consumer-minded Christians been led from the narrow road, drawn by promises of an impotent spiritual commodity masquerading as the power of God? Welcome to the church of Brand Jesus.

Praise from Others

Paul offers us the missing link necessary for such a diagnosis. Look at how he shifts from the stunning accusation of 2:24 to a relatively straightforward statement about circumcision in 2:25. This is a surprising move, if we stop to think about it. After all, Paul hasn't spoken about circumcision at all up to this point. He's talked about a failure to live up to the law. He's talked about a presumption of privileged religious identity, of being a teacher of God's ways. But he's said nothing about circumcision. So why now?

Perhaps Paul is trying to head off the obvious objection to the condemnation he has just made. Biblical scholar Joseph Fitzmyer speculates about the response Paul might have been anticipating, which could sound something like this: "Perhaps we Jews do not observe the law as we should, but at least we are circumcised.... Did not God himself set up the covenant with Israel and make circumcision [its] seal, the very shield against God's wrath?"[4] In other words, even if the self-proclaimed Roman Jew hasn't fully walked the walk, hasn't he taken the one outward step that does guarantee his spiritual status?

No, says Paul. As the seal of the covenant between God and Israel, circumcision "is of value if you obey the law." And, indeed, the circumcision of male infants marks the passage of the law from one generation to the next. But Paul's point is that a man cannot simply rely on the obedience demonstrated by his circumcision as sufficient for inclusion in the covenant. If one breaks the covenant by disobeying the law, then the seal that was a blessing becomes an indictment. That which gives Israel its glory also magnifies its sin. It has become like the wedding band on an adulterer's finger.

So circumcision becomes uncircumcision to the lawbreaker, a mark of honor turned into a mark of disgrace. Indeed, such a person will be condemned by one who, though physically uncircumcised, obeys the law (here Paul reinforces the point he has made in 2:13–15). True circumcision, by contrast — that is, the real mark of obedience to God — has nothing to do with what was or was not done physically. No, true circumcision "is of the heart, by the Spirit, not by the written code," and the praise of the spiritually circumcised is from God, not people (2:29).

The point in all of this is the devaluation of external identity. "Look," Paul says, "your circumcision hasn't enabled you to keep the law. The gift of the *law* hasn't enabled you to keep the law. The religious status you claim for yourself is a sham, because you're basing it on external things." The critical error made by the self-proclaimed Jew is that he imagines his Jewishness to rest on what he has rather than what he does. In other words, what he believes to be his Jewishness is based on commodities like his circumcision (which, though an action, wasn't one he took willingly) and the law (which was a divine gift). Now, it would be silly to imagine that we could find twenty-first-century consumerism in first-century Rome. But the principles of the self-proclaimed Roman Jew's error do indeed translate to our day and help in our understanding of what has gone wrong with American Christianity.

We've already explored this a bit while drawing the parallel of hypocrisy between 2:17–24, above. Just as the self-proclaimed Jew thought himself righteous because he possessed the law, so many Christians imagine themselves righteous because they possess Christ. But neither the law nor Christ is a *possession* to be had. Neither is a commodity. The law is meant to be followed. And Christ is the Lord, who should be obeyed by all who name him as such.

When Christians treat the one they call Christ as a spiritual commodity, then the one they believe to be Christ is not actually the living Lord. How could he be? The Lord is not a good to be purchased or a brand to be adopted. When Christians imagine that we "have Christ," what we actually have is Brand Jesus — the idol for Christianity in a consumerist age.

Brand Jesus is the starting point for most contemporary American Christian hypocrisy. We claim to live "in the world but not of it," and mouth aspirations not to "conform any longer to the pattern of this world." So why, as the subtitle of Sider's book asks, "are Christians living just like the rest of the world?" Like everyone else in contemporary America, we have bought into the idolatrous notion that we are what we buy. Our answer to consumerism has not been a vigorous counterinsistence that we are who God has given us to be. No, we have agreed to Mammon's terms, consented to be what we consume, and then happily gone about manufacturing Brand Jesus, the god of a Christianity that is a commodity for consumption.

This is why, despite all her claims to distinction, the mainstream Christian's lifestyle is essentially no different from that of her secular neighbors. Like them, she finds her identity in consumption; the only difference is that she buys different stuff. Yuppies are yuppies because they buy Ralph Lauren and Lacoste and BMW; in the same way, many Christians are Christians because they buy Brand Jesus. (This purchase is not always a financial or material transaction, though — as we'll see below — it is often manifested that way.) We may do different things, but we live by the same consumerist rules. We are, in fact, *wholly conformed to the pattern of this world.* So, while Christians should be radically different from everybody else, we find that Christians are no more different from practitioners of other lifestyles than those folk are from each another. We've made discipleship into one option (and, on the face of it, a not that appealing one) among many, when it ought to stand separate, as different from other ways of living as Christ was from the world.

This is no idle danger, because Brand Jesus will lead would-be Christians — who are filled with the best of intentions — whistling down the path to destruction. On the specifics of this point I will no doubt part company with any nonreligious and even a great many sympathetic Christian readers. When I refer to Brand Jesus, what I mean is not some psychological, social, or political phenomenon that, while unhealthy and not advisable, exists only as the group action of certain Christians. No, what I name Brand Jesus I believe to be a malicious spiritual force. It is there whether we name it or not: a Jesus-shaped scarecrow, the crucified puppet. Brand Jesus is a trick of Mammon for our age, our original sin molded roughly into a cruciform homunculus.

And, like dogs returning faithfully to our own vomit, to Brand Jesus we slink.

There is no great mystery why this is the case. Like a stage magician, Brand Jesus takes the promise of the kingdom of God and offers another pseudo-Christian vision instead, from the voyeuristic action thriller of the premillennialist *Left Behind* to the generic saccharine of *Touched by an Angel.* Brand Jesus takes the tragedy of sinful life and, without asking us to change our behavior in the plot, promises a happy ending. Brand Jesus takes everything our species' depraved imagination wants to believe is true about the world and feeds it back to us.

Brand Jesus does all these things — is able to do all these things — because it is the spiritual equivalent of a consumer good. We have already seen the way in which our collective imagination enables consumerism by giving a transcendent value to material things. To buy a Mercedes car or Nike shoes is not simply to buy a vehicle or footgear. Along with the material product that is purchased, one acquires a bit of the mystique of luxury or the triumph of athleticism. These transcendent values of luxury and athleticism do not abide in the objects themselves, however, as much as they do in the imaginations of the buyers making up the consumerist economy, who give consumerism power through their devotion to it.

Like brand Mercedes or brand Nike, then, Brand Jesus carries a host of transcendent values provided by the imaginations of the consumers in the spiritual marketplace. Instead of financial or athletic success, however, Brand Jesus provides the consumer with a sense of spiritual privilege as well as membership in a group of like-minded folk. As George Barna's polling indicates, personal salvation is the essential guarantee of what I am calling Brand Jesus religion. At its most profound, this is a sense of eternal security in the face of death and meaninglessness; at its most banal, it is the well-being that attends being one of the "saved" instead of one of the "lost."

For Brand Jesus to be a viable commodity, however, the transaction must be completed at a price. If you have spent any time in Christian circles, you will have been asked about the moment of your salvation. The most common way in which this is asked of you will describe Jesus Christ in the form of a commodity: "When did you accept him as your personal savior?" (An only slightly better form of this question will include the title "Lord.")

There are more charitable interpretations of such questions, to be sure. Jesus is Lord and God, savior and teacher, and his disciples can hardly recognize him otherwise. But when someone you asks such a question, he or she is not interested in hearing about your lifelong discipleship but about a single moment. And the answer you will be expected to give is to name the exact time you first decided to buy Brand Jesus. The day and hour and condition in which you made the sale by handing over your belief. The day you decided to let Brand Jesus — which promises infinitely more cleansing power than Tide, Oxyclean, or Era — start working for you by washing away your sins.

Unsurprisingly, buying into Brand Jesus bears demonstrable results. Such is the power of all great brands. A man dressed in an Armani suit will probably walk a little taller. A kid who gets her first pair of Nike shoes might run a little faster, simply from the psychological boost. As we have explored above, in a consumerist age the problem is not that brands are powerless, but that they are power*ful* in their own right. That is, they are powerful in the same way that all idols and demi-idols are powerful. It would be a dangerous delusion indeed to imagine them as harmless fallacies at worst. Idols are anything but impotent, as any reading of the Old Testament reveals. To take just one example, though Baal was powerless to ignite a pile of wood, *devotion* to him led 450 of his prophets to chant all day and to cut themselves ritually "until their blood flowed" (1 Kings 18:22ff.).

The problem with idols and brands is not that they are ineffectual, but that they cannot effect what we want them to effect. They cannot give back according to the measure of transcendent devotion we give to them. That Armani suit will not keep you attractive forever. The Nike shoes will not ensure that you will always be able to run and jump. And, while none of us, if asked, would admit to believing that such brands could offer such rewards, the way we treat them certainly reveals that they cannot, in the end, give us what we want from them.

Douglas Atkin is a marketing executive who works with commercial brands to increase their "cult appeal." In his how-to book, *The Culting of Brands*, he observes that the draw of any cult is the sense that membership in the group "means becoming more me."[5] The paradox notwithstanding, one's individuality emerges through the sense of group identity. In a consumer society, successful brands are highly effective in communicating meaning, and *cultic* brands offer self-actualization. That is, they offer us an enhanced and often comprehensive version of what we believe ourselves to be.

This is true whether the product is commercial or ostensibly spiritual. In fact, Atkin's unabashedly mercenary analysis — his final sentence is an exhortation to his business-minded audience: "The next cult brand could be yours" — would scarcely distinguish between the two. The primary difference, to Atkin, seems to be that cults of yore were spiritual, whereas today, commercial cults have sprung up alongside them. Both, in Atkin's view, traffic in an economy of meaning, rendering meaningless any distinction between sacred and secular.

Atkin writes: "Beliefs are well and good in theory — scriptural truths, mission statements, enduring values and beliefs. In the end, however, ideas fade and only action remains. We are what we do, not what we think."[6] Paul seems to be arguing a similar point by locating being in one's doing rather than in one's group identity. But for Paul, one will never be *able* to do righteousness without the "righteousness from God" that is in Jesus Christ. Yes, Paul replies to Atkin, our being is our doing, but this is a curse. We depend upon the gift of an alien righteousness in order to do righteousness ourselves.

This step is of course where Atkin will not go, because Atkin's account is atheistic. "We are what we do," Atkin writes, so those who recognize this point might as well make the most of it. The world he describes in his analysis represents a complete acceptance of the vision that Mammon offers for our existence, namely, one in which our original sin — the promise of being wealthy rather than dependent on God — defines every aspect of life. In writing what he hoped would be a top-selling book, Atkin is engaged in the same unspoken project as the readers whom he advises: making money. He offers tips toward the conscious participation and manipulation of an economy of meaningful symbols. This will presumably result in greater profits, which will in turn give Atkin's acolytes greater resources to partake in the economy of meaning that they have partially created. (Atkin is not scornful of cult devotees, since they make the consumer world go 'round, and in our brand-saturated economy it would be entirely possible to be both a brand cult member and a creator of brand cults.) But there is no escape; there is only the endless cycle of consumption and meaning.

No matter whether or where Brand Jesus enters this cycle, it interrupts it not one bit. Brand Jesus is always one commodity among many, wholly contained within the cycle of consumption, which does not in any way change the consumer's position. Brand Jesus, in other words, fits quite nicely into a world without God.

The reason Brand Jesus works this way is that his ecclesial pitchmen, concerned for the salvation of the drifting masses, have spared no effort to get people to buy into Jesus. Now, many have observed that contemporary churches are endemic to cheap grace, that is, forgiveness of sin without repentance. Sider puts cheap grace forward as a culprit for much of the widespread immorality he chronicles. But despite the various cries for reform, critics rarely conduct self-examinations and ask what it is that would lead to such a phenomenon. The offer of cheap grace is coming from people with integrity and deep belief: our pastors, preachers, and theologians. They aren't just conducting some scam in order to fill pews. In other words, the problem is not so much that cheap grace is being offered to non-Christians, but that Christians buy their own advertising.

Most observers do not go nearly far enough to uncover the root issues behind our church's problems. Doesn't the lament that grace is too cheap, for example, imply only that it ought to be more expensive? In other words, we don't seem bothered by the commodification of Christ, but the asking price! The step that I have not seen any Christian critics take is to go beyond the individual failures of Christians and churches to acknowledge a pseudo-Christianity that is inextricably entangled in the American church. It is a pseudo-Christianity because something of infinite value cannot be cheapened. Only a commodity can be sale priced, and true Christianity — like circumcision — is not a commodity.

Therefore, a Christianity that *can* be cheapened was never Christianity to begin with, but rather one of many knockoff attempts. Even if we emphasize that salvation entails a costly discipleship, we remain concerned with *price* and thus fail to recognize grace as the free gift that is God's renewal of humanity's pre-fall existence. That is to say, in doing so we continue to reckon ourselves — and the world — as Mammon would have us do.

There is no point in history to which we can point and exclaim, "Aha!" — having found the start of an infernal conspiracy to market a product called Brand Jesus. No, Brand Jesus is, in our own time, the particular form of that in history that continues to be opposed to God, and that adapts along with our changed and changing world. Brand

Jesus is something of a composite product, in fact, incorporating a number of disparate economic, technological, political, philosophical, and yes, theological movements over the past several centuries. Tracing its history is beyond our scope here.

Moreover, there is no complete deliverance from it. Unlike many who might make a similar charge about the faith, I am not suggesting that we can now draw bold lines between the authentic faith and the bootleg copy. If true Christianity — like true circumcision — is a matter of the heart, then judging between them is not ours to do (thank God!). Efforts to separate the wheat from the tares have been the source of innumerable schisms, a great many of them in my own Baptist tradition, which at last count was nearing a hundred distinctive varieties in North America alone. I confess to being uninterested in the project of devising a system to divide authoritatively that which God appears content to leave together for the time being. It is enough to recognize some of the distinctive markers of Brand Jesus as we embark on an exercise in self-criticism and renewal.

Part IV

BRAND JESUS

Chapter 14

Consumer Theology
in the American Church

Here's the rub that qualifies everything I've written in the previous section: I do not doubt that God has actually given grace to every person who has genuinely invited Jesus into his or her heart, regardless of whether doing so has meant commodifying him. I'm positive that it is the living Lord himself, and not a pretender, who looks in favor on us in those moments. I could spend pages and pages looking at every little theological problem I could think of and, in the end, even an analysis that was watertight and bug proof would be rendered as nothing by the actual working of God in the world. God creates the possibility of God's own moving. It is not ours to define.

Furthermore, a clear understanding of God is not a prerequisite for salvation. Humankind's spiritual perception is so flawed that we cannot make the first move toward God. Indeed, the very goodness of Christianity's "good news" is that God has made the first move toward us and — mercy and grace! — has done so once and for all in the person of Jesus Christ. If the only true Christians in this day and age were the ones who had extricated themselves from the trap of consumerism first, then church rolls would probably need to be reduced forcibly by about 100 percent — and, speaking for myself, I certainly wouldn't be around. In fact, it is by definition the case that the place from which we convert is a sinful spot. The significance of the incarnation itself is that God has entered the prison that our sinfulness has made of the world: "God demonstrates his own love for us in this: while we were still sinners, Christ died for us" (Romans 5:8).

Though God necessarily meets us as spiritual infants, however, we're not meant to remain immature. And the evidence that Ron Sider presents, for example, demonstrates that sanctification is not

111

happening as we might expect. For some reason, the genuine conversion that people are having is not blossoming into the fruit we hope for. There is a crisis. And this crisis is happening along the lines described in Romans. The parallels between then and now are too striking to be coincidental. What's going on?

There's no way to answer that question conclusively, but my theory is that at some point between our conversions and today — whenever today may be — many of us unwittingly begin to follow a "changeling" religion. You may be familiar with British legends in which fairies steal a human infant and leave a fairy look-alike — a changeling — in its place. In other words, it looks like the original, but secretly it is not. So it may be with Christians who have received the grace of God but now find that their discipleship consists of being loyal consumers of Brand Jesus.

I've met Christians on the verge of falling away who remember their coming to faith with befuddlement. They can't deny the reality of what happened, but they can no longer make sense of it. It is like a dream now past. They find themselves holding onto something different from what they initially received. This phenomenon has ample biblical attestation. The most notorious example is probably the churches of Galatia, to whom Paul wrote, "I am astonished that you are so quickly deserting the one who called you in the grace of Christ and are turning to a different gospel — not that there is another gospel, but there are some who are confusing you and want to pervert the gospel of Christ" (Galatians 1:6–7, NRSV). The Galatians certainly didn't imagine that they'd now converted to a new religion. Their error was not so obvious. Rather, while still considering themselves followers of Christ, they had become followers of a neo-legalism. Like the church in Ephesus, they had "forgotten [their] first love" (Revelation 2:4). They had, in effect, become followers of a changeling faith. On the outside, it looked similar to the truth, but internally, their devotion was not to the grace in which they had initially been called.

There are a number of interconnected reasons why it is unsurprising to see the widespread consumerization of American Christianity today.

Heaven Bound

The first reason is doubtless the exclusive focus on salvation that in many churches comes at the expense of discipleship and sanctification. I'm sure you've visited churches in which every single sermon is explicitly evangelistic. (I've often wondered what it's like for members to sit in those churches' pews year after year, continuously being fed the message that the high point of their faith — that is, conversion unto salvation — is behind them.)

In such a context, the only form of discipleship *is* evangelism, and perhaps even turns into proselytism. In other words, what it means to be a Christian in such situations is, simply, to make as many other Christians as possible. As I've heard one pastor put it, Christianity becomes pretty stale and curiously unappealing when the sole goal of we who are on Team A (Christianity) is to get as many people as we possibly can from Team B (i.e., everyone else) to come onto our side.[1] ("Come to church! Why? Umm...so you can be saved, join, and then spend your life getting *other* people to come to church!") Such a strategy, which is neither based in the truth of the gospel nor especially fun, is dually disadvantaged.

Now, I certainly don't want to discount evangelism. I come out of a tradition where every single sermon ends with an invitation, and this is my practice when preaching as well. As sinners, we *need* salvation, and have nothing without it. But it is only one aspect among many that are indispensable for the Christian life. It is possible to overemphasize salvation to the point that the congregation becomes rather frantic to win new converts. In other words, they're desperate for others to experience the same inbreaking grace that each of them once experienced. In these situations, it almost seems like evangelism becomes vicarious spirituality that hampers spiritual maturation, with older Christians trying to touch in new converts the zeal that they once knew firsthand.

The problem, of course, is that grace can't be manufactured. It can't be packaged. And it's not ours to bestow. So churches that are unhealthily obsessed with evangelism are, in fact, determined to give something that's not theirs to give in the first place.

I know that many brothers and sisters will disagree with the notion that a church could *ever* overemphasize evangelism. I can readily imagine protests about the impossibility of being too concerned with reaching "the Lost." (As an adult convert to the faith, I feel compelled to point out here that Christianity is rarely so off-putting to non-Christians as it is when they discover this in-house designation — and it only gets worse when they find out that we use a capital L.)

This issue cannot be thoroughly explored here. In my defense in the interim, however, I will point out that Paul the apostle, the greatest missionary in church history, spent exactly zero percent of his letters exhorting his flock to go out and make new converts. His emphasis was on doctrinal truth and living together as the body of Christ. He certainly didn't set up churches like those that we see today, which might as well be called "The Church of Matthew 28:19" or the GCC (Great Commission Church), since not much else seems to get taught at all.

In such churches, I am not at all surprised to find a cottage industry producing a homemade version of Brand Jesus. They need people to come to the Lord, but they can't make the Lord show up when and where and how they want. So, in his place, they offer a much more predictable and highly realistic substitute. The wonder of it all is that the Lord meets people even in idols such as these. But when we are met by Christ, we are called to follow him out of the situation in which he finds us. So, when we continue to cling to the salvation-centered Brand Jesus, we invariably fall away from the path of spiritual growth.

The reason most Christians don't live an active discipleship in such situations is because we're too comfortable resting on our personal savior, the Jesus-brand La-Z-Boy we got at church. "Now that's what I call salvation!" we sigh, contentedly sinking into the plush leather. "How beautiful *are* the feet of those who bring the good news!" we exclaim, as the footrest guides our slippered tootsies to a fully horizontal position. And our last words as we drowse off to our nap? "Praise . . . the . . . zzzzzzzzzzzzzzzz."

For insight into this dilemma, reflect on the way in which we talk about conversion. The most standard language is, of course, "inviting Christ into your life" through some version of the "Sinner's Prayer." Take the following text from an evangelistic Web site affiliated with Campus Crusade for Christ, www.4stepstogod.com:

> Step 4: If you want to accept Christ, you can ask Him to be your Savior and Lord by praying a prayer like this: "Lord Jesus, I believe you are the Son of God. Thank you for dying on the cross for my sins. Please forgive my sins and give me the gift of eternal life. I ask you in to my life and heart to be my Lord and Savior. I want to serve you always."

   Now, it is true that Christ has graciously answered countless such invitations. But if we persist in thinking that our righteousness comes from Christ entering *our* lives, we perpetuate an upended understanding of the ways of God. It is not Christ who enters our lives, but we who enter his. In fact, the Apostle Paul never uses the term "Christian," and instead favors the designation "in Christ" for those who have become disciples. For example, his letter to the Romans reads, "There is therefore now no condemnation for those who are in Christ Jesus" (8:1). It is not, as common versions of the Sinner's Prayer would implicitly have it to be, "There is therefore now no condemnation for those whom Christ Jesus *is in*!" The popular contemporary understanding of salvation reinforces a spiritual self-centeredness in which Jesus comes to the unmoved convert.

   Christians who continue to think of their salvation in those terms will invariably maintain their own lives as the center, with Christ entering from the periphery. Consider, for further confirmation, that classic evangelistic text from Revelation 3:23, "Behold, I stand at the door and knock." The popular treatment of this passage demonstrates the degree to which consumerism has co-opted Christianity. In most treatments of this passage that I have encountered, we are led to imagine Jesus standing on the front stoop of the mansions of our lives. The moment of conversion in this depiction is that glorious moment when we deign to let him in, that salvific Fuller Brush man or Mary Kay rep who stands ready to make the sale that will change our lives. But this understanding is an inversion of reality. The one who crosses your threshold in such a case will not be the Lord but a Brand Jesus pitchman. The real, living Lord does not wander the scorched suburbs of our reality, a lonely figure trooping door to door in search of houses that could use a spiritual sprucing up.

   Rather, in reality, we are occupants of cells that have no exit — no exit, that is, until his knock makes a door where before there was none. Our lives are not six billion points of reference between which he wanders; no, he is the one point of reference onto which all doors open. And his invitation to "come in and eat with" us and we "with him" is not the plaintive wish of one begging for scraps, but the offer of a minister offering to share a meal with a condemned person in his or her cell. Jesus offers to come into our lives, not because our lives are *his* proper place, but because his life is *ours* — and until he enters, we cannot be led out into the kingdom of God.

A Personal Relationship

The second reason why many Christians wind up with the changeling faith of Brand Jesus is that church leaders offer so little concrete spiritual instruction. This is certainly the case with the Great Commission churches described above, but it is true even in churches with more active discipleship. Many Christians don't have much of an idea what discipleship entails, beyond the guilt-inducing requirement of daily "Quiet Time."

Their predicament is understandable. Put yourself in a new (or even lifelong) Christian's shoes. You are encouraged to have a personal relationship with Jesus Christ, who died nearly two thousand years ago. Moreover, you are told that if you want to evaluate the quality of your spiritual life, you should do so by the intimacy of that relationship. Now, if we can all agree to set aside, even for a moment, our knee-jerk attempts to maintain a hyper-spiritual image, we can admit that Jesus Christ is, on the face of it, fundamentally *unrelatable to,* in any normal sense that we understand the word relationship. He's not physically here. He doesn't reply audibly to most people. He's not available to spend time with or, since he's actually always available, you're always neglecting him (bad Christian that you are). That is, you're neglecting him until you do decide to spend time with him, and then, to all outward perception — including that nagging doubt that lingers from your pre-conversion self — you find yourself sitting alone in a room, talking to yourself.

In summary, in an effort to make Christianity appealing, we tend to describe discipleship in everyday, hyper-contemporary terms (i.e., that of "relationships"), all the while ignoring the fact that the subject of that relationship is unlike anyone else with whom anyone has a relationship (i.e., everybody else who's *not* the resurrected Son of God).

Despite this difficulty, how many church leaders tell new converts — at a point of complete immaturity as Christians — that what they need to do is to exist continuously in this state of invisible, spiritual communion? Never mind that such a communion is what mystics in centuries past worked a lifetime to achieve. Never mind that an active sense of relationship with the invisible God (invisible!) is the result of years of spiritual discipline. Never mind that prayer is perhaps the hardest part of Christian life, one with which spiritual giants have wrestled and sweated. You've just kicked a drug habit and a lousy relationship?

You were at rock bottom and you heard the voice of God calling — really calling! — you out of it, and you want to know what to do next. And despite the fact that you lack any tools to understand or interpret your experience of God, all that so many churches have to offer is the useless imperative: "Stay there — on fire for Christ!"

What's a new Christian to do, for pity's sake? It is utterly unsurprising that the unfulfillable longing we evangelicals have cultivated would — indeed, *must* — find its outlet through the material world and consumer patterns in which we live the entirety of our lives. The church isn't offering any alternative models for how to live. Small wonder that many of us would cling to anything substantial, including Brand Jesus. This is understandable and even forgivable. But such a lack is unacceptable as a standard practice for church leaders because it fosters a spiritual sense that will not grow and, not growing, will not endure.

One Brand among Many

The fact that the church treats spiritual disciplines as if they were just like every other life skill brings us to our third reason why so many inadvertently trade their calling for the changeling belief in Brand Jesus. We make it all too easy to compartmentalize our lives and keep Christianity in its proper place. We don't want our religion to transgress the boundary lines of our lives. But a bounded Christianity is not Christianity at all — it is the devotion of Brand Jesus.

The undeniable marker of Brand Jesus is that it fits the cycle of "meaningful" consumption that encompasses our self-understanding. It does not generate any friction with our other patterns of consumption; instead, it fits neatly into the open part of our lifestyle marked "spirituality." I don't know how many Christians I've met who are outraged at the marketplace of religions in twenty-first century America; they are nostalgic for an era when pluralism meant having a Methodist and a Baptist in the same room. But our response to this marketplace has not, for the most part, been to insist on the incomparable Christ. Instead, faced with a competitive market, we have done our best to brand Christianity as the most attractive product available.

This may be the most significant and irremediable problem facing the church today, and it is one that leaves me reeling at the scope of our disease. Simply put, for the vast majority of American churches, becoming a Christian is as painless as adding a new brand to the repertoire that already forms your identity.

We've already seen the impossibility of extricating ourselves from consumerism for those who live in contemporary Western culture. Regardless of personal morality, we are tainted by social sin. So, when self-proclaimed Christians are not so much disciples of the living Lord as they are consumers of Brand Jesus, this represents the wholesale acceptance of the sinful order of the world — by the very group which imagines itself standing in opposition to the domain of "the prince of this age."

Here's the litmus test: Jesus Christ asks that we give up everything and follow him, living in the renewed creation of God's original order. This is the kingdom whose citizens are constituted by their radical reliance on the gifts of God. In other words, Jesus Christ cannot be a brand because he forbids the presence of any competitors. Christians are to find our identity in him and him alone. As Paul writes to the Corinthians, "For even if there are so-called gods, whether in heaven or on earth (as indeed there are many "gods" and many "lords"), yet for us there is but one God, the Father, from whom all things came and for whom we live; and there is but one Lord, Jesus Christ, through whom all things came and through whom we live" (1 Corinthians 8:5–6).

But Brand Jesus, like all so-called gods, is willing to be one member of a brand family. Brand Jesus baptizes consumerism and is utterly amenable to the presence of other brands. Are you a Christian yuppie? Enjoy Brand Jesus alongside Mercedes, Dom Perignon, Lacoste. How about those Christian punks? Brand Jesus rocks hardcore with P.O.D., Kerusso, and NOTW. For all the Christian patriots out there, know that Brand Jesus salutes you, along with manifest destiny, partisan politics, and anything that combines crosses with flags and/or bald eagles.

Brand Jesus, in other words, simply wants to add a tiny, harmless adjective — "Christian" — to whichever consumer identity you've already invested so much time and money in. In this, Brand Jesus is nothing like that horribly demanding Lord. Not only is that taskmaster Jesus Christ unwilling to be an adjective tacked onto your life, he insists on supplying the only noun — "Christian" — with which you name yourself.

Think about how utterly easy it is to live by the standards of modern American Christianity. How many churches in America would insist on any lifestyle changes, beyond adherence to the code of personal morality already mentioned, as part of membership? In fact, how many churches would offer a story of salvation that requires membership in the church at all?

This relative unconcern with authentic and wholly integrated Christian living is perhaps the strongest possible indictment of the American church. It says that despite tough talk about making Christ the Lord of our lives, we are actually perfectly content to imagine him as Savior only and relegate him to one corner of our existence.

Take Christians' employment as just one example. Would your leadership take even a marginal interest in the effect of a prospective member's job on his or her discipleship? (Unless, of course, the prospective member was in some egregiously immoral line of work that would facilitate the opportunity to make grave, deliciously self-righteous pronouncements about the danger of Satan.) We might be interested in helping the Christian cultivate a spiritual attitude toward her employment; this move would never be compounded, however, by daring to critique *what* the Christian did for a living — if it involved undue focus on wealth, say. Our situation is very different from the early days of the church, when Christians were forbidden employment that would require them to commit or be directly complicit in violence of any sort.

Brand Jesus makes the perfect chaplain to the American way of life because he gives it his uncompromising support — regardless of what it consists of. He is the ideal spiritual yes-man, permitting much while forbidding a few sacred cows so that his flock can maintain delusional pretensions at moral rigor. In this sense, he bears all the odium of the Pharisees' moral blindness, but without any of their rigorous discipline. (This same principle drove masses to hysteria about Janet Jackson's breast — and *only* about her breast — in the midst of that completely sexually explicit and violent dance routine.)

I can almost hear the retort: "Well, what are you going to do? Ask people to move, change careers, upend their whole lives? Following Jesus *can't be that hard.*"

Certainly not. Jesus would never ask his followers to leave their livelihoods, their hometowns, their families. Would he?

Well — *Brand* Jesus wouldn't.

Remember, we live in a symbolic economy where meaning is the primary commodity — but this symbolic economy is fueled by very real money. That's the currency of sacrifice that is offered up to Mammon. Now, I am not necessarily suggesting that Brand Jesus is a commercial commodity (though it can be, as we'll see below). But we overlook the role of actual money — hard currency — to our peril. For it seems that the materially poor are less likely consumers of Brand Jesus than are wealthy Christians. If one is poor, Jesus may be the only meaningful thing one can claim. As such, this Jesus is more probably the Christ, the living Lord. He is less likely to be one among many competing for the loyalty of his disciples — and when one's Christ is one among many, rather than himself alone, the Jesus known is not Christ at all, but Brand Jesus.

Such a phenomenon is more likely to be found among the rich. (If you balk at this, then is it the case that you really think material abundance comes without a cost?) The greater your material wealth, the greater your ability to configure a consumer identity through the strategic allocation of resources. If you are rich and Christian, then Jesus is certainly not the only significant commodity that you consume.

We can understand Jesus' lament in the Bible, that it is easier for a camel to pass through the eye of a needle than it is for a rich person to enter the kingdom of heaven, in contemporary terms. For the materially well off, Jesus must always be in competition with other brands. Thus, there is always the temptation to think secretly that he is simply a commodity communicating spiritual excellence, in the same way that a mansion or luxury car or country club membership communicates financial excellence. A Mercedes, for instance, invariably contributes to its owner's self-understanding in a way that a more utilitarian vehicle does not. This is unavoidable, because the brand marketers at Mercedes have gone to great lengths to make their brand as significant and meaning loaded as possible. But any space in your self-understanding that is claimed by Mercedes is space that Jesus will have to fight to reclaim. And we're not always disposed to give him the edge in that battle. In a material existence where we only give Jesus a section of our identities, rather than the whole pie, there is always a significant danger that the Jesus we know is nothing more than another brand in our lives.

There is not much hope that this situation can ever be adequately addressed. Our churches simply do not have the gumption to do so.

Despite the fact that following Jesus Christ clearly changed not only the moral situation but the *economic reality of every single significant disciple recorded in the New Testament,* the most that churches even bother to ask of our economic selves is that we tithe. Most ministers aren't known for their athleticism, but there's not a gymnastics competition in the world that can match the back flips and contortions of a preacher explaining to his "Bible-believing" church why Jesus was speaking ever so figuratively about wealth.

Chapter 15

The Righteous Shall Live By . . .

The final and perhaps most fundamental reason why Brand Jesus is allowed to thrive in the American church is because we have profoundly misinterpreted the meaning of "faith." Faith is and should be the core of Christianity. In today's popular Christian parlance, however, faith is frequently nothing more than a synonym for belief. And belief is as easy to define as it is to have. That is, belief consists of internal convictions about God. In many churches, the bare minimum of belief is the conviction that because we know Jesus as our personal savior, recognizing that he died for our sins, we are going to heaven when we die.

Faith, by contrast, is considerably more challenging to define and to have. In fact, you can't *have* faith. You live it. But our everyday understanding of faith as belief has drained any quality of action from the idea of faith. We speak of faith as if it were a noun to be possessed, rather than a verb to be enacted. So — how should we think of faith?

Outside of church, we use the word most frequently when talking about marriage. And, as it turns out, the way we use faith in that context can teach us a great deal about how we ought to use it in church. Everybody knows that keeping faith in a marriage is about fidelity or faithfulness over the long haul.

In other words, *faith takes time* in a way that belief doesn't. Imagining that belief is sufficient for Christian living is as absurd as imagining that a good wedding day will ensure a happy marriage. The bride and groom may believe their wedding vows with all their hearts and speak them clearly with their lips, but their convictions on the wedding day are only the beginning — not the end — of the story of their marriage.

From the wedding onwards, faith will be the day in, day out enactment of the couple's relationship. And a faithful marriage is one in which both spouses actively live out their wedding vows, in ways large

122

and small, throughout their years together. The wedding day only asks that we believe. But vows are easy to say and celebrate. The faithfulness of marriage, with its having and holding, loving and cherishing, sickness and health, and riches and poverty, is hard. So, too, goes our Christian faith. But the way that we commonly read scripture has distorted our understanding, leaving us with the profoundly unbiblical idea that faith is no more than belief.

Let's look at one of the most important biblical passages about faith, the thesis of Paul's letter to the Romans in 1:16–17. Translations invariably make as neat a package of this passage as they can, though the Greek is distinctly difficult to pin down, especially in terms of what is usually translated as "faith."

Observe below two reputable translations. In each of them, I have italicized the English rendering of the Greek *pisteuonti*. Notice how in each that the gospel is the "power of God for salvation" to the person who *has* something—the possessor of a spiritual commodity:

> For I am not ashamed of the gospel; it is the power of God for salvation to everyone *who has faith,* to the Jew first and also to the Greek. For in it the righteousness of God is revealed through faith for faith; as it is written, "The one who is righteous will live by faith." (NRSV)

> I am not ashamed of the gospel, because it is the power of God for the salvation of everyone *who believes:* first for the Jew, then for the Gentile. For in the gospel a righteousness from God is revealed, a righteousness that is by faith from first to last [or: that is from faith to faith], just as it is written: "The righteous will live by faith." (NIV)

In many standard evangelistic presentations, these verses are read alongside the great promise of Romans 10:9, which pledges salvation to the one who verbally confesses Christ's Lordship and internally believes that God raised him from the dead. This combined reading produces an exhortation to *a singular moment of belief,* usually marked by something like the Sinner's Prayer. After that, the conventional wisdom goes, if the person meant it, he or she is saved. In other words, Paul is understood to be describing the work of an instant.

If Romans 1:16 is read in this way, then the reader is already predisposed to interpret "faith" as a possession when she reads Paul's quotation from the prophet Habakkuk in the next verse: "The righteous will live by faith." And because this verse from Habakkuk is the climax of Paul's thesis in 1:16–17, the reader is then left with an understanding that faith is something that she is supposed to *have,* rather than *do.* If we read Romans like this, we can come away with the idea that being a Christian is fundamentally about what one believes in heart and mind.

The Apostle James wrote scathingly about such "faith": "Show me your faith without deeds, and I will show you my faith by what I do. You *believe* that there is one God. Good! Even the demons believe that — and shudder" (2:18–19, italics mine). In the false understanding of faith, one's Christianity can (in theory, at least) be an entirely internal and private matter, never requiring a connection to a church or any outward change in life. If Christianity simply requires belief, then Christ is technically no more significant than Santa Claus, the Tooth Fairy, or any other object of belief.

Many churches will put every emphasis on your conversion and the belief — the coming to a conviction about Jesus as savior — obtained in that moment. This belief is your possession, effective for salvation whether you act on it or not. And the only way you can *give up* that belief is to replace it with some other belief. Such a reading makes for easy conclusions to evangelistic tracts.

The problem, of course, is that a reading of Romans 10:9 that understands it to mean the work of an instant is a reading that ignores the rest of the New Testament context. Coming to faith is actually about joining the family of God, the body of Christ, and living out this new relationship faithfully. The biblical understanding of faith bears no resemblance to the quick belief that we so often sell. No, in the biblical understanding of faith, the righteous one will live by *fidelity,* or even *trusting obedience.*

To be sure, faith as fidelity or trusting obedience incorporates and even begins with belief, just as a marriage begins and often finds its inspiration from a wedding. One cannot be faithful to that which one does not first believe. Thus, the connotation of belief is clearly present in the classic definition of faith of Hebrews 11:1 — it is "being sure of what we hope for and certain of what we do not see." But, as Hebrews 11 goes on to describe, the faith for which "the ancients were commended" is an obedience over the long haul, not a spiritual possession that they acquired once and for all.

The way we use belief is not the way the Bible uses it. In the biblical usage, belief is what we would call faith, endurance based on a confidence in the final righteousness of God, regardless of one's present circumstances. Take Hebrews 10:39 as an example: "We are not of those who shirk back and are destroyed, but of those who believe and are saved." Faith, in other words, is lived in and over time. It is not something to hoard, but something to do — or, to be more precise, it is a way of living life.

This understanding of a way of life is consistent with the New Testament portrayal of conversion. Someone coming to faith in the biblical context was one who began to follow the way of the disciple — with all its stumbling and missteps (Mark 10:52). The book of Acts even refers to the early church as "the Way" (Acts 9:2; 19:9). And this in turn resonates with the message of the Old Testament prophets, who called the people to "ask where the good way is, and walk in it," and so "find rest for your souls" (Jeremiah 6:16). Contrast this with the life *style* offered by Brand Jesus. It is a belief to be worn, showed off, even posed in. But it is not the way of life that is biblical faith.

Biblical faith is the way in which God instructs the prophet Habakkuk: not only belief, but rather an active, lived trust in the sovereignty and final judgment of God. Habakkuk — one of the most honest figures in the Bible — cries out to God with a Job-like complaint: Why does wickedness prevail? God's answer does not offer immediate satisfaction, to say the least:

> . . . the revelation awaits an appointed time; it speaks of the end and will not prove false. Though it linger, wait for it; it will certainly come and will not delay. See, [the wicked one] is puffed up; his desires are not upright — but the righteous will live by his faith. . . . (2:3–4)

Interestingly, the comment on the faith of the righteous is merely an interjection in the middle of a longer judgment against the wicked. Both Habakkuk and the wicked one perceive the same situation — that evil goes unpunished for now, and that violence and greed run unchecked for the gain of the few. The wicked one is "arrogant and never at rest . . . greedy as the grave," God tells Habakkuk. But whereas the wicked one sees the situation and exploits it, Habakkuk cries out to God for relief. God's answer to Habakkuk — that God will be faithful to God's own character, which promises justice — points out the flaw in the perception of the wicked, who acts as if the present is all there is, with no judgment to come.

By contrast, the righteous one will live in the continual, present expectation of the future judgment of God — that is, in fidelity or trusting obedience to the dependability of God. Thus, the "by faith" of the righteous seems to refer both to God and humankind. The faith of people finds its home in the faithfulness of God. God is faithful. The Lord has not abandoned the world, the wicked do not build to their own lasting glory, and the righteous do not suffer without the sure knowledge of a final vindication. This emphasis on faithfulness is especially helpful in our present context, when it is difficult even to hear the word "faith" without simply thinking "belief" — given that the saying "have faith in Christ" usually means "believe such-and-such about Christ."

According to Habakkuk, the righteous one's life has everything to do with waiting for God with trust. This understanding of faith is beautifully expanded by the illustration in the final verses of his concluding hymn of praise:

> Though the fig tree does not bud and there are no grapes on the vines, though the olive crop fails and the fields produce no food, though there are no sheep in the pen and no cattle in the stalls, yet I will rejoice in the LORD, I will be joyful in God my Savior. The sovereign LORD is my strength; he makes my feet like the feet of a deer, he enables me to go on the heights. (3:17–19)

It is not the case that Habakkuk sings his hymn because all is well with the world. He is not deluded about the quality of his present circumstance. Neither is it true that Habakkuk simply believes a set of propositions about God. No, faith is the way Habakkuk *lives.* He enacts the faith of the righteous by rejoicing in the Lord and being joyful in God his Savior. He does not trust in his own strength (such trust being the imperative to Mammon's devotees) but relies upon the steadfastness of the Lord.

Taking the original meaning of faith in Habakkuk and applying it to our Romans text leads us to a very different interpretation than that of the status quo as described above. Notice that Paul's "from faith to faith" makes explicit the dual implication of Habakkuk's faith, which leaves faith as a shared action between God and humankind. Faith is the double-sided character of the divine-human relationship. We believe that God is believe-able, trust that God is trust-worthy, and have faith that God is faith-ful. An expanded paraphrase of Romans 1:16–17 along these lines might read as follows:

> For I am not ashamed of the gospel; it is the power of God for salvation to everyone who *trustingly obeys [God],* to the Jew first and also to the Greek. For in it the righteousness of God is revealed *by [God's] faithfulness to the faith [of those who trust him], just as it is written: "The righteous will live by faith/fulness."*

In summary, faith is something we are to live, rather than something we can have.

Let me say for the record, in anticipation of the inevitable criticism, that I am not advocating works righteousness. I hold to the traditional Protestant assertion of justification by faith alone. However, I am arguing that, while the formulation of "faith alone" is correct, in such contexts we often proclaim an emaciated "faith." Faith alone — always. But *belief* alone — never. The righteous one does not live by belief.

But if faith is something we do, then am I not making it a work? Am I not somehow saying we can earn our way into heaven? (The assumption that the question of heaven ought to be primary for the Christian is itself dangerous — see above.) The answer is no. To begin with, we have to remember that, during the Reformation, our Protestant forebears drew a stark line between faith and works in part because of the ecclesial situation they found themselves in protest against. We have inherited their (justifiable) hostility toward labeling *specific* works, like indulgences, as the effective work of faith. But the fear of backsliding on this issue has led many of us to shirk any connection whatsoever between faith and action.

Such a distinction is unbiblical, however, since James himself connects the two when he contends that belief, if it is something possessed but not enacted as faith, is not salvific (2:14). The fundamental truth of the Reformers was that good deeds neither constitute nor prove a saving faith. With them, we affirm that no one can work his or her way into God's favor. But though deeds cannot prove the positive presence of faith, their absence can and does prove the negative: A life without deeds is a life without faith. "By their fruits you will know them" (Matthew 7:20). Belief that is an internal quality — an assertion or conviction regarding a set of principles or propositions — is therefore an unbiblical faith. This is bad enough on its own, but in our age, the understanding of faith as possession of belief has resulted in the rise of an idol, Brand Jesus, a commodified Christianity.

So how can we understand an enacted faith without making it a "work"? Our trouble comes out of an inability to think past the presuppositions that accompany the compartmentalized life (spirituality | family | job | finance | politics | etc.), which is so hospitable to Brand Jesus. This fact is yet another indicator of how deep our problem is as a church. It is not true that the church body is healthy overall, with the exception of some doctrinal error called Brand Jesus, which we can excise as easily as an isolated tumor. Our problem is rather that the very way we live makes such a fertile soil for the false gospel of Brand Jesus. To paraphrase Pete Rollins, our problem is not so much that we believe the wrong things, but that we believe the wrong way.[1] We think of our lives in much the same way as we do belief; in other words, as something we have. And, in having life, we take actions — works — in the various spheres or compartments of our lives. In this manner of thinking, it is entirely possible to fall into the error of attempting spiritual works to gain the grace of God.

This course of action is based, however, on a false view of life. Life is not truly a possession because it cannot be hoarded. It must be lived. So, too, faith — which is no more contained in the moment of coming to belief than a marriage is contained in the video of the wedding day. Those events, frozen in a DVD and a hundred photographs, can be possessed. But the faith of the marriage, like the Christian faith, cannot be.

Life and faith, in other words, are enacted without being "works." To get to this understanding, we have to extract belief and faith from the compartments in which we have stuffed them. They are too big and too complex to fit there. Faith enacted is not a work; it is the basis for all works. Faith is not an action, but it is unrecognizable if not through one's actions.

Put grammatically, faith is an adverb. It is life lived *trustingly*. Faith takes the life that everyone possesses — good and evil alike — and commits it to the inbreaking dominion and final providence of the Lord Jesus Christ and the God who raised him from the dead. Faith is therefore enacted, but it is not an action in the way that obedience to the law is an action.

Recall the first of the parables that Christ told to the chief priests and elders in the Temple courts (Matthew 21:28–32). There was a man with two sons who told them each to go work in the vineyard. One refused, but later repented and went; the other assented, but did not go. Which did the father's will, Christ asks? And the religious leaders condemn themselves, correctly identifying as righteous the one whose repentance led to action, though they were more like the one who agreed and did nothing. Charles Spurgeon, preaching on this text, assailed the "deceptively submissive" in his congregation as latter-day examples of the religious leaders:

> You utter a polite, respectful "I go, sir," but you do not go. You give a notional assent to the gospel. If I were to mention any doctrine, you would say, "Yes, that is true. I believe that." But your heart does not believe: you do not believe the gospel in the core of your nature, for if you did, it would have an effect upon you. A man may say, "I believe my house is on fire," but if he goes to bed and falls to sleep, it does not look as if he believed it, for when a man's house is on fire he tries to escape.[2]

Those whom Spurgeon addressed, like many today, had an un-enacted belief, a propositional possession that was like a jewel in a safe, beautiful in shape, but worthless for the fact of its being locked away. They were, as Spurgeon quipped, as religious as the seats they sat in, and as likely to get into heaven. "Notional assent" — in modern parlance, belief as commodity — is not faith. Because the correctness of one's belief is not simply its content but *how* one carries it, a belief that is doctrinally correct but merely internal is *not* a correct belief. Internal belief that remains internal is faithless. Many cry, "Lord, Lord," but the only true belief is the one that is lived out in accord with the will of the Father who is in heaven (Matthew 7:21–23).

I realize that the above account will not satisfy some whose primary concern is avoiding works righteousness. It seems to me, however, that our desire for clean and simple answers can lead us astray. A paranoia about works righteousness that leads us to conceive of faith as merely one of faith's components — belief, and that simply as propositional assent — imposes an unbiblical sterility on the complexity of the actual biblical witness.

We may not resolve for our leisure what the Bible leaves as a challenge. The narrow way is surrounded on both sides by unavoidable slippery slopes. And discipleship, like it or not, is the hard task of avoiding a fall in either direction.

There is certainly the danger that talking about faith in action will lead to the errors of works righteousness. But divorcing faith from action *has* led to the error of desiccated belief. And we were never promised an easy road. Jesus did not tell us that two thousand years into the game someone would come up with a foolproof, ten-point church strategy that would suddenly make it easy to follow him. Christians are supposed to stay awake, so it is counterproductive to weave the doctrinal equivalent of a hammock on a sunny afternoon. Faith as belief, a possession to be had — who wouldn't be ready to put his or her feet up and relax on that?

Given our comparison with weddings and marriages, American Christians' overemphasis on belief is perhaps unsurprising. After all, the wedding industry has become a huge business in the United States. We subscribe so readily to the fantasy of that single, perfect, "magic" day; entire magazines are dedicated to perpetuating this myth, and our infatuation with reality television shows about weddings (Who Wants to Marry a Millionaire?) demonstrates that we fall for it completely. The average expense of weddings continues to rise. Yet so do divorce rates. Is it any coincidence that our infatuation with the magic of a single day corresponds to an inability to consider the span of a lifetime? And can the church therefore be surprised when so many take the plunge of making their baptismal vows to Christ but are unwilling to live them out over the long years of faith?

Chapter 16

Evangelical Brand Ascendancy

What does it means to be an evangelical Christian in America today?

This is a subject of much debate and a variety of theories, and it is a question that may be up for grabs. In their October 2006 editorial "Save the E-Word," the editors of *Christianity Today* wrote that for the word "evangelical" to be functional today, "it must be as a set of ideals and commitments around which to rally rather than as a partisan label."[1] *Christianity Today* has as good a claim as anyone to an authoritative definition of "evangelical": as a "magazine of evangelical conviction" founded by Billy Graham, there is a plausible argument to be made that an evangelical is a *CT* reader! But the very fact that the mainstream evangelical publication assigned the E-word with a subjunctive or imperative meaning ("it must be . . . "), rather than an indicative one ("it is . . . ") indicates that the word seems destined to continue as a work in progress.

As a self-identifying evangelical, my favorite definition is the Trinitarian set of theological emphases put forward by John Stott in *Evangelical Truth:* the threefold uniqueness of the Father's revelation in scripture, the Son's cross, and the Spirit's regeneration. However, while this is my favorite definition, it is certainly not the only one out there. For that matter, not all who describe themselves as evangelical assent to it, and many who would assent to it would not call themselves evangelicals. Other theorists have suggested four or six qualities that are uniquely evangelical, and a great deal of ink gets spilled by theologians and pastors trying to set out boundary lines by which evangelicals can reliably recognize their own ilk.

For all this effort, however, theological definitions of evangelicals don't seem to work very well. There is no creedal statement that identifies one as an evangelical, no single denomination to which we all belong, no liturgical pattern to which we all conform, no single evangelical leader whose teaching and administrative authority is universally recognized, and no ecumenical gathering (for evangelicalism is ecumenical, though with a lower-case "e") to which we can point as our shared origin. (The World Congress in Lausanne, with its resulting Covenant, is a viable but not unchallengeable contender.)

This mess of confusion, however, does not stop Christians and non-Christians alike from speaking authoritatively about who evangelicals are and what we are up to. The secular media have reported on evangelicalism mostly as a political phenomenon ever since *Time* magazine proclaimed 1976 the "Year of the Evangelical" after Jimmy Carter was elected as the first "born-again" president. But perhaps they are to be excused for this attitude, when the group that claims to represent the evangelical center (if there is one), the National Association of Evangelicals, exists to promote the united *social* and *political* goals of its theologically diverse members.

We are a fractious bunch! I suspect that if you pushed most evangelicals, they would likely be forced to admit that evangelicalism is a lot like pornography, as (not) defined by the U.S. Supreme Court: You just know it when you see it. But this un-definition does not offer a stable center.

Because we are more attitudinal than doctrinal, and because the movement, whatever it may be, has consistently emphasized an engagement with the "outside" world to convert nonmembers, we have always run huge risks of cultural syncretism. Alarm at this co-option by secular interests has been increasingly voiced in magazines like *Christianity Today* in recent years. But it seems from many indicators that the damage has already been done.

We have not understood the parallels between our rise to positions of cultural influence and our decreasing claim to authentic piety. Distracted by the prospect of "gaining the world," we have failed to confront in any adequate way the cultural dominance of consumerism. As a result, it has adhered to the very heart of our self-understanding, so that evangelicalism itself has become consumerist phenomenon, defined by allegiance to Brand Jesus.

What does it mean to be an evangelical in America today? Where, if it exists at all, is the site of evangelical unity? The reality, unfortunately, is that *American evangelicalism has become primarily a marketing demographic.* At our heart, we are that Christian section of the country that can be relied upon to consume in significant numbers any commodity to which advertisers can adhere the Brand Jesus sticker.

Searching for Security

For disciples of Christ who are concerned for the faithful witness to God of the American church, the latter half of the twentieth century has not been kind. A historical overview reveals a series of events that compromised the integrity of our testimony to God's faithfulness.

Immediately after World War II, it seemed to some Christians that things would be all right. This was, after all, the decade of suburban expansion, anchored spiritually by church attendance, and the emergence of neo-evangelicalism along with Billy Graham's rise to national prominence.

The social turmoil of the sixties, however, revealed the shallowness of Christianity's preeminence as a value system in postwar America. Many factors are cited as flash points, including the rise of the hippie movement, the Roe v. Wade decision that legalized abortion, and the rejection of Bob Jones University's tax-exempt status due to its racist policies.[2] Many Christians saw all of these as markers of a world come undone and a country turned against its historic faith. And so, confronted with the pluralism of ideas filling the social vacuum, American Christianity marched to (culture) war. Christian organizations and churches reacted to their loss of influence, both perceived and actual, by attempting a cultural power grab. In doing so, they hoped to reclaim the tradition's uncontested historical pride of place in American life.[*] The resulting culture war has been the social context for much of American Christianity over the past forty years.

This effort to cement Christian influence took place in a variety of operational theaters, all of which centered on politics and commerce. In the former, Christians rallied around several hot-button issues that — regardless of their theological validity — were guaranteed to elicit knee-jerk dogmatism in many. Thus, they built a political machine to fight for the codification of Christian values in all levels

---

[*]This was not equally the case for mainline or liberal churches. Though such a broad historical treatment cannot help but fall into the inaccuracy of generality, the liberal churches' response was generally to attempt an accommodating relevance to evolving social mores.

of government. A number of factors led to the near-complete alignment of this political movement with a single party, in which they
came to own a dominant, though not uncontested, share. Not least
among these factors was the perception that the other political party
was wishy-washy, a cardinal sin among evangelicals.

Though political engagement has attracted far more media attention, the commercial is actually more pervasive. After all, most
Christians aren't year-round political partisans. But a great many
Christians regularly and increasingly participate in the Christian material economy. This economy's first outlet was the cottage industry
of a specifically Christian trade in movies, books, music, and broad-
casting, sustained by the growing numbers of the demographic. As the
movement grew, the flush economies of the latter part of the twentieth
century presented the opportunity for the Christian trade to coalesce
as a potent, crossover market force, able to make — and sometimes
break — secular products, corporations, and media enterprises.

Focusing mostly on the political, secular woe-sayers have raised a
great hue and cry over the increasing cultural dominance of a group
they (wrongly, it turns out) imagined to have been in its grave since the
Scopes monkey trial. Conspiracy theories abound. But virtually none
of them links the commercial and political gains of Christianity with
one another, let alone the historical context that has given rise to both.

In fact, I would argue that nearly everyone — including its own
partisans — fundamentally misunderstands the roots and goals of this
Christian cultural power grab. Micro-machinations notwithstanding,
the movement as a whole is completely decentralized. It is not the
product of a cabal (though there are cabals), nor is it born out of malice
or sinister intent.

No, the Christian assault on culture is born from fear. It is the manifestation of collective terror at a world that seems to have spun out of
control. The movement emerges out of a set of presuppositions that
run so deep as to be rarely examined: Back when things were "Christian," the world was sane. (As conventional wisdom would have it,
this means the time before the wars and in the 1950s, the decade believed to have replicated that idyllic antebellum state.) Now that things
are not "Christian," the world is terrifying. "Things would be okay,
things would be stable," whispers the terrified and hunted Christian
unconscious, "if we could just make our culture *Christian* again."

The Brooksville experiment is a perfect example. In the late 1990s, this small rural community in Alabama sought to form a "Bible-based town." The idea was for a utopian Christian community that could survive as an anachronistic enclave in the midst of modernity.* In the context of our historical review, the words of the founder, James Henderson, speak for themselves:

> "It's so basic. When I was a child in the 1940's and 1950's, we had a sense of community, built around the church, on people helping each other. Over the years, that's gotten frayed around the edges. I've watched the issue of the separation of church and state get out of control. What we are trying to do, with this little country crossroads, is bring together the church and state. We want to make life make sense again, for people."[3]

The common thread between Brooksville and other efforts in contemporary Christian cultural engagement is the struggle for the dominance and representation of Christian *identity*.** The battles reflect the need to make things Christian, no matter what that means (in Brooksville, at least, that meaning seems to be a hybrid of a mythic "unspoiled Southern community" and certain Christian social principles).

But the Christian identity being fought for is largely devoid of theological content. The fight is not for Wesleyanism or Calvinism or dispensationalism or Orthodoxy or Catholicity or anything else so sectarian. As Brooksville campaigner Hubert Porter remarked, "We're not trying to make anybody Baptist or Methodist. Just live by Christian principles." The comfort — and proof of a rootedness in culture, rather than theology — of this Christianity stems from its very anti-denominationalism. This is not to say that there are no doctrinal battles. There are, but they are largely internal to the faith and inscrutable to outside observers, as Christians of varying eschatological

---

*The *New York Times* article on the town records that "The King James Bible would be the town charter, the Ten Commandments, its ordinances. The people who live here would look out for one another, would look in on the elderly, would watch for children in the crosswalk. They would not buy or sell alcohol or pornography. They would not steal. They would vote — every woman and man — in the churches instead of a city hall, but there would probably not be many votes because the aim of the town would be to preserve the slow life that exists here, not mess it up with change...."
**The goals of this battle are therefore actually quite similar to those of the representation wars of the 1980s and 1990s, which were fought by racial, ethnic, and sexual minorities.

and ecclesiological stripes vie for influence. And the Christian campaigners certainly have distinct goals in commerce and politics, the achievement of which they mistakenly imagine to be the historical basis for the overall struggle. While interior skirmishes are fought and won without attracting any serious notice, however, the victory in the culture war goes to the most generic Christianity.

For this stripe of evangelicalism, the dominance of Christian identity — glorious, nominal Christianity — is the prize. To be sure, this Christianity has boundaries. But the outlines of the camp are drawn almost entirely with cultural categories, exactly as one would expect of a culture war. Indeed, the rise of the social, economic, and political capital for the victors' generic Christianity is directly proportional to the thoroughgoing inoffensiveness of their gospel — which is, in fact, simple social conservatism dressed up in the rhetorical iconography of the historical faith. While theological distinctives get lip service, the movement's willingness to collaborate with anyone toward the advancement of its conservative cultural goals — the likes of the Unification Church springs to mind — demonstrates that its true loyalties are politically demarcated.

The Christianity that has emerged as the lead campaigner in this culture war has a distinct gospel that bears little resemblance to the biblical version. The good news it promotes is the prospect of safety in this lifetime through the destruction or suppression of anything that feels threatening; the result is an evangel that is pro-family, pro-life, pro-America, pro-military, pro-capitalism, anti-feminist, anti-sex, and anti-gay. The whole thing is sealed with the promise of heaven, to boot.

The result is a culturally triumphant Christianity in the form of a Mayberry-esque market demographic. When pressed, defenders of this Christianity will say they are fighting to create a culture that is hospitable to people receiving Christ as Lord and Savior. The cultural battles are thus construed as being vitally linked to the church's historical emphasis on evangelism. Only rarely is this root issue ever actually debated, however. Do evangelism and discipleship depend upon — or, more strongly, do they bear any relation whatsoever to — a friendly host culture? Was the Roman Empire hospitable to Paul and the Christian gospel? Is there even such a thing as a culture that is naturally hospitable to the gospel?

Despite this outward link to evangelism, the real appeal of this Christianity is cultural. For significant numbers of people, the uncertainty of late-twentieth-century life has understandably generated a nostalgia for the supposed once-was certainty of a mythic, safe, faithfully Christian America (the latter an imaginary construction itself, as we discussed in chapter 1).

Moreover, we are now at a turning point, the outcome of which has yet to be fully revealed. The mass popularity of this brand of the faith was based on the appeal to restoring a vanished security. But Christians coming of age now are thoroughly untroubled by the existential angst that their parents felt. They have inherited their parents' mandate for social conservatism, but *not* the fear that generated it, or the intuitive longing for a mythic, bygone Christian America. As a result, we are left with a form of Christianity gathered around the call to culture war, but which has no immediate knowledge of the conflict's *casus belli*. Will latter generations, untroubled by the ambiguity of late modernity, maintain the ferocity of their forebears' cause? Or will we see a new incarnation of Christianity emerge from the old, one less concerned with historical markers of Christian triumph than with the viability of Christian brand identity?

The Quest for Brand Saturation

When we look at twenty-first-century American Christianity, much of what we see is a cultural fortress that has been under construction for a long time. It is the ongoing end product of a long struggle to manufacture the safety of tradition in the midst of a frightening world. And the stronger this Christianity is, the safer its adherents feel.

The problem lies, as problems are wont to do, at the beginning, when the Christian response to the vacuum of meaning was to position itself as one among many of those cultural players striving for social dominance. *One player among many* — this is what Christ was and is not, and neither is his church. As John Stott is fond of saying, we may not refer to "Christ the Great" as we would "Charles the Great" or "Napoleon the Great." Christ is not the great, he is the Only! He is incomparable — and so is his church.

But our response to the culture war of the latter twentieth century has not testified to the uniqueness of Christ or his church, no matter what we claimed with the exclusivist words of our doctrine. We were afraid of going the way of cultural irrelevancy, like our fundamental-ist forebears, and, in fear — itself a peculiar and particular species of faithlessness — we determined to claim the prize. So Christians took on the culture with all the dignity of one more brawler in a bar fight or another stray dog battling the pack for a bone. To summarize, we have demonstrated with every action the (false) conviction that the fate of the church is ours to win or lose. And so we have dishonored the God who called and commissioned us.

In the process of our doing this, Brand Jesus has gradually taken God's place. He is a God on the ascendancy if we get enough spiritual consumers and brand adherents, but his fortune can just as equally ebb if our efforts lag (unlike the supremacy of the Lord Jesus). The battle-ground for Brand Jesus was the selling floor of the cultural marketplace that our society had become. We beheld a world where everything was for sale and thus where everyone was a shopper, and our response was to manufacture what we imagined to be a more competitive product.

Now, on the one hand, the *appearance* of being one option among many is unavoidable. There is a marketplace of ideas, we do live in a pluralistic society, and Christians have no governmentally estab-lished pride of place in this country. (And thank God for it, or the radicalism of our already diluted gospel witness would be irrevoca-bly compromised: A Christ that requires Caesar's authorization is no Christ at all.) From the point of view of any social observer, Christian-ity *is* simply one option among many. There is no getting around this cultural state of affairs. But this de facto situation poses a challenge to Christians, namely, are we to accept and confirm this pluralist social prescription?

If we were to stand in the middle of the religious mall that is Amer-ica, we would see an array of storefronts presenting competing brands and lifestyle choices. But this vision would be flawed — not because there is something wrong with our sight, but because we would be standing in the wrong place. Christians should not be standing in the middle of the mall. We do not occupy this neutral ground from which all options seem equal and equally valid. Everyone has his or her own perspective, to be sure. Our perspective is that of a people under the authority of the living Lord. From this vantage point, and only from this vantage point, we can and must recognize that Jesus' is the name high over all.

In contrast to this perspective is that of the religious shopper, strolling the aisles of the existential mall in search of personal meaning. He *cannot help* but perceive the one we know as the living Lord as just another branded commodity to be evaluated and — if judged to be lifestyle enhancing — perhaps consumed. From the shopper's vantage point, the one we know as living Lord cannot be anything *but* Brand Jesus, a god among gods. Because the shopper has not accepted Jesus' Lordship, his perspective is flawed, and Jesus must appear less than he is — that is, as one branded lifestyle choice in competition with all other branded lifestyle choices.

It is worth pointing out that from the shopper's perspective, any claim to exclusivity at all will appear equally deluded. Why such brand zealotry when there is such a wide and colorful array of options to explore? The two perspectives cannot argue fruitfully with one another because each lacks the ability to communicate its perspective with the other. From where we stand, Christ is the Lord Jesus; from where the shopper stands, he is Brand Jesus. There is no convincing either of the other's perspective, because the internal logic of each is self-supporting. One cannot stay where one is standing and think differently; no, changing minds requires changing the ground that one occupies.

So, though there is one Jesus Christ, there are two perspectives for him in our consumerist time and place: (1) the Lord Jesus, as he is recognized by those who follow him; and (2) Brand Jesus, as he is believed to be by those who do not acknowledge his lordship. The betrayal comes when — as has taken place in the past half century — *Christians begin to treat their Lord as if he were the brand option that non-Christians believe him to be.* When, in our zeal to draw in the shoppers, we advertise Jesus as if he were indeed a commodity for sale, as if he were in truth the Brand Jesus that he appears to be to the existential window shopper, we forsake the Lord.

The reason that we allowed our witness to Christ to conform to the demands of a consumerist culture is the fear described above. Our link to the imagined stability of an antebellum world was the dominance of Christianity. And so, in an effort to secure Christianity's dominance in the contemporary West, we have accepted the world's terms for what sort of Jesus he must be — namely, a brand or lifestyle enabler.

This would be a bad enough move, however understandable, on its own. But compounding our error is the fact that the "believer's

Christianity" central to evangelicalism requires the evangelism of each generation, including the children of Christians. One cannot inherit one's parents' Christianity. It is not as though there were parallel bloodlines of Christians on the one side and "shoppers" on the other, with the former waging an evangelistic war of attrition-cum-conversion on the latter. No, in each of the generations of late-twentieth-century America — by which time inherited stories had been rejected for good — the children of Christians were themselves up for grabs, and therefore became the target demographic for a new evangelistic sales pitch. Because of this, several consecutive generations of American Christianity have bought and then sold Brand Jesus as the object of their devotion. But while we have done this, we've lost the intensity of the fear that first motivated our Christian forebears — we've inherited the Brand Jesus that came out of it, but not the fear itself.

In a rather counterintuitive way, the problem is not that we do not believe in the product that we're selling (as the allegation of nominal or hypocritical Christianity is sometimes phrased) but rather that we have come to believe in our product so very strongly. We have come to believe in it to such a degree, in fact, that we tend to forget that the Lord is not actually a product at all. We're actually all too happy to buy ourselves the goods we have on offer. Like the happy president in that old Hair Club for Men advertisement, each of us can exuberantly claim that we don't simply work for the company — we are its customers, as well!

As a result, a sizeable segment of the national exercise of Christian faith is now firmly established around consumption of Brand Jesus, toward the goal of establishing the dominance of Christian identity as a cultural force. What we now appear to be after as a whole is domination of the culture market through brand saturation, achieved forcefully in the commercial and political spheres of life.

My claim in this chapter is *not* that all evangelicals are shallow or wicked consumers of Brand Jesus. The daily lives of most evangelicals are not spent in obsessive religious consumption or culture war strategizing; no, most evangelicals I know are good, generous, and decent people, and devout disciples of Jesus.

The problem is, instead, with evangelicalism as a phenomenon. And that *phenomenon* — the site or center of evangelicalism — is increasingly rooted in consumptive patterns. It has bought into the consumerist pattern of this age. And so, just as a voter is complicit in the goods and ills of his or her political party's platform, whether or not he or she thinks about them very much, so those of us who understand ourselves to be evangelicals are affected by developments and trends in evangelicalism. This movement in evangelicalism as a whole affects the theology and biblical interpretation we hear preached, the shape of our community life, the causes advocated at our churches, the style and content of our worship, the books we read, the things we buy, and the religious jargon with which we speak to one another. Evangelicalism has become a consumerist phenomenon based on Brand Jesus. And in so doing, it has baptized the consumerism that we already had in abundance.

Chapter 17

We Preach Ourselves

As described in the first pages of this book, the Christian retail market does not, itself, constitute wholesale Christian consumerism. But it does serve as a strong indicator, or a symptom, of this broader spiritual reality.

Christian retail has been in existence for many decades. But the claim that Christians have followed in secular footsteps is proven by the fact that Christian business has been booming ever since the country as a whole moved toward our contemporary consumerism. Even including factors such as the millennium, which fueled popular interest in end-times themes, and the terrorist attacks of September 11, 2001, which produced an increasing interest in spiritual books, the growth in the Christian-products industry corresponds directly to the explosion of brand-based advertising and consumption that followed on the heels of Marlboro Friday, 1993.

As with other brand-centric industries, the 1990s turned out to be a good decade for Christian retail. In 1993, the industry hit $3 billion in sales; 1998 saw a *USA Today* cover story on Christian retail and record-breaking attendance at the annual CBA conference; and 1999 saw the decade close with a ground-breaking ceremony for a new, five-acre CBA headquarters in Colorado Springs.[1] Perhaps most tellingly, the CBA officially changed its name from the historic "Christian Booksellers Association" appellation to its current acronym in 1996. That was the year that nonbook, "Christ-honoring resources" like apparel, jewelry, music, and the like outsold books in the member stores. The industry center, which had been literary resources for discipleship, had now shifted to Christian lifestyle accessories.

The recent entry of big secular chains like Wal-Mart into the Christian resources business has been hard on local mom-and-pop Christian bookstores, but great for the industry overall. Business is on the rise.

And the large Christian vendors are doing just fine. Take LifeWay Christian Stores as one example, which has 126 locations in twenty-three states, more than two thousand employees, and record revenues of $432 million in 2005. If LifeWay's success is any indicator, it appears that Christians are enthusiastically buying more and more Christian stuff in these early years of the twenty-first century.

To put the above in context, at exactly the same time that consumer identity emerged as the singularly dominant mode of understanding one's place in the world, Christians started buying more Christian goods (and the Christian bestseller became a regular industry occurrence, instead of an aberration). The phenomenon is likely all too familiar to the American consumer. After all, we buy our way into whoever it is we want to be. It appears that Christians are not bucking, but embracing, the trend. The difference between Christian and non-Christian Americans, it seems, is not found primarily in the heart, but in what we bring to the till.

Change Your Shirt, Change the World

Your standard Christian bookstore will have plenty of Christian T-shirts, for the T-shirt is king among Christian accessories. Jewelry, the only other potential contestant for the title, is too diverse in type (earrings, necklaces, bracelets, rings, brooches, pins, etc.) and materials (gold for grandma, silver for girls, and pukka-shell and bone for boys) to examine in depth. But the Christian T-shirt is a phenomenon in its own right, instantly recognizable as such (until recently, as we will see below) by virtually all Americans.

Helen Hendershot begins her book on Christian media by recollecting her "first encounter with 'witness wear,' evangelical clothing, mostly T-shirts, targeting teenagers."[2] Hendershot is likely not alone in her experience, which was the sight of an adolescent boy wearing a Lord's Gym shirt in a mall. This design, still a popular seller, is the product of the grandaddy of Christian T-Shirt companies, Living Epistles, which began in 1983. The "Lord's Gym" design is an early example of Christian brand appropriation — taking from the popular Gold's Gym shirts — which features a bulging Christ doing a push-up under a cross inscribed with the words "the sin of the world," and the slogan "Bench press this!" On the back is a bloody hand pierced by what looks to be a railway spike, crowned with the motto "His Pain

Your Gain." The ubiquity of these shirts in readers' memory will give credence to Living Epistles' claim that the message of the shirts they sell is spread far and wide by their wearers.

As Hendershot reports, "The marketers of [witness wear] claim they are not shallow ads for Jesus but rather useful evangelizing tools.... [They] would have us believe that thanks to witness wear and other Christian lifestyle products, purchases can have a justified, holy purpose."[3] The ostensible point of witness wear is to spread the message of Jesus to anyone who sees the shirt. As any evangelical will tell you, it's hard to start up a conversation with someone and then talk about your faith until you can get them to a point of making a decision for Christ (this being a fairly representative paraphrase of the popular definition for evangelism). The thought of doing what amounts to a religious cold call has filled many a believer, regardless of age, with fear. Witness wear removes your obligation toward that difficult first step, the conventional wisdom goes — instead of you having to start a conversation, your shirt will be so provocative that viewers will be motivated to ask *you* about it, thus giving you the opportunity to share the gospel with them. The erstwhile motto* of the apparel company — "Put on the Lord Jesus Christ" (pun intended) — describes the quasi-metaphysical ambition that is behind the witness or "share [your faith] wear."

Toward this soul-changing, provocative end, the consistent formula for Christian apparel until recent years has revolved around taking familiar secular images and giving them a Christian twist. The Kerusso brand, which began in 1987 and has made a veritable science out of brand appropriation, appears to have overtaken Living Epistles as the leading manufacturer of this type of shirt.** A casual count of Kerusso's vast online inventory of shirts, sweatshirts, hats, and wristbands revealed at least twenty-five designs based directly on widely recognizable secular brand images and slogans. The most popular designs on Kerusso's adult bestseller list (with the original brand source in parentheses) include: "Army of [the] One" (U.S. Army); "A Blood

---

*Hendershot lists this as Living Epistles' motto, but I have been unable to find any evidence for this still being the case.
**Kerusso claims that "our name is our mission," *kerusso* being Greek for "I proclaim." Their motto is less metaphysical than Living Epistles' "Put on the Lord Jesus Christ," but hardly less ambitious: "Change your shirt. Change the world."

Donor Saved My Life" (Red Cross); "He Saves" (Hershey's, identifiable by the brown background and distinctive font); and "Jesus Christ" (written in the Coca-Cola logo script on a red background).* The majority of the designs are based on food brands recognizable to teenagers, including knockoffs of Crush soda, YooHoo chocolate drink, Pepsi, Mountain Dew, and Reese's Peanut Butter Cups.[4]

This baptizing of images from secular consumer culture, with application toward a Christian end, might seem reminiscent of the anti-corporate activism recorded by Naomi Wolf's section on culture jamming in her *No Logo* (pp. 279–309). One main form of culture jamming, or "adbusting," involves turning familiar imagery against its original purpose. So, in the common parody form of culture jamming, one might see a billboard for Kool cigarettes that reads "Forever Kool" over the image of a toe-tagged corpse in cold storage.[5] Christian T-shirts from Kerusso and Living Epistles, likewise, attempt to "[borrow] visual legitimacy from advertising itself." Klein's acclaim for the work of culture jammer Jorge Rodriguez de Gerada could be a verbatim description of what Christian vendors of witness or share wear hope to be the case with their shirts. They "look like originals, though with a message that takes viewers by surprise."[6]

The critical distinction between culture jamming and Christian brand-based T-shirts, however, comes down to a question of edginess. Culture jammers attempt to invert the message of advertising for industries they see as corrupt — so, the lively image accompanying the Kool slogan becomes, in the hands of culture jammers, the corpse that will presumably come from using cigarettes.

With brand-based witness wear, however, there is no inversion whatsoever. The images used are chosen for their popular familiarity, not because they are attempting to contradict the specific, original content of their message. In fact, witness wear does not critique consumer culture at all. That would be biting the hand that feeds it. Christian T-shirts rely on the complete familiarity of the observer with consumer culture. A "Jesus Christ" shirt written in Coca-Cola font would be nothing more than a red shirt with a name on it if seen by someone who had never encountered Coca-Cola marketing imagery.

---

*The historian Randall Balmer, reporting from a Christian Booksellers Association conference, makes a similar observation in "Bible Bazaar," chapter 8 of his fine book, *Mine Eyes Have Seen the Glory: A Journey into the Evangelical Subculture in America* (New York: Oxford University Press, 2006).

The currency of these Christian T-shirts is the viewer's fluency in a brand-saturated society.

As a result, while culture jamming attempts (albeit failingly) to undermine the influence of branding and marketing on us, Christian T-shirts depend on it. And this is where we get into theological trouble, because in the totally uncritical adoption of consumer imagery, Christian T-shirts run the risk of simply substituting Brand Jesus for the original commodity — omitting the living Lord completely. The frequent play on the original content only exacerbates the problem. For example, the sub-slogan of Kerusso's "He Saves" Hershey's mock-up ("Taste and see that the Lord is good") seems to say, "If you like Hershey's chocolate, you'll like Jesus even better, and in totally the same way!"

It would be an overstatement to claim that Christian T-shirts are resulting in the wholesale spread of Brand Jesus. They are made, marketed, and sold by people that I assume are decent, honest Christians, who are serious about their faith and view their work as ministry. I am sure this is the case. But while witness wear of the Kerusso and Living Epistles stripe may not be causing the spread of Brand Jesus, it is certainly indicative of Brand Jesus' dominance in the American church.

The mode of evangelism that the T-shirts are designed to facilitate is precisely the sort that commodifies salvation. The shirts are supposed to help people "get" saved, plain and simple, and the transaction requires a purchase. While witness wear makers would doubtlessly and wholeheartedly insist that the purchase was that of humankind from sin through the blood of Christ, brand-based T-shirt evangelism only helps to invert the proper understanding of that gospel message. It is advertising to lead us into buying Christ, just as we would a can of Coke, a pack of Reese's Peanut Butter Cups, or a bottle of YooHoo — and we imagine we get heaven as a freebee bonus. The cost, meanwhile, has nothing to do with the price of discipleship, but only the credulity of the consumer ("taste and see").

Moreover, the above scenario is only true if we grant that witness wear works like its manufacturers and retailers claim that it does. And this is far from uncontested territory. In many ways, shirts from the likes of Living Epistles and Kerusso actually work against themselves. They are designed to provoke a reaction in the viewer so that he or she will approach the wearer and ask what the shirt is all about. But shirts from Living Epistles and Kerusso leave no doubt as to the message of the shirt. They are not so much provocative as they are varying degrees of clever.

If, for example, I see someone wearing the Jesus Christ/Coke knock-off shirt, I have no questions whatsoever of him. His shirt tells me all I need to know about him and what he's selling. If the Coca-Cola-esque "Jesus Christ" didn't give away the show, then the subheading "Eternally Refreshing" and accompanying Bible verse, "Whoever drinks the water I give him will never thirst" (John 4:14), surely would do the trick. Assuming I'm not already a churchgoer, I'll have no desire at all to go talk to him about his shirt, because he's so obviously an evangelical Christian who's just waiting to get me saved. The online catalog copy for this shirt reads: "If you have tasted this water you know nothing else can compare, so why not share a drink with those around you." But there's nothing about this shirt that makes a viewer want to share what its wearer is drinking. The shirt's effectiveness depends on the presumption that there are vast numbers of wandering souls who know they are lost and are just wondering how they can be saved. The idea that such a demographic actually exists, however, represents a profound misunderstanding about the state of American religiosity in the twenty-first century.

Now, any wearer of a witness T-shirt would quickly retort that the shirt is worth it if even one person comes to faith as a result of it, and I am certainly not going to argue against the pricelessness of conversion. The protest of the witness gear wearer seems somewhat disingenuous, however, as I suspect that many buyers know full well that their shirt will almost certainly not have the desired spiritual effect on the people who will see it. As Hendershot remarks, "It is unlikely . . . that many evangelicals honestly expect a T-shirt to provoke a profound spiritual transformation. A person already receptive to religious questions might stop and talk to the T-shirt wearer, or a lapsed person might be spurred to start going to church again."[7] But that's about all the response one might even hope for. Furthermore, such a speculative ambition does not mitigate against the guaranteed downside of promoting a Brand Jesus spirituality to every one of the thousands of people who will see your 100 percent cotton testimony. Will you promote Brand Jesus and risk the stumbling of thousands for the sake of the one whom God does not seem particularly inclined to save through your T-shirt?

Though I admit I can rely only on anecdotal evidence, I suspect that many readers' personal experiences will confirm the secret disbelief held by wearers of Christian T-shirts regarding their clothing's evangelistic potential. For example, while Christian youth groups abound with zeal for reaching the unsaved, their members mostly seem to bring their witness gear to Bible camp and church events. Usage decreases in the public school setting and, by the time these same students gather with non-Christians at someone's house for the weekend party, the witness wear all but vanishes in favor of more fashionable clothes. To summarize, the prevalence of witness wearing falls in inverse proportion to the number of the unevangelized likely to see the shirts.

The shirts' failure to live up to their evangelistic promise actually seems to be built into the theological rhetoric around them. Every wearer knows, after all, that evangelism is actually the work of the Holy Spirit. There is nothing that mortals can do to manufacture salvation (though church talk about evangelism, like "soul-winning," clearly implies the opposite). Instead, our job is simply to open ourselves to the possibility of being used by God. Enter witness wear! Then, when the wear designed to provoke witnessing results in nothing more than a couple of sneering double takes every now and again, the absence of conversions is indicative of the mysterious will of the Holy Spirit, rather than any problem with the shirt.

It seems that brand-themed Christian apparel fails to live up to its evangelistic promises and, on the negative side, actually demonstrates faith commitments of the sort that are more inclined toward Brand Jesus. Shirts like Living Epistles and Kerusso do, however, unfailingly make that explicit evangelistic pitch, and sacrifice a certain amount of desired provocativeness by doing so. Consider the effect of Kerusso's "Jesus died for Pedro" knockoff of the *Napoleon Dynamite* movie merchandise. It could border on hip irony, and perhaps lead a non-Christian observer to rethink her conviction that Christians have no sense of humor (a worthy goal!). But Kerusso ruins any such effect by scrawling "and he died for you, too!" along with a citation from Romans under the main slogan. One does not have to check to know that the wearer of such a shirt washes behind his ears. This omni-present evangelistic earnestness makes the shirts instantly recognizable as evangelically Christian, as opposed to the host of ironic secular T-shirts that festoon other teens. Say what you will about Kerusso and Living Epistles, you need not look twice (or hard) to know where they stand and what they're about.

By this everyone will know that you are my disciples...

By way of contrast, a newer breed of Christian gear seems to be changing the nature of the Christian apparel game. Brands like NOTW ("Not Of This World"), One Truth, Souldog, Ezekiel, Ephraim, and Disciple are producing hip, artistic designs like the cutting-edge styles favored by board- and extreme-sports-based companies. (Not coincidentally, such sports enjoy a wide following among evangelical youth, based on the assumed correlation between extreme sports and extreme faith.) NOTW appears to be the most dominant of these brands, selling widely among Christian retailers, and is itself the flagship brand of the C28 chain of stores (standing for Colossians 2:8 — "not of this world and all about Jesus," as paraphrased by the C28 Web site).

C28 has expanded to six stores in California since its first retail storefront opened in 2001. As such, it is far from being a dominant retail presence like LifeWay. But, as a Christian store founded explicitly to reach the much-coveted youth market, it has a growing influence — demonstrated by the two new California franchises and a Florida location that opened in November 2006. Even more significant in the increasingly competitive Christian market, C28 and NOTW's cache of cool far outstrips Kerusso and Living Epistles, which show their age by comparison — and which C28 evidently does not sell, despite their carrying the more hip Christian brands like One Truth and others, listed above.

The transition from the Kerusso/Living Epistles era to the NOTW era is simultaneously one of image and mission. Gone is the dorkiness inherent to the earnest evangelicalism of brand knockoff T-shirts. In its stead is the visually ambiguous, often obscured Christianity of NOTW and — even more so — the likes of One Truth, Disciple, and Ephraim. And, while the founder of C28 and NOTW claims an explicitly evangelistic mission for the clothing, if it is being carried out, it is happening in far more subtle ways than occurred with the first generation of Christian shirt makers. That generation bore all the cleanness and obviousness of the secular brand logos, designed to be instantly recognized, that it poached for evangelistic purposes.

NOTW's designs, by contrast, are visually compelling, frequently ornate, and mix different fonts, colors, and images — to the point where the viewer may need to examine the shirt to discover any evangelistic or even identifiably Christian content. (In this way, NOTW might actually be considered to succeed in Kerusso's stated mission — of provoking a long look — in a way that the older brand fails to achieve.) Other brands' Christian content is even more obscure, if it is there at all. Shirts by Ezekiel, for example, are overwhelmingly *not* recognizable as Christian. And Cobian sandals, though known by insiders as a Christian brand, bear no visible attestation to that fact — let alone something like an evangelistic pitch printed in reverse on the sole.

What this change represents is the movement away from blatant evangelism and toward Christian apparel that often proclaims nothing more than one's own Christian identity — and that only to those other consumer aficionados who recognize the brand's religious identity. This is a massive theological shift. Kerusso shirts, for example, are ostensibly geared toward the viewer to whom the wearer is trying to witness. By contrast, NOTW shirts seem far more concerned with establishing the identity of the *wearer,* as would be the case with a shirt bearing the Nike swoosh or FUBU logo. (This emphasis on personal branding is even more extreme with less obviously Christian brands, like Ezekiel and Cobian.) The audaciously named Disciple Clothing, for example, began out of precisely such a concern with the unfashionable design behind older Christian clothing. According to co-founder Andrew Garcia:

> One day we were all sitting around eating burritos … talking about different clothing companies and styles, we did not really see anything that we thought represented our passion. We continued to talk about it and decided that Disciple Clothing would help us reach out and at the same time be fashionable. In other words be cool to wear.[8]

Be a disciple? Buy Disciple. A very recent move is the advent of Christian clothing emblazoned only with the brand logo, instead of any evangelistic or even Christian imagery. One recognizes the shirt as Christian only because one knows the brand to be religious. NOTW has a number of products branded with nothing but the NOTW logo and perhaps a nondescript design; other brands make nothing but such products.

Such goods would be unthinkable coming from the older T-shirt makers, which would never design clothing that was marked only with the Kerusso or Living Epistles brand. Now, it may be that the older brands are headed in a similar direction, as Kerusso's line of accessories includes items with no evangelistic appeal, but only a cross or crown of thorns design — that is, they only proclaim the wearer's religious identity. But such products are not substantially different from religious jewelry, as they employ identifiably Christian images, like the cross, toward their purpose. This is a far cry from the move by the branded clothing companies to add their own symbols to the historical iconography of the faith.

When Constantine adopted Christianity as the imperial religion of Rome, he added the Christian Chi-Rho symbol to his battle flag. Now, with brands like NOTW, we are seeing an even more remarkable step, as the corporate logos of branded Christian companies are themselves becoming symbols of the faith. Perhaps this is the foretaste of a theo-corporate Christianity to come. Or perhaps it is already here.

One could argue that NOTW and its ilk are simply being more honest about what Christian apparel has always done. Given that Kerusso's "share wear" so infrequently results in "sharing," and that Christians seem to wear it mostly around one another, the purpose its wearers put it to seems primarily to declare their Christianity.

But admitting this would be to confess a dangerous self-centeredness. "Worldly" things like designer clothing gained acceptability with evangelicals because of the evangelistic intent behind them, and the potential to win souls is still at the heart of the Christian apparel industry. Perhaps the muted evangelistic appeal of the newer brands is why C28 is the only Christian apparel manufacturer I could find that would claim a specific number of conversions as a result of its ministry.[9]

The FAQ on C28's Web site demonstrates a bit of this implicit defensiveness, along with oddly unsatisfying answers to the questions posed there. Asked about the "positive effects of mixing fashion and faith," the FAQ responds that " 'witness wear' convey [sic] a clean and positive lifestyle," which C28 alleges will "encourag[e] people to share the gospel with others." In answer to the allegation that people might wear the shirts simply for the " 'cool' factor," the Web site offers the reader the pithy reply: "In either case, the Lords [sic] word (scriptures) never returns back void" — this being exactly the sort of aphoristic non-answer provided when one needs to take a theological punt to avoid the spiritual responsibility of one's actions. And, instead of simply offering an honest affirmative to the question "Are you making money off of teenager's [sic] need to fit in?" — C28 is a business, after all — the response brushes the inquiry aside by citing the 6,280 people who are reported to have been saved by praying the sinner's prayer in C28 stores (a nifty presumption at knowledge of final election!).[10]

It's easy to imagine a likely counterargument to the critique I'm making here. C28 might argue its case, for example, by citing evangelistic zeal. Take Paul to the Philippians, for instance — "the important thing is that in every way, whether from false motives or true, Christ is preached." C28 could say that no matter what, its clothing is valuable because it preaches Christ to a world that needs to hear about him.

But there's the rub. More and more — and maybe this has always been the case — it seems that Christian apparel doesn't preach Christ nearly so much as it preaches its wearer, the consumer. The value of Christian apparel's "preaching," if that is even what it does, would be akin to the value of standing in the street and yelling, "I'm a Christian!" Paul's comment in Philippians 1:18 is about the unimportance of the preacher's motive, but I'm not questioning the motive behind Christian apparel. I'm questioning the content of the proclamation. The movement that is apparent in Christian clothing is clearly in the direction of proclaiming Christian identity *only* — that is, buy a Christian T-shirt to tell the world that you're a Christian.

This is a matter of critical importance, because while the preacher's motives might not matter, it must be Christ who is preached. And when brands proclaim the wearer — when one consumes Christian apparel to set oneself apart as a Christian, when Christian clothing simply consists of "special garments" that announce the Christianity of the wearer to anyone who looks hard enough or is hip enough to recognize the obscure Christian logo — then the proclamation is not of the Lord Jesus, but of Brand Jesus. Proclaiming our own Christian identity turns the Christ-centered focus of the gospel on its head, and places ourselves, through our brand idol, in the Lord's rightful place. Proclaiming our own Christian identity *makes being Christian first and foremost about being known as a Christian,* which is a description far too close for comfort to Paul's indictment of the Roman Jews.

I remember the first time I saw a NOTW product. It was a wristband with only the NOTW logo, worn by a teenage boy — the sort of branded, self-advertising product that Kerusso and Living Epistles would never make. I was virtually sure it was Christian, due to the vaguely cruciform "t" in the graffiti-esque acronym. But even though I've grown fairly attuned to the Christian pop aesthetic, I wasn't certain, and I didn't know what the NOTW meant. It communicated a pretty cool, skater punk vibe, and Christians of a certain age bracket and class doubtlessly would have recognized it in an instant. But, contrary to NOTW's claim, the wristband was not "all about Jesus." It was all about that kid.

The peril of clothing that marks its wearer as Christian is that none of us deserves to bear Christ's name. In the course of a day spent wearing a Christian T-shirt, the odds are good that the wearer will dishonor the name that he or she bears. I'm sure if I'd watched that kid for long enough, I would have seen something that made me question the connection between his interior commitments and the brand affiliation he wore (literally) on his sleeve. And I'm sure the same would have been true if I had been wearing the wristband, with someone watching me. The ever-popular memory argument — that such exterior labels "remind" the wearer to be good — simply doesn't hold. Circumcision was a lot tougher to undergo than changing one's shirt, and it didn't help the Roman Jews to remember the law.

In light of the above, the irony of NOTW's name is really rather spectacular. The NOTW consumer aspires to be "not of this world," even though there is hardly anything *more* of this world than proclaiming one's identity through the clothing one buys. The irony only thickens when the whole of Colossians 2:8, from which NOTW is derived, is considered. "See to it that no one takes you captive through hollow and deceptive philosophy, which depends on human tradition and the basic principles of this world rather than on Christ." As we've explored above, "human tradition" is all too evident in the consumerism of our time and place, with its "hollow and deceptive philosophy" that you are what you buy. This consumerism, which is a manifestation of the "basic principles of this world" — namely, the idolatry of our own original sin through Mammon worship — has indeed taken us "captive" to the point where we cannot find a safe, nonconsumer space. And here are Christian clothing companies — NOTW being only one example, albeit significant, of a broader trend — proving with their actions and products the very fact of our captivity, because with every best intention they have only buttressed a system of self-understanding through consumption, enslavement to Mammon, and the promotion of self over Christ that is the mask of Brand Jesus.

I sympathize with the good intentions of Christian gear manufacturers. But I cannot, for the life of me, figure out *any* overall positive effect that Christian clothing has toward the spread of the gospel or discipleship. Defenders of efforts such as Christian T-shirts invariably fall back on the sacred cow of evangelistic zeal and point to isolated moments of grace that supposedly justify the entire endeavor. But this is really no defense at all. Grace abounds, and it will appear even in the midst of darkness, like fireflies on a summer night. But such fragments do not prove the righteousness of the situation in which they appear. So, when C28's Web site testifies to the "young girl on a wheelchair" who came into a retail store and asked, "Is this the store that prays for people?" — it does not indicate anything more than the store's reputation as a religious place. And it certainly does not indicate God's favor on the store or the clothing, nor, as the Web site claims, "[say] it all!"

Jesus told his followers that "you must love one another. By *this* everyone will know that you are my disciples, if you love one another" (John 13:35). Elsewhere in John, Christ links this love to sacrificing for one's friends. In other words, such love has internal origins with external enactment. It is not a simple sentimentality, but a love that finds expression in daily life and is a testament to the love that God has shown to the world in Christ. But such a proclamation of one's discipleship bears no resemblance to the consumerist phenomenon of buying goods that declare one's spiritual identity. There is no room in Jesus' ordinance to love one another for a booming Christian accessories market that expresses wearers' discipleship.

Sola Scriptura, Many Features

Despite the financial dominance of nonbook items that led the Christian Booksellers Association to change its name to CBA, books retain at least a nominal pride of place at Christian stores. At LifeWay, for example, bibles appear to be the biggest single product group, as one might expect from a store that grew out of an evangelical denomination's Sunday School Board. One large store I visited had row upon row of bibles, offering an array of options in terms of binding color and material, page-edge gilding, print type, and translation. They occupied a dominant segment of the store, eclipsing other book categories like Christian fiction, Christian psychology and self-help, Christian spirituality, and so on. (Theology, once recognized as "Queen of the Sciences," occupies one solitary bay at the rear — one can actually find more theology books at the local Borders.) The rows of bibles were like a fortress wall, the bays filling the section of the store nearest to the window — a visual and spatial affirmation of the priority of the Bible to the mission and values of the store.

The selection of bibles at the LifeWay retail outlets is daunting. But, assuming that even this large store could not carry all of the bibles that LifeWay carries, I looked at the LifeWay online store and discovered I was correct. The online store offered twenty-six different cross-referenced *categories* of bibles (i.e., Wedding, Family, Pew, Award, Women, Men, Study, etc.). A search using the "Advanced Bible Search" tool, set to "no preference" in each of the thirteen search parameters, turned up a dizzying 1,000 bibles for sale, sorted by order of sales popularity. Even this total proved to be only an artificially limited fraction of the total available options, however. The Boolean "red-letter" parameter — that is, a Bible can have the words of Jesus in red, as some do, or not — reveals that LifeWay offers 1,683 red-letter and 1,659 black-letter titles, for a whopping total of 3,342 different bibles (plus, I suppose, audio versions). And even LifeWay is trumped by the online giant, christianbook.com (known also as CBD), which boasts 4,256 varieties of the Bible.*

Lest we forget, as we reel at the sheer numbers at play, it is worth reminding ourselves at this point that these numbers represent different versions of *a single book.*

The most striking implication to this staggering number of bibles is hidden in plain sight; that is, publishers wouldn't print, nor retailers carry, so many kinds of bibles if there weren't consumers willing to buy them. But why is there a market for such variety? Some differences matter a great deal, of course — foremost being language and translation, followed by the inclusion of aids for study/devotion/research, as well as large-print and audio versions. But even the large inventory that could be compiled out of *substantively* distinct versions would come nowhere near the thousands that comprise the LifeWay and CBD

*Accurate as of October 4, 2006.

catalogs. In the LifeWay stores, approximately 500 titles represent non-English editions (the majority of them Spanish), leaving about 2,800 different titles that are spread across the twenty-four main English translations.

One reasonable conclusion, therefore, is that this lunatic proliferation of Bible versions is an evangelical expression of consumerism in a buy-to-be era. Evangelicals often verge on a totemistic relationship with our bibles, given the centrality of scripture to our religious self-understanding. With the current explosion of customization as a consumer priority — a necessity given the tension inherent to individuals' attempts to invent, define, and understand themselves through the purchase of mass-produced items — it is therefore unsurprising to find that evangelical consumers' demand for bibles is rooted in the desire to form our spiritual selves through hyper-customized scripture.*

Baby's New Testament (with Psalms) is a perfect example. It is advertised in LifeWay literature as "a perfect gift for new parents to commemorate their baby's arrival," and I am sure it makes a lovely gift. But to what purpose? Is it a new translation that is magically comprehensible to infants? Is there baby-specific material that will help the parents and child grow spiritually? No. *Baby's New Testament* is essentially a pastel accessory that affirms, in Bible form, a couple's identity as parents. It is a quintessential example of a consumer product that, offering no inherent functional value, serves primarily and nearly exclusively as a vehicle of personal meaning and significance.

The principle of buy-to-be at play in *Baby's New Testament* seems an unavoidable fact of bloated bible inventories like LifeWay's. The free LifeWay brochure, available to aid customers' decisions in sorting through the store's inscrutable selection, simply confirms this. Titled "Picking your Bible is as easy as 1, 2, 3," the titular step 1 is "Choose your features." The store will help you in your search, the brochure proclaims, by determining features first, translation second, and binding third. Do you want a text-only bible, a youth bible, a reference bible, a chain-reference bible, or perhaps that New Testament for baby? Or some other sort?

---

*I would be surprised if this diagnosis does not hit close to home for many readers; for myself, I know that various moments of spiritual transition have been marked by the desire to have a new bible as an expression of that development. This is particularly unconscionable, given that both my wife and I have been to seminary and have worked in churches, and as a couple we have therefore acquired bibles the way folks in other industries amass convention tote bags.

The third criterion of LifeWay's brochure, binding, highlights the obsession with packaging that is endemic to the explosion of bible options. Today's options go far beyond hardcover, softcover, and leather. Take the dramatic examples of packaging innovation that are *Blossom* and *Revolve,* two versions of the New Testament in the New Century translation, formatted to resemble young and teen girls' popular magazines, respectively. (The publisher, Thomas Nelson, also produces boys' versions.) On the inside of *Blossom,* the biblical text is laid out in magazine style, with traditional devotional and study helps formatted and titled like the insets familiar to magazine readers; for example, "Why is God so AWESOME?" and "Meet 10 New Friends from Around the World!" *Revolve* takes the resemblance one step further. The cover teasers, cast against a photograph of three fresh-faced teen girls laughing, read like a squeaky version of *Seventeen:* "Guys Speak on Tons of Important Issues," " 'Are You Dating a Godly Guy?' and other quizzes," "Beauty Secrets You've Never Heard Before," and "200+ Blab Q&A's." The resemblance to secular magazines is precisely the point.

The publisher's rationale is that kids and teens don't read books, but they do read magazines; ergo, Nelson has produced a magazine-like New Testament to encourage younger Bible readers. As many of the reviews on Amazon.com testify, this strategy seems to have worked, and a number of relieved parents sing *Revolve*'s praises for piquing their girls' interest in scripture. Moreover, these bibles surely have the hyper-practical effect of making Christian schoolgirls feel less awkward than they might otherwise feel if they tried to read a leather-bound bible in the merciless social arena that is adolescent society. Both of these effects are surely good things and ought not to be disregarded as easily as some critics like to do. (After all, the critics' leather-bound "normal" bible is far from socially neutral itself, communicating as it does the seriousness and piety of the reader.)

Is this short-term advantage worth the inevitable price, however? The problem with such "Biblezines" is that they play directly into a consumeristic mentality. Everything about them screams "target audience." Girls can't be expected to read the Bible, the logic goes — why, they hate books altogether! So let's give them what they do want.

Today's young people are savvy consumers. They know precisely what's going on with a bible produced especially for them. These hyper-individualized bibles therefore perpetuate the very consumerist that their publishers, with every good intention, might hope that the biblical content would combat. The old saw of "changing the packaging, not the product" fails to consider adequately how, in a consumer society, the packaging is part of the product — packaging often *is* the product, in fact. And today's product-package is not simply the physical commodity being sold, but the very self of the buyer. Biblezines thus implicitly confirm for the teen recipient that she can indeed base her sense of self-understanding around the exercise of her personal consumer preferences. And the long-term problems with this way of life, as explored in previous chapters, can prove disastrous to authentic discipleship, encouraging a devotion to Brand Jesus instead.

These consumerist patterns are by no means limited to teens, either. Consider again the LifeWay Bible brochure, which is designed to help the customer "to help you find the one [bible] that's right for you." This appeal to hyper-individualism — the ideal of a consumerist culture — is compounded by the classic marketing strategy of planned obsolescence, which guarantees turnover. The brochure further advises the customer to pick a bible that he or she "can grow into" — the implicit message being that your bible will only be good for so long. At some point in your life, a youth bible will be most appropriate. You will graduate to a study bible. Eventually, this will be replaced by a wedding or couple's bible, and then by a women's or men's bible. If you're fortunate, the baby's bible will come along, followed by youth and study bibles bought as gifts. And perhaps your twilight years will be graced with a large-print — and eventually giant-print — Bible. Even the very conservative estimate of a five-bible consumer life will result in a pretty good business.

We can't blame the marketers, retailers, or any one publisher for leading us astray, however. It is not bible proliferation that has created religious consumers. No, our turn to consumerist Christianity has created a climate where such an industry yields financial fruit. Christian consumer demands for specialized bibles are to be expected in an accessory-crazed culture, where the binding of one's bible is akin to the faceplate of one's cell phone. Consider the lead paragraph from the *Publishers Weekly* report on a CBA midwinter "Advance" conference:

> One product trend on the show floor was the proliferation of high-quality gift Bibles with soft Italian leather covers, often imprinted with designs and varying color tones. These Bibles were all the

rage at the Crossway booth, and also at Zondervan, which went an additional step with its "Bible in a Bag" product. This small two-tone NIV Bible, marketed for young women and girls, comes in an easily portable pink tote. "There's such a trend in carrying bags," said Zondervan president Doug Lockhart. "We've tested this with consumers and the feedback has been very strong to have a coordinating case that matches their Bible."[11]

This state of affairs calls for plain language. There is no possible rationale for matching bibles and carrying cases (a phenomenon not limited to Zondervan) that is not fundamentally rooted in the ideals and values of consumerism. The concern for such an option to be available can have nothing whatsoever to do with the functionality of the Bible or the consumer's relationship with the textual content. It cannot relate whatsoever to enabling growth in discipleship. It can say *only* that the Bible in such a case (pun intended) is — whatever its spiritual use — a personal, consumer-defining accessory. It proclaims to a certain demographic the pious Christian identity of its carrier, just as a Louis Vuitton bag would proclaim to another demographic the wealthy, high-fashion identity of its carrier. The "Bible in a Bag" is a sure indicator — along with a host of others, including the examples above — that consumerism has surrounded and even permeated the Bible-centric heart of evangelical spiritual discipline.

Chapter 18

Called to Be a Demographic

While searching for the real money in Christian consumerism, one invariably winds up in media — especially music, best-selling books, and movies. The contemporary Christian music industry has grown nearly 900 percent over the past twenty years, and as a segment of the market exceeding the combined share of jazz and classical music, it currently reaps $720 million in sales annually.[1] The financial success in recent years of Christian books like the *Left Behind* series, *The Prayer of Jabez*, and *The Purpose-Driven Life*, as well as movies like *The Passion of the Christ*, has alerted the secular media giants to the lucrative potential of a largely undeveloped market. Sales like this cannot be generated merely through the Christian bookstore retail market. No, for this kind of money, big business needs to get involved.

Not everyone is going to buy a Kerusso or NOTW T-shirt. But if box office and retail receipts are any indicator, it does seem that a sufficient percentage of everyone can be counted on to see a properly marketed Christian blockbuster or buy that hit crossover Christian book. Christian titles comprised a whopping 15 percent of the $11 billion in retail book sales in 2001. And *The Passion of the Christ*, one of the least-regarded properties in Hollywood in the months before its release, received such support from American Christians that it became the highest grossing R-rated movie in history, with $370 million at the domestic box office.[2] As a result, corporations across the media spectrum are now frantically trying to get a slice of the evangelical pie.

Corporate attention to the evangelical demographic has meant greater attention to evangelical concerns. And this has manifested in the increased representation of Christian identity in secular spheres, as well as the promotion of media content that excludes content perceived to be in opposition to Christian values.

Because much of contemporary American evangelicalism understands its mission as cultural conquest, the fawning attention from secular commercial interests represents a massive victory — at least in the minds of many Christians. If evangelicals can make demands of media institutions and have them answered, the logic goes, then the tide is turning toward a more "Christ-honoring" culture.

But the opposite is actually the case. Not only do such conclusions demonstrate a false understanding of the forces at play — as we explore below — they also confirm that mainstream evangelical interests traffic in nothing so much as the blasphemous praises of Brand Jesus.

Take the supposed "war on Christmas," waged in 2005–2006. In recent years, Christian groups have launched crusades against companies like Wal-Mart and Land's End, who had changed the usual "Merry Christmas" of their winter retail catalogs to a generic holiday greeting. Some Christians fell into line by patronizing only those stores that would wish them a merry Christmas.

But when secular retailers are forced by Christian interests to bend the knee, they do not bow to honor the name of Christ, but the dollars of his self-proclaimed followers. They are willing to change their marketing tactics in order to get Christian business. Does this bring any honor to Christ's name? The very thought that it might is theologically bankrupt. No, what is being honored in this patently stupid "war" is Brand Jesus.

Wake up, Christians! The sheer hypocrisy of our venom is staggering. How on earth can we justify getting angry at retailers for failing to help us cultivate our own delusion that Jesus is at the heart of our midwinter retail binge?

This conflict was invented neither by pastors nor retailers. No, self-appointed television demagogues interested only in stroking their own outrage, who want their brand of faith fed back to them, manufactured it. What should the true Christian care if Wal-Mart, of all things, fails to pay lip service to Christ? But such lip service is of vital importance to the external Christian. Brand Jesus is all the Jesus he has! Behold: the anger of the one who knows no faith but that which he gets at a till, the one who obtains his spiritual identity from consumption and needs to have his brand choice affirmed. Such a one as this receives all his praise from men (cf. Romans 2:29). And the dishonor done to the Lord by a retailer's failure to acknowledge Christmas is *nothing* compared to the dishonor done to God by such a devotee, a supposed disciple who has instead made Brand Jesus his king. The greeting "Happy Holidays" does not insult the Lord, but the Brand.

Another example of this misguided culture war is the campaign for a family-friendly tier of cable channel offerings.[3] Theologically speaking, it demonstrates the exact same priority as the "war on Christmas" — our fear-based need to have the world around us reflect our personal preferences. I have nothing against a family-friendly cable plan, and the a la carte channel arrangement advocated by the likes of Concerned Women for America seems like a terrific idea. But whatever pragmatic function such an arrangement might serve, the fact that it is a top goal of the Christian lobby reveals that as a group, our primary interest is in having institutions bear the cost of discipleship for us. "Family-friendly" or "pro-family" are bona fide Christian sub-brands. And, like all good brands, they carry meaning for their consumers so that the consumers don't have to shoulder the weight of interior commitments.

After all, the easy answer to a repugnance for what is on television is to turn the thing off or throw it away. There would certainly be a biblical basis for such an action, and doing so would be far less painful than cutting off the hand or gouging out the eye that leads you to sin (Matthew 5:29–30). But getting rid of television isn't really an option for American Christians, is it? No, we want the comfort of an American lifestyle with Jesus to boot.

Well, we'll get what we demand. We'll get the family-friendly cable arrangement. And we'll get our Jesus. But the Jesus we get will be the Jesus we've asked for, namely, the branded version, packaged and sale priced, with Jim Caviezel's chiseled jaw and baby blues, and a remote control to pause or mute him if we need to pause for a snack or a nap.

Corporate Constantinianism for a Capitalist Christendom

Christian delight at the newfound evangelical cultural influence is dangerously delusional, because we have only the faintest idea of the forces that we're messing with. We've gained cultural influence because we've operated under the radar until recently. But now that industry has figured out that we're a virgin gold mine, we've become fair game. The same *BusinessWeek online* article that cites Christian "gains" with the war on Christmas and family-friendly cable arrangement also points out the discrepancy between Christian perception of events and the practiced realism of secular moneymakers. The author writes:

> [Signs] of progress may be misleading. While the Christian Right has more political power now than it has enjoyed in decades, American society has never been more secular. Many of these [perceived Christian gains] stem more from a long-overdue recognition of the importance of the Christian consumer market rather than a decision to bow to the Christian thought police.[4]

The key phrase here is "recognition of the importance of the Christian consumer market." We have become one among many marketing demographics, right up there with "18–34–year-old males" or "urban Latinos." In other words, American Christianity has positioned itself as a demographic on par with the mortal categories of divisions, like age, gender, ethnicity, which it is supposed to transcend. Now, Christians might protest — and I would be at the front of the picket line — that there is more to our Christian identity than can be encapsulated in a market study. Well — at least there *should* be. But are we acting like this is the case? And if not, what's going to happen?

The funny thing about demographics is that they aren't independent, sovereign entities. Yes, the marketers have to do a bit of chasing to figure out what teens want — but they play an equal if not greater role in forming teens' desires. So, now that the market has discovered evangelicals as a target audience, we should expect that the Christian marketing effort will start playing a significant role in defining how and who evangelicals believe themselves to be.

This is why we can understand laments like that of Concerned Women for America's Lanier Swann, despite the fact that CWA's corporate and governmental lobbying has helped to create the evangelical demographic that now faces exploitation. "If you allow the cable industry to define family-friendly," she complains, "you'll end up with packages that contain programming like ABC Family Channel, some of which promotes premarital sex and infidelity."[5] Isn't that just the trouble with brand slogans like "family-friendly?" If you make them definitive of a group, as "family-friendly" surely is with the evangelical brand, then they carry cachet for anyone who wants to use them.

Some critics will doubtlessly hang the blame for our vulnerability at the door of ecclesiastical phenomena like the seeker-friendly movement, which has helped to proliferate free-market tendencies, ideals, and practices in church governance and evangelism. Pioneered by the likes of Willow Creek Church and the Willow Creek Association, seeker churches often advocate the use of market-based techniques to give churchgoers the church experience that they want. This movement is rooted in brand savvy. Willow Creek began by using polls to discover what the Chicago suburbanites of the 1970s disliked about traditional Christianity — and then offered them what they did want, instead. (There are certainly ecclesiological problems with this. Most notable is the observation that people will follow the God to whom they convert, and a Brand Jesus conversion is unlikely to be followed by a living Lord discipleship — because nobody likes a bait-and-switch.)

However, not every attempt to meet non-Christians where they are demonstrates unrepentant marketeering, and at times, the traditionalist critics' alleged orthodoxy looks more like simple obstinacy. No, the flaws in the seeker-friendly movement are not native to that segment alone — they are endemic to the national church. The danger we face from corporate attention is of our own making. Because we have failed to form our lives in any meaningful resistance to the worldly patterns of consumerism, we ourselves have bought the discipleship of Brand Jesus at nearly every level. As a result, the American church has compromised its own immune system and left itself essentially defenseless against modern marketing.

But it's not enough that we've created ourselves in the world's own image. No, because we are star struck at the prospect of even more cultural influence, we're opening the sheepfold gate to commercial giants — not only that, we've sent the wolves an embossed invitation. It's this delight at receiving the attention we believe we so richly deserve, this hubristic glee at having Hollywood come knocking, that leads Bob Waliszewski, a media specialist with Focus on the Family — a group that has struggled as much as any to wage and win a culture war — to crow that "Mel Gibson did us a favor."[6] The media industry has come hunting for evangelical pocketbooks, and our response has been to declare open season on the flock.

Consider the invitation from Frank Breeden, president of the Gospel Music Association and the Christian Music Trade Association, in a statement to the *New York Times:* "If marketers are looking for a niche that's working, we know from market research that the largest affinity group in the nation, second to none, is the 100 million people who go each week to a house of worship."[7] *Affinity group?* Have the shepherds fallen asleep? Wolves and lambs don't lie down together — at least, not in this age. And the integrity of American evangelicalism (such as it is) will prove easy prey for the greed of big-money media.

What we're seeing is "Corporate Constantinianism" — a contemporary, consumerist version of the alliance formed between the Roman emperor Constantine and the church in the early fourth century. Until Constantine, the church had been a persecuted, though growing, minority; so, when the emperor decided to institute Christianity as the state religion, Christians understandably rejoiced. But this move of acceptance, while it had its good points, also put the church under the emperor's thumb. The moral of the story, to paraphrase our Lord's saying, is that gaining the world entails losing one's soul. And the world is beating a path to the American church's open doors like never before.

"There's definitely more of an awareness," says Russell Schwartz, president of theatrical marketing at New Line Cinema, referring to Hollywood's sudden discovery of evangelicals' spending potential. And, faced with this new cash cow, it's no mystery how they regard us. Continues Schwartz: "[It's] just another group to be marketed to." A virtually identical statement from Universal Pictures' vice chairman, Marc Shmuger, pegs us perfectly: "It's a well-formed community, it's identifiable, it has very specific tastes and preferences and is therefore a group that can be located and can be directly marketed to."[8]

Would that the marketers' claims were not true! Would that evangelicals were culturally heterogeneous enough that we could claim our true identity lay in the Lord Jesus Christ. But we are an affinity group. As both Christians and executives realize, we are a demographic "second to none." And as a consumer group, our true master is Brand Jesus, Mammon's crude puppet.

The proof of the developing commercial-ecclesial hybrid — which amounts to the institutionalization of Brand Jesus — is the explosion of cooperative efforts between secular business and popular Christianity. This has resulted in a two-way street between the institutions. We give them our money, and they give us their Jesus.

For example, Chevrolet came under fire in 2002 for its title sponsorship of a sixteen-city contemporary Christian music concert tour, which showcased artists Michael W. Smith and the band Third Day, with Pastor Max Lucado preaching between the musical acts. Abraham Foxman, national director of the Anti-Defamation League and critic of Chevrolet's involvement, named outright what must have been the company's quiet hope: "Evangelical Christians believe they have the truth, so are they selling a product because it's God's product?"[9]

I hope none of us clings to the notion that such corporate involvement with the church will result in corporations or the culture being more Christ honoring. Such is the delusion of the Catholic League's William Donohue, notorious for his role in the Christmas wars, who said, "The battle is a long way from over, and the culture is still up for grabs."[10] The culture is not up for grabs; it has already been grabbed by the prince of this world. If we keep on clutching at it, we will only wind up holding hands with him. Instead of corporations honoring Christ, we can expect to see churches honoring corporations with their consumption.

The corporations know it. This was certainly the case with Disney, which stole directly from *The Passion of the Christ*'s marketing playbook in its heavily church-based promotion of *The Chronicles of Narnia*. In fact, the company went so far as to sponsor a drawing for pastors to win a trip to the Holy Land. To enter, a preacher only had to submit proof that he or she had mentioned *Narnia* in a recent sermon.

For-profit Mediators

As might be expected, an industry that is almost completely ignorant of such a shiny new demographic has to channel its efforts through entities that can translate between the two. Thus, the "newly minted" job description of "experts in Christian marketing." Firms like Grace Hill and Motive Entertainment, which help the movie industry navigate the unfamiliar world of the church, are tapping into Hollywood's newfound and lucrative interest. The goal of such firms is ostensibly to benefit the church, first by directing Christians toward good, "family-friendly, biblical values-affirming" content; and second, by encouraging studios to produce more content like it. Unfortunately, despite what are the doubtlessly authentic Christian commitments of such middlemen, their rhetoric confirms Christ's saying about Mammon. It is impossible for a person to serve two masters — in this case, the church and Hollywood — for he must necessarily love the one and hate the other.

One might hope that the result of such efforts would be the reining in of an ever more sexual, ever more violent Hollywood. But Christian entertainment preferences don't give much reason to hope that this will be the case. As a *New York Times* report on evangelical media revealed,

> ... a new study by a leading Hollywood marketing firm, Market-Cast, suggested that not only do Christians watch mainstream entertainment, but the most conservative among them are also drawn to violent fare. ... The researchers found that "when it comes to popular movies and popular shows, tastes don't differ at all" between religious and nonreligious, said Joseph Helfgot, president of MarketCast. "What you find is that people with conservative religious doctrine are the most likely to see movies rated R for violence. If you compared it to liberals, it's a third more."[11]

This tells us that Christians aren't willing to subscribe to an either/or market share. We like our family-friendly, Mayberry fare to reinforce our Christian identities. And then we'll put the kids to bed and rent the latest shoot-'em-up action thriller. The point is, the explosion of Christian entertainment is likely to do little more than make a lot of money for movie studios that can produce content that is the Christian thing to see. As a result, we will see the confirmation and solidification of Christians as a mere market. The more successful that firms like Grace Hill are, the more evangelical Christians will be identifiable, targeted, and defined by the media we consume. What effect can we imagine that this will have on our evangelistic witness?

A similar partnership is occurring in sports, spearheaded by Third Coast Sports, which serves as a middleman between churches and professional athletic teams that are interested in hosting promotional "faith nights" around a ballgame. The comments of Third Coast's president, Brent High, offer an unwitting testimony to the current state of church-world integration and hybridization:

> The current climate has everything to do with the success of our events. The 2004 Presidential election, the success of Christian movies ... the crossover hits in pop music by Christian bands and the popularity of Rick Warren's book, *The Purpose-Driven Life*, have made it easier for sports executives to wrap their arms around these events. They see the smart business in aligning themselves with these large, influential groups.[12]

The problem is not these faith nights, which seem harmless enough and are probably a good time for families wanting mild, safe fun.

The problem is the growing trend toward identifying Christianity with brand attributes, and where that leaves the faith. As Professor Timothy Beal observed of the faith nights at the ballpark, "From a business perspective, it looks like a no-brainer. I mean, does it move product or not? For evangelicals, it's hopefully a more complex matter, requiring some serious reflection."[13]

But Beal's insight, that efforts like Third Coast occupy "a dilemma that goes to the heart of evangelical Christianity: getting the Gospel message out by whatever means necessary versus protecting and preserving the sacredness of the tradition," is likely to go unheeded. Third Coast's mission statement — "I have become all things to all men so that by all possible means I might save some" (1 Corinthians 9:22) — demonstrates the company's decision for a "whatever means necessary" zeal for evangelism.[14]

Unfortunately, this attitude, which Third Coast shares with brands like NOTW, is virtually immune to external criticism, since any critic can be written off as less than fully committed to the Great Commission. Such a closed circuit of logic is theologically perilous, however, precisely because there is almost no evangelistic method that falls out of bounds. Thus, there are no real barriers in place to stop business values from streaming unhindered into the church.

Concerns like those of Chris Carpenter, Catholic priest and movie critic, are starting to sound more and more like prophecy: "I think there's potential for us to be taken for a ride."[15] We are seeing the consequences of that corporate ride play out with increasing rapidity and intensity, and in various arenas of life. Even the theologically dubious goal of proclaiming one's religious identity through one's clothing is becoming more and more difficult, as corporations increasingly employ religious imagery to market secular products.

This has long been the case for Eastern religions like Buddhism and Hinduism, which have had their sacred symbols pillaged by Western companies wanting an exotic feel. The author Chuck Palahniuk, speaking with *Christianity Today* about the inspiration for his novel *Lullaby,* said that his inspiration came from a visit to the chain store Bed, Bath & Beyond, where he "started seeing all of the sort of beautiful religious symbols of every other culture suddenly being used on bath mats and toilet seat covers and wallpaper borders."[16]

The same is now true of Christianity, as America's once domestic religion becomes increasingly foreign on its own soil — especially to the young. Commodities like Teenage Millionaire's million-selling "Jesus Is My Homeboy" T-shirt, popularized by celebrities like Ashton Kutcher, have effectively helped to erase for younger generations any distinctions between sacred and secular representations of Christ. Is this a Christian T-shirt? An anti-Christian shirt? It's neither. It's both. It doesn't matter. The point is, it sells.

The credibility of representing oneself with Christian iconography has rarely been more divorced from internal reality. How faithful can our testimony to Christ's care for the poor be, for instance, when the cross is employed everywhere from the oversized platinum and diamond jewelry favored by hip-hop artists, to the jeweled, torso-sized embroidery of a Derek Lam couture blanket wrap?

Given such usage, products from Christian companies like Reliance skateboards — which uses the familiar "praying hands" image and the slogan "skateboarders who love Jesus" — could be worn equally well by a dedicated Christian or an atheist showing off her ironic detachment from the avowed message of her clothing. In this light, the move by some (usually younger) Christians to abolish the sacred/secular divide becomes a bit more alarming. Given our propensity to dishonor God, when barriers between sacred and secular fall away, it seems that the latter colonizes the former, rather than vice versa.

Chapter 19

Consuming Politics

I close this section with some concluding reflections about the political ramifications of the consumerism that we've seen in the previous pages. The relationship between consumerism and politics, like that between consumerism and religion, is rarely explored in depth. This is an inexcusable lapse, given the totalitarian grip that consumerism has on our culture. We are either blind or foolish or both to imagine that our consumerism stops when we are dealing with politics.

So how does consumerism — especially that of Brand Jesus — affect our engagement with government? To begin with, remember that American evangelicals have become accustomed to understanding their Christianity through consumption of Brand Jesus. We have come to enjoy our externalized faith. We know it when we see it, and when we see it, we grab at it. If we accept that this is the state of Christian consumerism, then it is worth considering that this consumer reflex, so to speak, might play out in politics.

Imagine, for example, Joe Candidate, a politician who can label himself with Brand Jesus. He can brand himself with it. If he can wear the logos, speak the lingo, and walk as if he were listening to the jingle in his head — well, he is a formidable force, indeed. Such a politician reaps the benefit of stimulating people's religious reflexes in ways that neither they nor he might even realize. The very way of living out our spiritual selves would come into play with Joe. He would appeal on an almost visceral level to voters. He could command zealous devotion and perhaps even the aura of divine anointing. And he would do so not because Christians are easily duped or essentially theocratic, but because we are so habituated to consuming Brand Jesus that we will reach for it, almost compulsively, wherever we find it.

Now, I don't want to make too much of this possibility. I still believe that the nitty-gritty issues of politics do in fact matter, and can trump branding in the end. This may not be the case in ten years, given that our political parties are becoming brands themselves. But in the meantime, though I can ruefully acknowledge the role that image plays in our political process, I hold out hope that it's not yet the end-all and be-all of our electoral system. I have pointed out in another chapter that voting is in and of itself a small act of resistance to consumerism, because the voter has to live with a result that she may not have chosen for herself — a phenomenon that distinguishes the polling booth from the cash register. There's still a hope for the polls.

Oddly enough, however, as a political feat, branding doesn't seem all that difficult to pull off. The basic political "brand family" for Brand Jesus consists of positions against abortion and gay rights — and anomalies only prove the rule. Depending on one's local situation, the Brand Jesus family also might include being in favor of school prayer, or of teaching intelligent design theory. To win his race, Joe Candidate expresses these positions in the evangelical crypto-vernacular, that curious jargon by which we can instantly recognize one another. (President Bush is fluent in it, for example, as was his primary speechwriter for six years, Michael Gerson.) If Joe can add to that mix a general resonance with the cultural priorities of our contemporary Christianity (patriotic, militaristic, and hating sin but not sinners), then the job is basically done, assuming he has a modicum of political ability and his life is absent scandal.

The standard counterargument to this idea of political branding is that people actually care very passionately about issues like banning abortion and opposing civil rights for gay men and lesbians. It's not simple consumerism that motivates them, but personal, heartfelt opposition to what they see as immoral practices. The political activism of many individuals is certainly based in such convictions.

But when I read a book like Thomas Frank's *What's the Matter with Kansas*, the overall political phenomenon he describes sounds a lot like brand zealotry. Kansans, Frank reports, vote overwhelmingly Republican based on whether a candidate is pro-life and anti-gay, and thus vote against the sensible choice for their economic self-interest (Democratic, according to Frank).

What's strange is not that people would vote their moral consciences even if it would hurt their pocketbook (and this is what Frank fails to see). To discount that possibility is to cede the field to cynicism. No, what is strange is that people would vote "values" despite the obvious and continuing fruitlessness of doing so. As Frank observes, voting pro-life candidates into office has not resulted in Roe v. Wade being overturned. Nor will it. A constitutional amendment against gay marriage is a nonstarter now, and its prospects grow weaker with every *Will and Grace* or *Queer Eye* fan who reaches voting age. The two-issue "values candidate" will *never* be able to deliver measurable advances on either one. So, why, oh why, does Joe Candidate get elected?

Frank's answer — that Kansans have been bamboozled into a culture war — seems both overly simplistic and condescending. Though the cultural conflict is real, voters haven't been tricked into anything. The roots of the culture war run deep in the existential crisis faced by modern America. Today's "values voters" are pushing a platform based on the conviction (articulated as such or not) that only reestablishing the preeminence of Christianity — or its cultural forms, which is to say, Brand Jesus — can make the world safe again.

What Frank doesn't address is the connection between this culture war and consumer identity (his failure to do so is surprising, given that he has written extensively on the subject). The simple truth is that in a consumerist society, we like to see our own brand win out, because brand dominance makes brand loyalists stronger. And when "values" come into play, it is voter identification with Brand Jesus that drives sympathetic candidates straight to Washington.

It would be an easy mistake to assume that Jane Consumer-Voter is primarily concerned with Joe Candidate's accomplishments. She is not. No, Jane is concerned with representing herself. As a consumer, she is accustomed to acting in a way (by buying things) that express who she is as a person. She is accustomed, in fact, to *creating* herself as a person by what she consumes (though she would deny this). And this way of living is going to carry over into Jane's voting.

So, as an evangelical voter — which has come to mean a pro-life and anti-gay voter — she is, in effect, a political consumer of Brand Jesus. Despite her patent sincerity on those issues, Jane Consumer-Voter is interested in expressing her individuality through voting. If Joe Candidate is Brand Jesus too, then that looks pretty good to Jane. She sees her own brand in Joe Candidate, "consumes" that brand by voting for him, and Joe Candidate becomes Congressman Joe. As infuriating as it may be to many, that shared brand identity is far, far more important to Jane's decision-making process than anything Congressman

Joe will do or fail to do once he arrives at the Capitol. (This is unless his behavior smirches the brand. There is no forgiveness for the apostate.)

Of course, brands are about image, and legislation, however frustrating, is about substance. It is about real action and real people and — most importantly — people's real money. So the brand that Joe Candidate rode to Washington actually comes into play hardly at all when he faces the work of lawmaking. The issues that Brand Jesus exploits are basically resolved. And this leaves a lot of spare time to legislate around a lot of other issues.

This is, by and large, an admittedly oversimplified theory for how the concerns of the Religious Right have led to the rise of a Republican party that has been essentially unable to deliver on them. But it appears to be true in theory and in actual practice. Consider the 2004 presidential election, after which conservative commentator William Kristol remarked that Bush political guru Karl Rove's "singular achievement" was to isolate inflammatory social issues like abortion and homosexual rights as a way to attract swing voters.[1] In other words, Rove either consciously or intuitively realized that the brand appeal of social conservatism would override, for many, more substantive opinions that might diverge from those of the Republican platform.

I say this in part to point out that evangelicals are not the ideological theocrats that the conventional secular wisdom imagines us to be. It's just that our consumptive patterns lead us to act that way. (Lest nonreligious liberals scoff and snigger at this, I would point out that there's plenty of room for similar self-criticism on that end of the political-consumer spectrum, as well.) In a world where the strength of consumer identity is directly linked to brand domination in the meaning market, evangelicals' desire to see Brand Jesus ascendant has led to theocratic pursuits. And our zeal for it has resulted in a general acceptance of the legitimacy of Christianizing the government, a sort of "theocracy lite."

This is actually a surprising state of affairs, historically considered. Take the Baptists, for instance, who make up a sizable portion of American evangelicals. We have a rich history of rigorous separation between church and state. But that history is all but forgotten now, as we march in virtual lockstep to the beat of Brand Jesus' tune. Is that song an ad jingle or a campaign fight song? Hard to tell these days.

In waging our current culture war, what evangelicals need to realize is how far we are straying from the bounds of orthodoxy. It's one
thing to want society to be safe and decent. It's another to take the
steps we have, through which we have inadvertently supported the
aims of the fundamentalist lunatic fringe. We're getting the job done
for groups like Christian Reconstructionists, who actually do want to
see a Christian theocratic rule in America and the abolition of de-
mocracy. I cannot think of a single evangelical who I personally know
who would support a Reconstructionist doctrine — which includes,
among other things, the death penalty for homosexuality or for striking
one's parent. In fact, most evangelicals I know would rightly consider Reconstructionism to be rank blasphemy and a defamation of
the grace offered in Jesus Christ. But *a great many* of the evangelicals I know are unwitting soldiers for the Reconstructionist cause,
due to their conviction that it is the job of Christian citizens to see
"Christian values" legislated — regardless of what the common good
may be.

To be sure, there are a thousand shades of gray differentiating
thoughtful Christian political conservatism from the likes of Reconstructionism. But we should pay attention how we move through that
mottled field, because we are not quite as distinct as we might like
to imagine. Consumerism's grip on our lives is pervasive throughout
faith and politics (in fact, consumerism's wholesale dominion over our
society makes the Reconstructionist ideal of theocratic dominion —
which is pretty sweeping — pale in comparison).

The thing is, though I've talked primarily about evangelicals, that's
just because they're my people — my infuriating, frustrating, beloved
people. But we're all implicated. So for any nonevangelicals who are
tempted toward self-righteousness, I'll say right now that it's simply
not good enough to write off huge sections of the family of God.
Liberal Christians, whose outrage at the Religious Right leads them
to disinherit conservative Christians without any interest in actually
knowing or understanding them, infuriate me. And vice versa. God
chooses God's family, not you. And not I. All the more reason for
the family's shared shame at being guilty of Paul's allegation to the
Roman Jews: The name of God is blasphemed among the nations
because of us.

Derailed

The overwhelming grip of consumerism on our lives, even (and especially) as Christians, is the take-away conclusion of this chapter and of Part IV. The way we live demonstrates our surrender to it and its dictates for who we can be. When we try to invite Jesus into our lives as just another brand, even if he is the dominant one, we treat him as if we were not under his Lordship. We make him out to be a lie.

I have a great deal of respect for Billy Graham and the tireless evangelistic work he has done over a long career. I do not doubt for an instant that the Spirit of God has worked through his preaching to convict the hearts of thousands or even millions. But I'm afraid that a great many people have failed to move beyond the particular kind of conversion moment that he has popularized. I worry that the very way we have come to conceive of conversion is part of the problem. A writer's account of Dr. Graham's final New York crusade brought this fact home to me:

> ...I am reminded of [the] power [of Graham's invitation]. His sermons have never dwelt on the evils of the world, like the old-style preachers; nor has he presented Christianity as a success religion, like the younger ones today. His approach has been almost purely existential. His ideal listener is someone whose life hasn't gone too badly: no bouts with cancer, no rap sheet. Billy simply looks that person in the eye and says: I know what you know. That you aren't happy. You may have a decent job, a loving spouse, healthy children, a pension plan. You might even be a "professor" like Nicodemus. But there are moments when you sit out on your lawn and wonder, Why do I feel so empty inside? What does it all mean?
>
> I know you feel this way, Billy says; I also know what you need. I'm not asking you to forsake father and mother, wife and children. I'm not even asking you to forsake your car and vacation home — not because those things are valuable, but because they are irrelevant. All I'm asking is that you hear Christ's simple invitation, that you accept him as your personal savior and start your life anew. So come forward, come forward now while the organ plays.[2]

It's inevitable that Americans are going to meet Christ for the first time as full-blown consumers. That's who we are, and grace is that he meets us where we are instead of demanding that we cross the impassable divide of God's holiness on our own. But there is a way of considering conversion that will, unless challenged, forever lead us to treat our discipleship in the same consumptive ways that we have understood our "secular" lives. And part of the problem is that so many of us believe we can claim Jesus existentially without any corresponding demands. If the Jesus that we claim remains the Jesus whom we worship, then over time we will truly be left only with Brand Jesus.

Let me say very clearly here that the problem is *our* problem as the American church. I fear that the dominant individualism of our culture will lead many Christian readers to assume my complaint is with individual, "nominal" Christians — the isolated person reading this book. It is not. My complaint is with you and with myself, but it is more with the entirety of the church and the (stunted) consumeristic discipleship it teaches. A solitary rededication to be "all about Jesus — the *real* Jesus, not Brand Jesus" would be a wholly inadequate response. We are so mired in consumerism that there is no easy way out. And there is no way out at all for a Christian on his or her own.

That's the point. This book isn't an invective against individuals' sins, as if the train were on the right track but oh, look how some have jumped off at the wrong stop. No, the whole assembly is derailed, and it started with the locomotive. We've seen that the whole way we understand Christianity, and ourselves as Christians, is too similar to the way that Paul's Roman Jewish audience understood their Jewishness, as "hearers but not doers." An entire group has misunderstood its position in light of God.

This systemic sickness has metastasized throughout the church because we have created and tolerated an understanding of Christian identity as a subset of consumer identity. Hypocrisy will always be endemic to this type of practice of the faith, because it is an externally generated, rather than internally generative, religion. I hear so many Christians railing against Christian hypocrisy as if the fault were simply with each individual's choice. Nothing wrong with our Christianity, the story goes, just problems with individual Christians. If only they'd get their acts together.

But our *system* is broken. We can't just order people back into righteousness. Telling the American church not to breed hypocrites is like telling a dead tree to bear good fruit. And telling American churchgoers to shun Brand Jesus in their churches is like telling swimmers not to get wet. The way that we have set up discipleship of the living Lord as a consumer identity is itself the problem.

This is a dour diagnosis, but the situation strikes me as being that grim. My hope is that there is a hope for the American church — that God will see fit to retain a remnant whose faithfulness will pass the true witness of the Lord's righteousness to the world and to subsequent generations. We turn, in the closing chapters, to some thoughts about what might be required of us if we aspire to this kind of faithfulness.

Part V

FAST AND PRAY

Romans 12:1–2

Chapter 20

Therefore I Urge You

Therefore, I urge you, brothers and sisters, in view of God's mercy, to offer your bodies as living sacrifices, holy and pleasing to God — this is your spiritual act of worship. Do not conform to the pattern of this world, but be transformed by the renewing of your mind. Then you will be able to test and approve what God's will is — his good, pleasing, and perfect will. (Romans 12:1–2)

At one point in Jesus' ministry, a distraught father brings his son to the Lord. The boy has been possessed by an evil spirit that is determined to kill him. It seizes control of his body and throws him into water to drown and into fire to burn. Christ's disciples, who have otherwise caused a stir with their healings and exorcisms, have been unable to do anything for the boy.

Jesus expels the spirit and leaves the boy whole. When his disciples ask why their efforts failed, Christ replies, "This kind can come out only by prayer and fasting" (Mark 9:29).

The body of the American church has been seized by Brand Jesus, which seeks to kill us. And this evil spirit will not be expelled by our continuing to do church business as usual. Our trusted methods, the old standbys — they will fail. It is business as usual that has opened us to such peril.

No, this kind can come out only by prayer and fasting.

We have dedicated ourselves in this book to diagnosing our problem along the lines of Paul's letter to the Romans. So it is appropriate to seek a prescription from the same text. We turn, then, to Romans 12, where Paul begins to lay out his instructions for how the Roman church ought to live. And the directions he gives correspond remarkably to the words of our Lord when he told the disciples how to deal with such destructive spirits as that which possessed the boy. Paul writes that we are to be a living sacrifice — and that we are to do so through the twin effort of nonconformity to the world's pattern (fasting) and transformation through the renewal of the mind (prayer).

Because of what I have written to you, Paul declares, *live like this.*

This is quintessential Paul, who — despite being employed by systematic dogmaticians throughout the church's history — is really a pastoral theologian. That is, he writes into specific situations with specific advice, stemming from intimate knowledge of the gospel and its implications, which is his by apostolic right. And Romans, his masterpiece, concludes with four chapters of exhortation about what it looks like to live as Christians together, given the grace of the good news that he has spent eleven chapters proclaiming. These instructions are as true today as they were for the Roman church then.

We have skipped a long way forward into Paul's letter from the end of chapter 2, where we left off. The reason for my doing so is that the need for translation between the biblical then and the contemporary now seems to me to be greatly reduced after chapter 2. It is one thing to understand ourselves in light of Paul's Roman audience, because there is merit to comprehending how we fit into the classes he so roundly condemns. But God's *answer* to our situation is the same for our consumerist era as it was in the apostolic age. Though there is no human claim to righteousness, nevertheless — oh, grace! — there is a righteousness from God, given through the faith of Christ, to *all* who are faithful (Romans 3:22). Though it can bear interpretation and exposition and application, this does not need translation. Nor, for that matter, does Paul's theological-historical argument about the Jewish covenant and Gentile inclusion into its promises that follows in Romans 4–11.*

_____

*Chapters 4–11 do, however, require a sense of context. One of Paul's most pressing issues in Romans — his primary concern, some might argue — is the reconciliation of Jew and Gentile in Christ. The material in Romans 3–11 is Paul's understanding of how the Jewish covenant ought to be understood in light of Christ, as well as the inclusion of the Gentiles into the historical privilege of Israel. This material is dangerous ground for overly metaphorical interpretation, because it refers to a specifically historical process in a specific historical time. We cannot draw easy parallels between then and now, such as an overly facile reading of the church as a new Israel. This is especially the case given that nearly two thousand years of church history — entangled with a history of violent Christian anti-Semitism that is quite nearly as lengthy — finds us in a situation where to be Jewish is de facto not to be Christian, and vice versa. (In saying this I refer to our socio-religious reality rather than making any theological claim. The former is plainly the case, given the patent [though understandable] refusal of Jewish groups to accept that a "Jew for Jesus" can be anything but an oxymoron, in modern times.)

One might wonder, given the perils of such analogical interpretations, how I have read the three categories of Romans 1–2 (degenerate Gentile, moralizing Gentile, hypocritical

When we arrive at Romans 12, however, we are plunged back into material that appears immediately relevant to our particular, twenty-first-century context. We who have identified with the ways of life that Paul condemns must pay attention to the advice that follows on his admonition. Because you are like X, writes Paul, do Y. The ethical imperatives in Romans 12–15 may be timeless instruction that Christians should follow in every time and place. But they are, given our parallel to the Roman Christians, instructions that we should particularly follow in our time and place, as they did in theirs.

This book has dwelt extensively on the nature of our problem and the ubiquity of our captivity to the sin — manifested in our day as consumerism — that makes us spiritual kin to Paul's Romans. Where could we turn for a solution but to Romans 12, and Paul's *therefore I urge you, brothers and sisters?* We look first at the significance of the text before turning to how it might be concretely manifested today.

The Living Sacrifice

Paul's exhortation in the first sentence of Romans 12 is a singular instruction to all Christians: "In view of God's mercy . . . offer your bodies as a living sacrifice, holy and pleasing to God — this is your true worship." This instruction looks both backwards and forwards within Romans. First, a living sacrifice is the appropriate, restorative response to the situation described in the first part of the letter — especially, for our context, that of 1:18–2:29. And second, "living sacrifice" looks forward to encompass and describe the whole set of Christian ethical behavior outlined in the rest of chapters 12–15.

Though Romans 12:1 is frequently cited as a pithy prooftext to describe the depth of Christian discipleship, the verse and its context

---

Jew) in contemporary — metaphorical — terms. It is an admittedly debatable move. But it is one that I think has exegetical merit, because I understand Paul's opening chapters to be dismissing *ways of life* that might be imagined as competitors to the gospel. And, while these ways of life were historical realities in ancient Rome, they also bear sufficiently general resemblance to our contemporary situation. Like Rome, our ways of life today are similarly perceived as sources of intrinsic righteousness. Given the socio-political parallels between imperial Rome and globally dominant America, drawing those links seems like a plausible application of Paul's argument to our own day. But the same would not be true of Paul's talking about Abraham, for instance, as he does in Romans 4. There he speaks of the historical and biblical Abraham in describing the nature of the Jewish covenant. Because Abraham is unique, Paul's treatment of him may not responsibly be ripped from its context and applied devil-may-care to a contemporary parallel.

need to be explored fully in order to appreciate the extent of what Paul is enjoining, as well as its specific implications for us. After all, "living sacrifice" isn't an everyday term for most of us; like much of the God-talk that we toss around so easily at church, it can easily be made into a lukewarm catchphrase. ("Bearing your cross daily" is my personal favorite among verses that are often radically misappropriated. I have heard it used to describe phenomena as banal and *un*-cruciform as one well-intentioned congregation member's Lenten vow of giving up pie.) So, "living sacrifice" bears some explanation.

Body

The first key to the living sacrifice is that which is offered — namely, one's body, which has a dual significance. First, "body" is noteworthy because it locates the Christian's sacrifice. Paul's term does not simply mean one's physical being as opposed to one's mind or soul.* Rather, as the commentator James D. G. Dunn observes, the body in question "denotes not just the person, but the person in his corporeality, in his concrete relationships within this world. . . . It is as a part of the world and within the world that Christian worship is to be offered by the Christian."[1]

We cannot imagine that the sacrifice we are to make is purely interior. In light of our tendency to view faith as simple belief, this is an especially important point. Convicted by the command to offer ourselves as living sacrifices, we might be tempted to undergo an inner overhaul with only personal ramifications — being more diligent in one's quiet time, for instance, or praying more, or combating some tenacious private sin. But this would miss the point. Our sacrificial offerings are our bodies, in all their relationships. We cannot pretend that the sacrifice is simply confined to our secret spiritual disciplines. Instead, the sacrifice must be of our selves in every aspect of life, whether at church, on the job, with family or friends, or alone. The Christian is to be a Christian *everywhere*.

---

*In fact, while Paul is happy to talk about one's exterior and interior faculties, or the flesh and the spirit, he also rejects any body-mind dichotomy that sees the former as worldly and the latter as holy. Our entire existence — whole and holistic — is spiritual, according to Paul. And just as our flesh and spirit are corrupted by sin, so the resurrection to glory will not be souls only but bodies also. This fact is especially important to note regarding a verse that might be misappropriated and erroneously preached to justify or excuse all manner of physical abuse, including domestic violence.

The second implication of "body" is its scope, which is related to the previous point. When we offer ourselves as a sacrifice in every area of our lives, we are to offer our *whole* selves. Dunn points out that this offers a contrast to Romans 6:13, in which Paul forbids the Christian "to offer any *part* of yourself to sin."[2] It is difficult to imagine a person who has given himself entirely and in every aspect to sin, with each area of his life wholly dedicated to evil. Even the worst of us — think on the great villains that history regards as monsters — cannot deface into unrecognizability the image of God that is our created nature. But though we cannot obscure that *imago Dei* entirely, nevertheless, there is no part of our lives that sin does not corrupt and tempt toward wickedness. Hence, Paul's warning in Romans 6:13 and the opposite urging in 12:1 to offer ourselves to God in our entirety. We cannot compartmentalize ourselves and give only the bits we imagine to be religious as our sacrifice to God. There are a good many ministers, for example, whose pastoral activity seems to contain a great deal of zeal for evangelism and fire against sin, but not an iota of kindness, gentleness, or compassion. This is not the offering of the whole body.

This realization is especially critical to our brand-crazed society, in which there is the constant temptation to treat discipleship as the "spiritual" aspect of our lives as if it could be divorced from the professional, familial, and so on. No, in addition to being Christians everywhere, the significance of offering our bodies means that we should be *completely* Christian in all situations.

Now, we certainly don't need a resurgence of Christian legalism, which usually owes much more to conservative cultural standards than to responsible interpretation of the gospel.* But the state of the church, which clearly demonstrates that we are not offering up our complete selves in every situation, demands that we take a serious look at how our teaching and behavior serve to excuse whole sections of life and self from the unrelenting sacrificial duty described in Romans 12:1.

---

*Otherwise, why would even the most legalistic branches of the faith turn such a blind eye toward Christians occupying positions where violence is required of them, for instance, or the massive accumulation of wealth? Such a double standard shows that the church is only too willing to sacrifice gospel integrity for the privilege of serving as the finger-wagging, bow-tied chaplain to the American way of life.

God

The second key to understanding the meaning of "living sacrifice" is the rightful identity of God, the one to whom the sacrifice is made. Notice that God encompasses our sacrifices, which are made "in view of God's mercy" and which are received by the Lord as "holy and pleasing." The former — our perspective of God's mercy — contextualizes the whole action of our sacrificial discipleship. This mercy is no abstract quality, moreover, but a concrete reality attested to and described throughout Romans:

> You also are among those Gentiles who are called to belong to Jesus Christ. (1:6)

> [The] gospel . . . is the power of God for salvation to everyone who believes. (1:16)

> [Apart from the law] from the righteousness from God . . . has been made known. . . . God presented [Christ] as a sacrifice of atonement . . . to demonstrate his justice, because in his forbearance he had left the sins committed beforehand unpunished — he did it to demonstrate his justice at the present time, so as to be just and the one who justifies those who have faith in Jesus. (3:21–26)

> [Jesus] was delivered over to death for our sins and was raised to life for our justification. (4:25)

> God demonstrates his own love for us in this: While we were still sinners, Christ died for us. . . . Through [him] we have now received reconciliation. (5:8, 11)

> The Spirit himself testifies with our spirit that we are God's children. Now if we are children, then we are heirs. . . . (8:16–17)

> For I am convinced that neither death nor life, neither angels nor demons, neither the present nor the future, nor any powers, neither height nor depth, nor anything else in all creation, will be able to separate us from the love of God that is in Christ Jesus our Lord. (8:38–39)

In other words, the mercy of God is the work of love done by God in Christ. It is the action of graciously drawing near to we who by our sins have pulled away from God. It is the justification at the cross of a world that has pulled condemnation upon its own head. It is the inhabitation of the Spirit to liberate us from the shackles that we diligently forged. The mercy of God is the love of God in spite of ourselves, shown in the person of the Lord Jesus Christ. Mercy is another word for God's kindness, which we know is the postponement of judgment that "is intended to lead us to repentance" (2:4).

No small wonder, then, that the appropriate response to this love is our imitation of its demonstration. We offer ourselves as living sacrifices in emulation of the one who first offered himself for us. And this offering orients us properly to God. Becoming like Christ means becoming "holy and pleasing to God." To employ a spatial metaphor, in our sinfulness we walk at cross-purposes to God. We have set our faces to our own purposes and our own destinations and, because they are of our own origination, they are false. We are following a trajectory that neither begins with a recognition of what God has done nor ends in a place pleasing to him. Repenting from this trajectory requires situating ourselves in relation both to God's present mercy and to his final ends. And thus resituated, we find ourselves walking the path that Christ alone walked without stumbling — that perfect orientation of the one who is himself the Way.

Worship

When we do this, Paul says — when we become such an offering — this "is [our] true/reasonable/spiritual worship." However the adjective modifying "worship" is translated, it points to a rightness in both action (offering our bodies) and direction (to God). This rightness is a stark contrast to the multifaceted and multidirectional errors recorded by Paul in Romans 1–2. The depraved Gentile (1:18–32) knew of God but refused to give God glory or thanks. The moralizing Gentile (2:1–16) was complicit in the very actions he imagined that he stood above, seeking to supplant God's place as judge. And the hypocritical Roman Jew (2:17–29) believed that his inheritance of divine privilege was irrevocable and entailed nothing in return from him. All three refused the right offering, and all three had a distorted relationship to God.

The mercy of God, the pleasure of God — there is truth here for a lifetime. As self-centered creatures, we cannot help but begin with ourselves and our bodies, and at the end, we have nothing more than that with which we began. But though we must start with the imagination that we are our own beginning and our own end, we are neither *the* beginning nor *the* end. God is the beginning; God is the end. His mercy allows and encourages the living sacrifice of our discipleship, and he receives it and is pleased by it. Long before we delivered the first of our daily judgments over a world not our own, God created it. And long after we and our petty judgments have been returned to the amnesia of the earth, God will judge at the last.

Our true worship is the very thing that the Gentiles would not do in Romans 1:21, which is to say, offer the sacrifice of our thanksgiving back to the divine giver. The act of offering a living sacrifice demands this perspective of humility, this disposition of gratitude that results from the knowledge that we own nothing. Mammon has lied, is a lie. There is nothing we can do to be wealthy. Though we work day and night, there will be nothing that is rightfully ours, no property free and clear that we might present as a gift to God. Even the air in our lungs is borrowed and will be returned for good someday. All that we can do is acknowledge that God gives and we have received — and, so acknowledging, dedicate God's gift, our bodies, our all, to the glory of the giver. So the only thing we ourselves can give is something that we in fact cannot possess, but only offer, and that indeed does not exist outside of being offered: that is, the disposition of sacrifice itself.

Conformation versus Renewal

Paul follows the urging of 12:1 with the instruction of 12:2, which both clarifies and expands our understanding of what the offering of our bodies as living sacrifices will look like — that is, the renunciation of the world's pattern and the renewal of minds. The result of this, he writes, will be the ability to discern the perfect will of God.

For our purpose of understanding what it will mean to be a faithful Christian in the age of Brand Jesus, the dual implication of 12:2 is especially important. Paul's clarification of the living sacrifice entails a negative and a positive action on the part of the Christian. Living out our faithfulness with integrity will mean changing our present location, which itself requires that we give up the old (the negative) and adopt the new (the positive). The faithful life requires both steps.

First, the negative. We are not to "conform to the pattern of this world." The initial interpretive danger here is to imagine that we automatically know what that pattern is. Language of "world/liness" is tossed around in churches as if we all know precisely what it indicates and are already doing such a good job at avoiding it. What "world/liness" usually refers to, in church-ese, is that terrain on the far side of the cultural boundary markers that evangelicals have set for ourselves. In short, the term "the world" often has no content in and of itself, but is most frequently used to mean whatever the church smugly believes itself *not* to be. This is why even churches that blaspheme the gospel with prosperity teaching* are able to rail against worldliness, despite the fact that they are concerned with nothing so much as flourishing materially and physically in the here and now — a definition of "worldly" by most any standard.

By "pattern of this world," however, Paul is not referring generically to the "not-church," but specifically to what might be termed the pattern of the present age, the order imposed by "powers and principalities" that is a concrete spiritual reality. In many ways, this entire book represents an attempt to discern what this spiritual reality is in our day. And our conclusion tells us that Mammon, in the form of consumerism, has established the pattern for our day.

This pattern cannot fully be understood simply as a sweeping cultural trend, such as those frequently listed by evangelical writers with a full head of polemical steam (materialism, consumerism, anything-goes-ism, oh my!). No, if we think of worldliness as an external trend, it becomes too easy to dismiss as irrelevant to the believer's life. (*"Those* things are after the pattern of this world. *I* don't believe in those things; hence, I am not conforming to the pattern of this world. Now . . . off to the mall!") But, as we have seen, the habits of consumerism bear an insidious influence even on those who imagine themselves to be immune. This ought not to be surprising; rather, it is

---

*The "prosperity gospel" is the heretical but increasingly popular teaching that God wants Christians to be "prosperous" in all areas of life, not the least of which is material wealth. Prosperity preachers point to their own lavish lifestyles as confirmation of God's blessing and favor on their teaching, though most Christians within historic orthodoxy would reply that the only thing such lifestyles conclusively prove is the existence of a well-fleeced flock. In short, being pretty lousy news, the prosperity "gospel" is actually not the gospel at all, and is a prime example of ostensibly Christian behavior that leads non-Christians to blaspheme the name of the God.

hard to understand why so many Christians seem to think that non-conformation to the pattern of this world is an easy — indeed, almost automatic by virtue of being a church member — discipline.

No, the "pattern of the world" contains those aspects of life that we tend to consider — in practice, if not in confession — to be on the same level as our Christianity. Race (understandings of identity, rather than actual skin color) is one such aspect; class is another; gender (roles, as opposed to biological sex) is a third such power. Which one of us does not have a race, a class, a gender? Who among us is immune to thinking of him- or herself in these categories? The few exceptions of each only prove the dominion of the rule. The "pattern of the world" consists of those forces like racism/tribalism, classism, and sexism, which infect us all. And if we doubt this, is it not proven by the fact that race, class, and gender are the three attributes that Galatians 3:28 tells us we transcend in Christ?

Now, into this group of worldly patterns has arisen consumerism, which threatens to become the king of all patterns, given that we increasingly understand all other aspects of our identities through our consumptive habits (including nationality, gender, race, class, etc.). This movement is all the more threatening for our lack of recognition that it is happening. We are becoming irretrievably consumptive beings, and this is true whether we want to or not and regardless of whether we ever give that fact a conscious thought. Now, *that* is a pattern worthy of the prince of this world, and one that gives due weight to Paul's instruction.

Paul juxtaposes the negative rejection of the pattern of the world with the positive exhortation to "be transformed by the renewal of your minds." As with the reference to "bodies" in 12:1, we should import neither a modern nor a dualistic (body vs. mind) understanding to Paul's usage of "minds." Dunn writes that Paul's reference to the renewal of minds points to "a transformation which works from inside outwards," which, while typical of prophetic exhortation, "becomes a way of distinguishing the Christian emphasis from the too ethnic, law-centered spirituality of contemporary Judaism."[3] In other words, "renewal of your minds" is Paul's prescription for the Romans, following on his diagnosis of the external religious sensibility that we saw in our exploration of Romans 2:17–32, the hypocritical moralism of

2:1–16, and the mental degradation especially in 1:28–32. The mind, renewed, is the beginning of the proper vision of God, which will come to undo and replace the spiritual glaucoma induced by sin.

We explore below some specifics of mental renewal. Perhaps the most important overall implication, however, is the way in which the inside-outwards change of "renewing your minds" is *itself* an example of nonconformation with the pattern of this world. After all, the patterns of our daily living reinforce nothing so much as the idea that change is an external commodity. How could it be otherwise in a buy-to-be society? What you consume — by definition, something external to you — defines who you are. If you don't like who you are, buy yourself a new identity, a new lifestyle. Thus goes the prevailing, if often unconscious, conventional wisdom.

This attitude is so endemic to our society today that even anti-consumerism is itself a consumer good. Take the popular magazine (and quasi-mail-order catalogue) *Real Simple*, which carries the implicit promise that fed-up consumers simply need to buy a subscription in order to figure out how to buy less. James Twitchell, noting this phenomenon of consuming anti-consumption, observes the "profoundly commercial nature of letting go" of commercialism, in that we seek the cure to the "social disease" of our consumerism by "buying a how-to-stop-buying book."[4] But in the end, all that's changed is what you buy — not your basic disposition to consumption. The pattern of this world is maintained.

The change that occurs through the renewal of minds, by contrast, does not begin by adopting any new external source of meaning. Paul's exhortation implicitly rejects consumerist logic such as that demonstrated, for example, in the Christian T-shirt makers' mottos. "Put on the Lord Jesus Christ [with our shirt]" and "Change Your Shirt, Change the World" are revealed as inherently false — or, at least, inherently inadequate for, and likely distracting from, the true work of Christian discipleship.

While the renewal of minds cannot begin with the external, however, neither can it be limited to internal change. "Coming to belief in Jesus Christ" is not something that simply happens *in* one's life. Our usual understanding of conversion is totally inadequate to the task of discipleship as presented by Paul, because all too often the essential transaction is "inviting Christ into your life," with anything that follows simply being viewed as sanctificatory bonus. But renewal of minds is not a goal in and of itself; no, if we look at 12:2, such renewal is the *means* of "be[ing] transformed." The necessary internal change that is the renewal of minds is incomplete — cannot, in fact, be claimed as valid — if it does not lead to the holistic offering of our "bodies" as living sacrifices in all their social, external, and especially ecclesial relationships.

The Will of God

The result of this nonconformation on the one hand, and transformation via renewal of minds on the other, is the ability "to test and approve what God's will is." These are dangerous verses for contemporary generations obsessed with discovering personal significance. The fact that a book dealing with personal purpose has become the best-selling hardcover book in American publishing history should tell us something of the nature of our era's spiritual angst.* Each of us wants to be special; moreover, each of us wants to know the nature of our particular specialness. That we feel this way is understandable given our modern rootlessness and the efforts that advertisers expend to make each one of us feel uniquely targeted as the right consumer for their brands.

But is this the way of God? Though it appeals to our culture's existential crisis, the idea that God has a particular, micro-managed meaning for each one of us smacks of an entirely modern, unbiblical individualism. Yes, God numbers the hairs on each of our heads, and yes, all lives are treasured in God's sight — but to imagine that we are each the center of our own, special, divine reality show fractures the redemptive work of God into as many fragments as there are believers, reinforcing the cosmic self-centeredness endemic to Brand Jesus Christianity.

We should also acknowledge that discovering God's individual plan for our individual lives is a pretty narrow spiritual ideal, given that it completely fails to account for the worst tragedies of human existence.

---

*I refer, of course, to Rick Warren's *The Purpose-Driven Life.* However, while I think that this fact is indicative of our unfortunate situation, I hope that I will not be misread here as criticizing Pastor Warren, for whom I have a deep respect. He understands the contemporary world and has written a book for people who live in it. So, while the title of *The Purpose-Driven Life* may attract people whose concern for purpose is profoundly self-centered, that's admittedly where most of us are. Furthermore, if read properly, Pastor Warren's book will not let its reader abide comfortably in his or her initial disposition.

That is, it may be what we're worried about in modern America, but it's certainly not the most universal human concern. Worrying about *which* job God wants you to take is, admittedly, high up on the list of desirable crises to have, given that it requires a fair amount of physical and economic security to indulge in the first place. Fussing about a meaningful job requires, to begin with, a *life* — which is why the poverty and misery of much of the world, properly considered, instantly reveals our particularly American quest as a relatively petty spiritual concern. And yet too many of us treat individual purpose as the highest goal of discipleship, demanding a significant portion of our spiritual (and, given the money we spend on self-help books, financial) resources.

Instead, we should read the final exhortation of Romans 12:2 — "then you will be able to test and approve what God's will is" — in light of Paul's unrelenting Christ-centered teaching. Without denying the particular value of each human life, it seems that the will of God for our lives doesn't require daily, special discernment. We're to become like Christ. That's it. We are not the center of God's redemptive drama, Christ is.

Our purpose, if we're given the luxury of worrying about it, is to enter into him. Becoming a living sacrifice is not about being the best me I can be. Though being a living sacrifice will not destroy one's individuality, neither will it encourage or strengthen it. While discipleship is a profoundly personal responsibility, it does not consist of the disparate paths of each person following his or her own individual purpose. Instead, it is the movement of every Christian toward the same center in the Lord. It is, in fact, the action of becoming more like one another as we each live into Christlike-ness, imitating imperfectly the one perfect living sacrifice. As we come into alignment with God — as described above — we thus achieve discernment regarding our conformity with his "good and perfect" will: not one individually tailored for us, but one given specially in Christ, whom we are then able to follow. (Notice that this is an inversion of the consumerist ideal of hyper-individuality.)

The fact that God's will is that we each become Christlike is confirmed by the description of behaviors that follows, in Romans 12–15. All of these conform to the self-sacrificial mission and teaching of Jesus. Consider the consistent double-sidedness of Paul's exhortation: Hate what is evil, cling to the good; never lack zeal, keep your fervor;

do not curse your persecutors, but bless them; do not be proud, but associate with the lowly. This duality of rejecting evil and affirming the good is itself an echo of Christ's life. Recall prayer and fasting — the two are a parallel of the renewal of minds and nonconformation to the worldly pattern. The former is the renewed intention and self-direction toward God; the latter, an abstaining from all mortal sustenance.

American Christians have a hard time pretending at radical faithfulness. The way we live doesn't appear to be substantially different from the way our non-Christian neighbors live, and even the few attributes from which we derive our proud distinctiveness — such as it is — seem to go largely ignored by much of the congregation. We appear to have embraced that emaciated, bumper-sticker theology of sanctification: "Christians aren't perfect, just forgiven." To be sure, none of us has arrived at pure holiness. But if our spiritual lives are satiated by forgiveness alone, we have no claim to a discipleship that includes the imperative of Matthew 5:48: "Be perfect . . . as your Father in heaven is perfect."

Part of the problem, I would suggest, is in the two-fold error of understanding our faith primarily through external, cultural factors, which has led to the commercialization and politicization of the witness of our discipleship. That is, we've replaced personal (both individual and church-body) commitments to self-sacrificial virtue with a legislative program designed to criminalize sin, and a consumptive pattern that we imagine will keep us from stumbling. And we have done so in large measure because we've accepted that cultural influence is tantamount to faithfulness.

Of course, we're not living any better than non-Christians. We're doing the exact same things under a different brand.

Chapter 21

Fasting and Prayer
in the Age of Mammon

I have a confession. When reading this or that piece of cultural or religious criticism, I am often tempted to skip straight to the conclusion. If I agree with a book's premise, I am mostly interested in the recommendations for change, the steps that can be implemented. I agree about the problem; tell me how to beat it.

But this section will not — cannot — highlight practical steps for churches or individuals to take on and beat Brand Jesus, as one might expect. Nor can it offer a study guide or the like for interested groups, with a catchy, alliterative title: "Make Mammon Moot," or "Boycott Brand Jesus! A Church's Guide."

There's no such thing as a plan to help us twelve-step our way out of consumerism because no consumer-free utopia lies on the far side. There is no far side to consumerism on this side of the veil. This doesn't mean that there's nothing for the church to do. But the sort of thinking that moves straight to problem solving — a program that, if consumed, will change our identity — is captive to the very problem we might hope to solve. The way of thinking that led us to serve Brand Jesus in the first place will never free us from it. So most of our instincts will steer us in the wrong direction.

I realize that many readers will, like me, always be itching to jump into problem-solving mode. For us, half of the battle is realizing that "How do we tackle Brand Jesus?" and "How do we get out of this bind?" are the wrong questions to ask. Even more important, however, is realizing *why* these are the wrong questions. There are two main reasons for our fundamental inability to come up with an actionable plan to combat Christian consumerism. The first is theological and universal in scope, while the second is cultural and particular to our situation.

First, speaking theologically, if we try to take on Brand Jesus, we'll be doomed to failure because taking it on *simply isn't our calling as Christians.* Paul's letters are full of martial language that encourages us to fight evil. But this type of exhortation is designed to equip us for defense against attacks of a hostile spiritual reality, not arm us so that we can lead the frontal assault that will rid the world of evil once and for all. Remember that consumerism and Mammon idolatry comprise, in the analysis of this book, a "pattern of this world," and perhaps the dominant worldly pattern, at that. And Paul didn't tell the Roman Christians to *destroy* such a pattern. No, he told the Roman Christians to *refuse* the dominion of the current age: *Do not conform.* Language of spiritual warfare is awfully popular, especially among boys' and men's groups at churches, because all that testosterone lends itself toward the imagining that one is God's own chosen champion, sent to smite the devil. (Look at the bios at any youth pastor conference and see if 90 percent of the participants don't list at least one, if not all, of *Braveheart, Star Wars, Lord of the Rings,* and *Gladiator* as a favorite film.) Such martial talk in our churches appeals a great deal to our sinful natures. Spiritually speaking, we're not called to wage war against consumerism. And because we don't win battles that God hasn't called us to, we'll fail if we engage in such a fight.

I'm not talking about a failure that will happen in mysterious, super-natural ways. No, this entirely predictable failure is due to the second cultural reason why an actionable plan against Brand Jesus is doomed. And that is because consumerism is better at cultural judo than any of us will ever be: It will take our own efforts and turn them against us. Any active attempt to resist consumerism can and will be packaged, branded, marketed, and sold back to us. And when we consume our own identity as the resistance — as we invariably will — we will have surrendered, in advance, the very battle that we aspired to fight.

The inevitability of our defeat if we attack consumerism head-on does not mean that we should try harder and come up with more innovative strategies. Rather, the fact that we cannot win is a cultural manifestation of the theological reality that this is a battle we're simply not supposed to fight. Secular folk have been way ahead of us in this type of guerilla, anti-corporate campaign, and when they have tried to take a bite out of Big Marketing, they've had their teeth handed back to them — whitened and polished and with a flourish that made them feel grateful for the service.

Consumerism doesn't strike back. It disarms you by giving you what you apparently want. There is "no real alternative to our culture of consumption," Carrie McLaren writes, "just a different brand."[1] Or, as James Twitchell puts it, "The faded Levi's, the rusted-out Volvo, the frayed Brooks Brothers shirt become a mode of subversion, a way of saying 'I do not comply.' However, even noncompliance is done via brands."[2] The same would happen to Christians. Mammon will take our passionately held faith and turn it into a label to slap on and thus define whatever alt-religious category we have larded with significance.

We can already see such branding happening in the groundswell of so-called "radical" Christian ministries that purport to rebel against the church status quo. Consider some recently reported examples:

> In the increasingly clamorous Christian marketplace rebellion is where you find it: in full-contact skateboard Bible study groups; in Christian punk, Goth and hip-hop CD's; in evangelical tattoo parlors; in sportswear brands like Extreme Christian Clothing and Fear God; in alt churches or ministries called Revolution, Scum of the Earth and Punk Girl; in a podcast called Xtreme Christianity, which turns out to be a fairly conventional weekly sermon delivered by a Baptist minister in a suburb of Kansas City, Mo.[3]

And:

> The actor Stephen Baldwin, a born-again Christian, has just directed a DVD called "Livin' It," pairing extreme sports with faith testimony, from which he hopes to spin skate Bibles, clothing, CD's and Bible-study guides, all tied to a nonprofit youth ministry. "This could be the first get-down rock 'n' roll, cool Christian brand," he said. "I've been to conferences with youth pastors, and they all said, 'Dude, we've been waiting for something that's cool and edgy and Christian.'"[4]

It's easy to see the appeal of such moves. Within any established system such as the church, there will always be those whose quest for authenticity makes them strain against boundaries both real and imagined. But when I read about many of these examples, they smack of nothing so much as marketed rebellion, with a peel-off Brand Jesus sticker on the price tag.

Take the increasingly popular "skateboard ministry" of the type championed by Stephen Baldwin. It's difficult to figure out precisely what it does *except* offer the hyped "get-down rock 'n' roll, cool Christian brand." In other words, the thing that makes it radical and revolutionary has absolutely zero to do with Jesus and everything to do with the astounding athleticism and tricks of the skaters. Tattoos, board sports, hard-core music — all of these things are edgy by secular social standards, the sort of things that set your grandparents' teeth on edge. But there's nothing *spiritually* radical or edgy about the faith of tattoo- or board-sport- or punk-based ministries. In fact, given its brand merchandise integration, this kind of Christianity seems positively — gasp! — suburban.

The frequent rhetorical appeals to Jesus' status as a rebel ("the original rebel!") mostly demonstrate little to no thought about the nature of Jesus' rebellion. He didn't get crucified for sticking his skateboard on one too many fakie grinds over the pristine steps of the Jerusalem Temple. No, he got crucified for saying things like the Sermon on the Mount. But as far as I can tell, the Christian skaters' rebelliousness *isn't* because they're living out Matthew 5–7 so perfectly and teaching all the other skaters how to do the same. No, they're living the pro-skater life, riding around on the tour bus, hanging out with other skaters, and doing all the other stuff that they'd do on a secular skate tour. Doing all the stuff, that is, except for the spindly ethical restrictions (no sex, smoking, drugs, parental disobedience, etc.) that we've come to imagine are sufficiently constitutive of Christian discipleship.

Now, I don't mean to be unduly negative. I'm sure that the skate ministers are good guys, and they've undoubtedly sacrificed what would be more lucrative gigs from secular sponsors. But it's hard to say what marks this kind of ministry as a Christian activity *beyond* all the hip Christian sponsorship brands (like NOTW and the others mentioned in the last section) and the "join Team Jesus!" style of evangelistic appeal that happens at the events. In other words, if you take away the packaging, what's Christian about it all? It seems that the only thing there, except for what might be a generally higher level of niceness than one would find elsewhere, is the Brand Jesus label.

It's hard to imagine that such ministries promote much more than another branded identity, which can be marketed to the sub-demographic of Christian skaters. There's nothing inherently radical to the faith at all. The plea of the youth pastors mentioned by Stephen Baldwin says it all: "Dude, we've been waiting for something that's cool and edgy and Christian." They want hip Christian brands. And the reason they want them is that the youth in their care — who, like most adolescents in American society, are unparalleled in their consumer savvy — are embarrassed by all the lame Christian retail options. There's just not the merchandising to support their lifestyle choices! *The bottom line is that you can be whatever kind of consumer you already are, whether skate punk or budding preppie, and Brand Jesus will make it all Christian.*

Personally, I've got nothing against skaters, Christian or otherwise. In fact, my biases there are actually probably less developed than my instinctive resistance to the preppie, J. Crew evangelicalism so prevalent on campuses today. (I would not be surprised to find that someone, somewhere, is wearing a "J[esus] Crew" T-shirt.) But the problem here is that the system of consumerism in which we live will take *any* identity that we hold dear — any noun, if you will: "I am a _____" — and turn it into an adjective that we have to buy.

Christian identity is in no way immune. The skaters who flock to the skate ministry events would be completely socially unmoored if they were denied the brands that held their social identity in place. But the same is true for all of us. In consumerist society, we're walking collections of such adjectives. The only noun we're allowed, the mother of all identities, is that of "consumer." And this is why, if we try to take out consumerism, we will doubtlessly lose without ever realizing that we've been beaten in the first place.

This kind of talk sounds rather defeatist, especially by contemporary standards of Christian rhetoric, which is usually peppered with all the go-git-'em spirit of a college fight song. It seems to me, however, that our standards have been corrupted by the same optimism with which the culture war of the past half century has been fought. We've become accustomed to the idea that if we can just slap a Christian label — and better yet, Christian *values* — onto an institution, it will shape right up. That's been our attitude toward individuals, so why shouldn't it work for politics, say, or corporations?

But our assumptions are based on a falsity. As we've seen, the culture war that American Christians are so determined to win has its roots in fear. Fear of a world come unmoored from history. Fear of the inability of human institutions to protect us from ourselves. Fear of a society that can end human life as we know it. Fear about the veracity of our origins, and fear about where we are headed. And this fear is, at its heart, faithlessness in the promises of God. We might well hear Jesus' rebuke to his disciples cowering in the storm-tossed boat: "Why are you so afraid? Do you still have no faith?" (Mark 5:10). For Christians who would live by our faith/fulness, then, it's imperative for us to realize that whatever chaos today's twenty-four-hour news cycle brings into our lives, God has established the beginning and the end of history. Win or lose the culture war, the story ends the same.

No Christian culture warriors would dispute this final point, of course. Their perfectly understandable response would be that the sovereignty of God does not negate human responsibility. As Christians, the call to culture war goes, we are called upon to use our talents well, and to be salt and light to the world. Furthermore, Part II of this book describes how our culture is endangered by the consumerist rejection of God. We need salt and light! Notice, however, how quickly we assume that being salt and light entails our effort to codify "Christian values" in society.

This leap of reasoning is embedded in contemporary American evangelicalism so deeply that it has become accepted as fact (and the coming years will tell whether it is so entrenched as to be constitutive). But it is not true. Being salt and light does not necessarily mean serving as God's attack squad in secular society. Light illuminates — it does the work of light — by shining, not by waging combat against the darkness. So, if our social activity looks more like the bloodletting of political trench warfare than it does like the blaze of a brightly burning lamp, we ought to ask ourselves whether we're perhaps engaged in the wrong type of venture. Where is the basis of a legislative agenda in Matthew 5:16: "Let your light shine before others, that they may see your good deeds and glorify your Father in heaven"? Our fear has led us to the radical misunderstanding of the church's role in society. We have imagined that our job is to *do* something: salt in the wound and a solar glare in the eyes. But the biblical imperative is simply to be. Be bright. Be salty. In other words, be who the Lord has permitted us to be — by grace, in Christ — as a testimony to God that others "may see and glorify [our] Father in heaven."

We are to be, in a word, faithful — that's it. And our instinctive disbelief at the simplicity, the deceptive ease of such a calling (where are the bullet points, wherefore the action plan?!) testifies to our fear, our hidden lack of confidence in the Lord. Our disbelief testifies to our impoverished vision of faith-as-belief, which is insufficient for Christian discipleship. We know it is insufficient because we have been forced to *add* to it. It seems that "the righteous" in our day will not only "live by faith," but also by reclaiming American culture for God.

For the righteous to live by faith and faith alone, faith must be a very great thing. Faith is the integrity of saying, I will live with full and constant trust in the promises of God, and God will do as God will do. The widespread lack of this confidence is demonstrated by the hurricane of books about the church that proclaim "the death of the church in a generation!" if we fail to adopt the author's proposals. As if the church were some obsolete charity in the midst of a funding crisis, and we its sentimental booster club. As if our success or failure at this or that church project will determine whether the church universal lives or dies. We demonstrate a peculiar faithlessness when we act as if the church's future is in our hands.

If we were ever to find ourselves in a situation where this were true, then we should all pack up and go home, because the promises of God would be void. But thank God that this can never be the case! The church isn't some college frat or sorority that we, its aging alumni, must now endow so that generations hence can enjoy the same happy memories we have. Congregations, buildings, sects, and national denominations — all these will come and go. But the survival of the *church* as the body of Christ, the house and family of God, does not depend on our efforts; indeed, it's not even properly our concern. *Only the faithfulness of its witness is.* If this holds, the church will endure.

I am not arguing for do-nothingism or for retreat from the world. It doesn't matter how right and good our doctrine is if we're just mumbling it to a handful of desiccated believers in a dusty church building at 8 a.m. every Sunday. It's not witness if someone doesn't hear it. But it's not witness if it's something we have to ram down people's throats, either. Neither retreat nor culture war: I am arguing for a show of faithful confidence from those of us who know that the battle isn't ours to fight because it was fought and won on our behalf at Calvary.

We're not supposed to take down the system of this world. We're supposed to testify to the one who has already done so.

If consumerism sounds a bit like a cultural prison (albeit of our own making) in which our only freedom is our ability to decorate our cell as we please, then we're getting the right idea about the pervasiveness of the system. However, this shouldn't lead us to despair. Indeed, the fact that we might feel inclined to despair is itself an indicator of misguided spiritual priorities. We'd feel despair because we want to fix the situation. And yet this desire to fix our problem is itself a powerful consumerist impulse. Consumerism wouldn't work, in fact, if we didn't (1) think we had problems, and (2) imagine that there is something we can buy (an "anti-consumerism Lenten devotional"!) that would fix them.

Consumerism isn't going anywhere, so the point of this conclusion is not that we have a problem we need to solve. *The point is that we have a problem we need to endure.* And when we start doing more enduring — a virtue of faith that demonstrates confidence in the final authority and judgment of God, not ourselves — we'll be a lot closer to the walk of faithfulness to which Romans calls us.

The crisis of meaning that plagues late modernity (i.e., the period of time we're living in) isn't going to go away. As I described in the first two chapters, we can't get our inherited stories back. There is nothing to do but come to terms with the fact that the world isn't ever going to make sense again, at least not in the particularly stable way that it did several hundred years ago.*

This is why fundamentalisms of every stripe are finally doomed. A fundamentalism, by definition, clutches desperately at an existence where perspectives other than its own are literally unimaginable. But

---

*This turbulence is the price we pay for having a world where the different races and genders are acknowledged as equally human — at least legally, even if we still have a long way to go on the ground. The turbulence might, in fact, be seen as the price we pay for the historic, earth-shaking claim that "all men are created equal," since the world that this statement began to create was one where the men (and women) acknowledged as equal could disagree with each other. It should go without saying that the price we pay for this is one well worth the paying.

such perspectives *are* imaginable, now, and cannot be unimagined. Like adolescent runaways longing to return to the security of the house we grew up in, we know that — having left once — it can never be home in the same way again. Our lives are now filled with a wealth of choice, and it is no good simply pretending that those choices do not exist. The cultural situation out of which consumerism has emerged as dominant will not go away.

Neither is there anything we can do to defeat consumerism. Commercial interests are well on their way to establishing global dominance as the preeminent way in which human beings understand themselves. Teenagers in Japan are starting to look more like teenagers in the United States than either group resembles their respective parents by virtue of what they consume: They wear the same clothes, listen to the same music, eat the same fast food, play the same video games, watch the same movies, and so on. In the same way that the modern nation-state has overtaken tribal and family identities (a rocky process, and one that is still in progress, evidenced by micro- and macro-conflicts worldwide), so too I suppose multinational commercial identities will eventually come to trump citizenship.

This is frightening, but thus is the nature of change. If our fear is all the more heightened because the pace of change today is orders of magnitude greater than it was in previous generations, we can only grit our teeth and wonder at the cultural aptitude — like fish born to water! — of children and grandchildren who seem to be flourishing in a world unrecognizable to us.

We began this chapter asking how to extricate ourselves from consumerism, to take on Brand Jesus. Those weren't very good questions, however, because any positive answers would deceive.

So, in the midst of our consumerist age, how can the church maintain the faithfulness of its witness to God?

Now *that's* the right question.

Chapter 22

How Dare We?

Consumerism has rendered the world we know into a marketplace of meaning. So, it is unavoidable that spiritual shoppers will perceive the church to be just another store with a product for sale. Furthermore, it has proven to be the case that Christians will conform themselves to the expectations of non-Christians, devising our own brand name religion to fit into the wider consumerist culture.

There is nothing we can do to prevent this perception from outside. But we *can* decide whether we will conform the church to their expectations and sell the Brand Jesus they're looking for. We can decide whether we will operate on the principles of the gospel, or on the idea that the customer is always right. We can decide whether our Sunday "service" will be a service of worship to God, or a product dished up to the consumer-congregation for the price of the offering plate. We can decide whether to turn storefronts into churches (those beacons of hope that sprinkle destitute neighborhoods), or let our churches become retail experiences. We can decide whether we will offer a theology and way of living that celebrates the kingdom coming, or one that conforms us to the consumerist rule of the principality present. We can tell people that they have already been bought, and at a price (1 Corinthians 6:19), or — like those who sold doves for sacrifices in the Jerusalem Temple courts — we can offer them what they expect: To get themselves right with God, they've got to pay, got to buy.

But if we choose the latter option in any of the above choices, we do not have to guess at Christ's response.

> In the temple courts he found men selling cattle, sheep and doves, and others sitting at tables exchanging money. So he made a whip out of cords, and drove all from the temple area, both sheep and cattle; he scattered the coins of the money changers and

overturned their tables. To those who sold doves he said, "Get these out of here! How dare you turn my Father's house into a market!" (John 2:14–16)

Christ's body is itself the new temple, is the church. What will we do with it?

The temptation of idolatry is ever present. It will *always* be easier to treat Jesus Christ from the point of view of the marketplace, as if we were outsiders looking in, window shoppers lusting after the promises of bargain-bin cruciformity. The temptation is all the more pressing for the fame, money, and power that come with it. But in the face of that temptation, our calling is to remember and testify that it is the Lord who has ransomed many, and through whom God has reconciled himself to all things (Mark 10:45; Colossians 1:20). The rejoinder to idolatry is not to address the idol, after all, but to bow before the true God.

It's impossible to provide generic directions as to how this should play out in practical terms. We can't construct a foolproof program or determine exactly what this will look like. The church's action in the face of consumerism will need to be lived, not theorized.* But we can talk about right and wrong directions for that living. We need to be nonconformed to the pattern of consumerism and we need to be transformed through that internal renewal of our minds. And if we do these things, it is possible to imagine what the character of our lives might look like.

Be Not Conformed

Given the pervasiveness of consumer values, we will have to maintain a posture of utter diligence to avoid the creep of marketplace ideals into the church body. Now, nonconformity cannot be the project

---

*I hope that this book does not simply add to the colossal mass of "Christian living" titles in print. Does our hunger for quantity stem at least in part from our inability to put into practice the concise instructions we've already got in the Bible? If Christians lived lives hospitable to the virtues listed in Romans 12–15, and did so with any degree of integrity and on a scale that was anything beyond the isolated saint, consumerism would be a nonissue for the church. Even if we just mastered the first couple of verses, we'd be well on our way: in gratitude for God's mercy, presenting our bodies to God as a living sacrifice, holy and pleasing to him; practicing nonconformity to the pattern of the world; being transformed through the renewal of our minds. The overachievers who managed to live out Romans 12–15 in the allotted time could turn to Matthew 5–7, which should keep them busy for the duration of their threescore and ten. The answer to the question "How are we to be faithful?" isn't hidden. It's just hard.

in and of itself. As mentioned in the previous chapter, rebellion too easily becomes its own idol. The "Church of Nonconformity to Consumerism" would be devoted to nonconformity, not to God. But nonconformity is nevertheless an integral practice for a church desiring to see the inner transformation working outward that is the "renewal of [our] minds."

One consumer ideal to be especially wary of is our rather blind acceptance of consumer demographics as the basis for the discipleship of the saints. Especially at many larger churches, the trend is to create ecclesial spaces for people with common interests, which wind up looking exactly like the results of market research (to wit, the "over-50-married-men's-weekend-motorcycle-riding" ministry). This move represents the adoption of an essentially commercial version of Donald McGavran's controversial "homogenous unit principle" (HUP), which is the utterly unsurprising revelation that people like to join groups, including the church, without crossing uncomfortable cultural lines, like race. Many churches rejected the HUP, claiming that if there is neither Jew nor Greek in Christ, the present church could not accept racial/caste segregation. But we have seemed all too willing to accept and affirm the identity divisions inherent to consumer society, thus allowing "ministry" to become virtually synonymous with "market," as in, "let's form the tweener girls' extreme sports [market]!"

Certainly, there is no crime in reaching out to people through the consumer spaces they already occupy. But those spaces are insufficient as a foundation for growth into a mature discipleship. One concrete example of this failure was the termination of Willow Creek's Axis program, a "Generation X 'church-within-a-church,'" in mid-2006. In its day, the Axis service at Willow Creek — a suburban Chicago megachurch, and a pioneer in the use of marketing methods — was groundbreaking. As *Christianity Today* reports, however, over time, "Axis didn't connect young adults with the rest of the congregation," and members "found it hard to transition" into the larger body when they grew too old for the ministry's age-based demographic. The analysis of Wheaton College professor James Wilhoit was that by "marketing to niche groups, such churches 'institutionalize fragmentation.'"[1]

The danger here is to imagine that such ministry marketing is simply bad church *technique*, when it is really bad *theology* that we're talking about. If the church leaves us to believe that we are what we buy commercially, then it is all too likely that Brand Jesus will find a welcome environment as a spiritual commodity to complete the believer's total consumer identity. Instead, the church should be a place in which worldly divisions are not finally affirmed. Given the power that consumer identities have over our self-imagination, the church should continually challenge them. Eventually, all our purchased identities will wither, leaving only our discipleship to Christ in their place.

The error of treating believers like consumers is compounded by the pervasive use of commercial principles and language in speaking of the church. A reader thumbing through any Christian magazine will be barraged with advertisements for professional conferences and seminars offering commercial "best practices" for running Church, Inc., promoting growth-oriented advertising, and reaching new markets. Willow Creek, which was built through the explicit use of contemporary marketing methods, pioneered the trend of making a megachurch into its own brand. As observers herald the death of denominations, the church-as-business model seems to be the new order of the day. Churches seeking to emulate Willow Creek's success can emulate their best practices by joining the Willow Creek Association (WCA) as quasi-franchisees run according to the proven principles provided by ecclesial HQ.

In illustrating this point, I don't want to come down too hard on the folks at Willow Creek. Their zeal is unquestionable, and I have dear friends who have grown in their love for God there. Furthermore, criticisms of that church are all too often based on an implicit glorification of amateurism, as if it is more pleasing to God to have a poorly run startup church than a smoothly operated enterprise. Given Willow Creek's size, I, for one, am glad that its leaders employ an unabashed professionalism in their supervision. It couldn't be led as if it were a small group Bible study. Furthermore, the approach is not without virtue. A number of churches now employ executive pastors, for example, which is an administrative title clearly appropriated from business. But their doing so simply reflects the very wise recognition that one pastor will not have every quality (or the time) necessary for the shepherding of a large church; the appropriation of business-talk in this case simply frees each to work according to his or her gifts.

The uniqueness of the church, a human institution both like and unlike all other human institutions, means that we will always require similes to speak of it. It is like a family, like a nation, like a service organization, like a lifeboat, and, in the twenty-first century, like a business. These similes are unavoidable and we should use them as need be. But we must also always remember that the church's origin and ordination is from God, and that we can never give in to the similes we employ. The temptation will be to let them have the last word, to turn the simile into a metaphor: Instead of thinking of the church as being *like* a business, we can wind up imagining that the church *is* a business.

Our similes thus tell us the particular temptations we will face. Is the church like a family? Then we will face the dangers of infighting and abuse. Is the church like a kingdom? Then we will face the dangers of monarchical hierarchy. And in our day, is the church like a business? Then we will face all the dangers that come with imagining God's people to be a commercial enterprise: planning primarily for growth; promoting brand loyalty; projecting future returns; adhering to a bottom line; prioritizing efficiency; and — most importantly — treating people as consumers.

This is an ever-present danger, especially given the glut of popular books that gleefully apply lessons and practices from our consumerist economy to the church. Some business practices may translate to church governance, and they should be adopted when they serve the church's calling. But our uncritical, wholesale appropriation of such techniques only encourages the already entrenched consumerist sense of selfhood in the congregation. This appropriation does nothing to challenge the message or media provided by the market culture — and so it leaves even the most well-intentioned disciples wide open to Brand Jesus' lures.

If we are not exceptionally diligent in preventing the slide from simile to metaphor, we will indeed lose the uniqueness of the church to the banality of the institution with which we describe it. Then people will talk about "church shopping" without grimacing at the comparison. Then we who are in positions of leadership will not blink at ordering the church organization after the latest models in corporate governance. Then we will not realize that the very structures of our church life provide safe haven for commercial idolatry. And then, at that point, we really will have failed in the task posed at the start of this chapter, having conformed ourselves to the expectations of the spiritual shoppers passing by — that we have a branded product for sale.

Be Transformed

The effort of nonconformity is only half of an ecclesial response to consumerism. It is important to recognize that consumerism is not an idolatry that has sprung up out of nothing and for no reason. Rather, it represents a desperate grasping for stability in a world where meaningfulness seems as if it must be earned or taken, and is never given. Consumer selves are the identities formed by people who have not inherited any other place in the world. So the development of consumerism is certainly understandable.

As a result, a church that strives not to conform to consumerist patterns cannot do so without offering an alternative story to take their place. Recall the man Jesus refers to in Luke 11, who was exorcized of a demon but who did not fill the resulting vacancy in the house of his spirit. The demon, returning to the man, finds his former dwelling unoccupied, swept and tidied, and so he goes back to dwell there with seven other spirits as well. There must be a positive counterpart — an inner-working outward transformation via the renewal of our minds — to any efforts at nonconformity. This positive counterpart will take the form of satisfying the existential hunger, characteristic of our modern situation, which has left us feeling adrift in history.

We can already see such a hunger within the church, especially by brothers and sisters in their twenties and thirties. The most dramatic expression of this seems to me to be the widely observed movement from free church evangelicalism toward the so-called "liturgical" traditions like Anglicanism, Roman Catholicism, and Eastern Orthodoxy.* On a personal level, I quite honestly cannot even count the number of friends who have made such a move. While my evidence is situational and anecdotal, the common thread in such friends' experiences seems to be a deep weariness with the individualism of evangelical piety. In traditional evangelical conceptions, God's engagement with the world tends to occur at the level of the individual believer. This is fine in terms of personal zeal, but the resulting doctrine of the church is rather emaciated. The church then tends merely to be the place where

---

*I believe that calling such traditions "liturgical" is something of a misnomer, since it seems to imply that "nonliturgical" traditions like free or charismatic churches do not have liturgies, or forms of worship. They do, of course, and their practitioners know these "low church" (another misnomer, in my view) liturgies in their very bones. In a nod to common parlance, however, I will employ "liturgical," as well as "high" and "low" church, according to their customary use.

a bunch of people get together on Sundays to commune individually with Jesus.

It isn't hard to see how this individualistic religious experience resembles consumer identity. First, it is something for which the individual is solely responsible, and second, it is devoid of any sense of historical context beyond the individual's own lifespan. Such an experience is highly attractive in a consumer society, given that it doesn't cut against any of the life patterns that consumers are used to operating within. But it is frequently unsustainable, as my friends' experience testifies. Such a faith often has little more durability than any other consumer identity. Ultimately, it does not satisfy the modern anxiety about meaninglessness any more than does buying a new jacket or car, because it does not provide a sense of place in history.

By contrast, the "liturgical" traditions anchor the individual believer in the historical body of the church. The Book of Common Prayer and the celebration of the Mass root a person in a life that preceded her and provide a sense of order to her faith. Moreover, because the doctrine of the church is so much more robust in these traditions, they are often much more enduring places to develop as a disciple. Our traditional evangelical churches, founded upon the sense of personal joy at conversion to salvation, frequently fail to account for people dealing with spiritual drought, grief, or depression. The liturgical traditions, by contrast, maintain that God is present to the *church,* regardless of how the individual believer is feeling. In other words, these liturgical traditions seem to represent to many Christians today a solution to the existential drift of the modern self.

The irony of this fact, of course, is that in making such a move, people are *choosing* tradition. We are choosing to limit our choices by placing ourselves in a historical lineage. Denied a direct inheritance from our ancestors, we are forced to seek it out for ourselves, like a woman who stumbles across and redeems her grandmother's long-lost set of china from a pawnshop. We thus claim as our own the filigree and patina of the historical church, but we do so *unavoidably* as free agents, as religious consumers. Now, we may of course insist — as I would about my own conversion as an adult — that we are chosen before we choose. Nevertheless, given that the world is a marketplace of meaning, from a mortal point of view, we necessarily come to our faith as shoppers. We cannot erase the contingency of our particular spiritual place, and the theoretical possibility of changing our beliefs cannot be unimagined out of existence.

In a way, however, the disinheritance of late modernity is its own blessing, however challenging. The theologian Søren Kierkegaard railed against the social Christianity of his nineteenth-century Copenhagen, a faith that seemed merely to be the inherited order of gentility. Just so, we cannot pretend to have any natural relationship to the church. We have no illusion that we support the root of the faith, rather than the root supporting us. It should be plain to every twenty-first-century Christian that we, though wild olive shoots, have been grafted in among the others and now share in a nourishing sap to which we have no integral claim (see Romans 11:17–20). Theologically speaking, we are well suited to recognize that our inclusion into the family of God is via adoption, rather than organic privilege.

In a consumerist age, therefore, the transformation through the renewal of our minds seems to me to be the very act of commitment to a church family and history that transcends our own time and place — however unavoidable it is that such a commitment be done as a consumer. One of the most insidious of all consumerist traits is the inability to have personal commitments to anything other than the space of one's own life. Though consumerism emerges out of and attempts to address a modern sense of meaninglessness, like any idolatry, it does not deliver what it promises. Instead, it simply sates the devotee through a cycle of consume/become/consume that distracts from — but does not solve — her existential crisis. In a world that suggests selves may be put on and taken off at will, pledging one's permanent identity in baptism is a radical step, indeed. So, in the wake of nonconformity to the solitary individualism of the consumer, the positive step of renewal is taken through a commitment to the church whose elders preceded us and whose children will survive us.

We face the open question, however, as to whether the church will be sufficiently faithful to God to merit such a commitment from its new members.

Living It

After the opening lines to Romans 12, Paul launches into a beautiful description of what it looks like to be a Christian: "For, by the grace given me I say to every one of you," do this and this and this.

Now, the attributes he lists aren't constitutive of discipleship, in and of themselves. As I mention above, the most critical thing is that we understand the problem. Paul has laid this out in the first eleven chapters of Romans; that is, no human identity has any claim to righteousness by virtue of its particular attributes. Despite the temptation to skip straight to the implementable steps, we can't simply begin with Romans 12:3 and distill from the text a systematic checklist that can be photocopied and bound and distributed for a marginal fee at pastors' conferences.

23 ATTRIBUTES OF A RADICAL DISCIPLE!

54 WAYS THAT YOUR CHURCH HAS FORGOTTEN THE LORD —
AND HOW TO REMEMBER HIM IN 5 SUNDAYS!

No. In chapters 12–15, Paul is simply giving some content to his instruction of nonconformity to the worldly pattern and transformation through internal renewal. In essence, he's saying that "a living sacrifice looks like this." Honor others above yourselves. Be patient in affliction. Share with those in need. Bless those who persecute you. Do not be proud. Live at peace. Do not take revenge.

Throughout this book, I've tried to identify a number of the dominant traits in the consumerist culture. Here, then, are some concluding thoughts as to what a church living in nonconformity to that culture would look like. These thoughts are insufficient and incomplete. We cannot describe a forest by listing the trees that comprise it. Neither do I intend the following as some sort of checklist-in-disguise toward anti-consumerism. But as we attempt to live as sacrifices to the Lord whose sacrifice is our all, it may be beneficial to have these markers to help guide our way through treacherous territory.

Interdependent

I have continually been struck by the testimony of American travelers returning from vacations, study, or mission trips to the poorer corners of the world. Without fail, we exclaim in wonder that those who have so little should be so unstintingly generous — indeed, far more so than we who have so much.

This is not to say that Americans are not generous. Largely, however, our generosity takes on the form of charity; that is, we give away surplus money to good causes. We give out of abundance. Others give out of poverty.

The difference between the two, it seems to me, stems from standards of independence that are taken for granted in middle- to upper-class America. Most Americans need a relatively large amount of money to live at a level they find acceptable. This is due neither to the higher costs of living in a leading industrial society nor to a simple addiction to comfort — though elements of both are surely present. Rather, this is a condition endemic to a consumerist culture. Simply put, to be a fully functioning member of this society, we need to possess a great deal: our own job, car, house, multifunctional wardrobe, bank account, investments, and so on. That is, as consumers we need enough money to function independently of anyone and everyone else. Once we have sufficient funds to obtain this security, then we can think about giving.

By contrast, life in "those other countries" (or, for that matter, in the impoverished rural and urban America that many more affluent citizens never see) is much more risky. In those situations, when you give you do so with the trust that someone else will supply your need when it comes (and it will). This continual and reciprocal giving-receiving-giving creates an interdependent community — the very interdependence of which is far closer to the kingdom of God than is the financial and personal autonomy of consumerist culture.

I'm not trying to romanticize the poor or to suggest that the ideal for humankind is material poverty. But it is very difficult to have in any true sense total dependence on God when we live lives that are so *in*dependent from one another. In this regard, consumerist culture perpetuates a false vision of humanity. The answer, perhaps, is in the church's encouraging a move toward an interdependent simplicity.

I don't know how most churches could facilitate this, built as they are around communities that have entrenched ways of living. For example, how could a suburban church counteract its members' autonomy, given that the physical layout of suburbia is actually designed to isolate people in the private domains of their single-family homes?[2] But I'm convinced it needs to happen somehow.

There is simply no top-down solution that any pastor can plug-and-play effectively in his or her church. Instead, the church needs disciples — leaders and members both — who see the ways in which our ideals of financial and personal independence are reflections of the autonomy sought by our first parents in the original sin. And for this to happen, the church will need to make every effort to cultivate disciples who are fluent cultural theologians; that is, men and women who can read the signs of the times alongside the Bible and understand the spiritual interplay between the two.

As members of a consumer culture, we want to live independently from one another. And we will bring this desire, without ever thinking about it, to our church life. The contemporary resurgence of small groups represents an attempt to counteract this, but too often, they simply represent one program among many that barely mitigates against a church structure that is otherwise overwhelmingly individualistic. We need to change who we *are* by changing the way we live. Paul's demand that we practice interdependence is rooted in the truth of the church's being: "In Christ we who are many form one body, and each member belongs to all the others" (Romans 12:5). As members of the church, we need to foster a communal life that will help people break the habits of desire created in consumerist existence.

Self-denying

Christians should not be rich.

In an age filled with chest-pounding rhetoric about "standing up for the gospel" on matters of sexuality and abortion, there is a stultifying silence on issues of material wealth. Oh, we're willing to talk about relieving poverty — just not about the other side of the coin. But God did not only say that the lowly would be exalted. He said that the great would be brought down.

So there it is. My colors are nailed to the mast. There is nothing in the Bible to justify a Christian merchant prince. And there are no rich men or women who can honestly say that their wealth means nothing to them compared to Christ. If this were the case, then why would we still be rich, given the screamingly obvious needs of the least of these — to whom an action is as unto the Lord — in the world?

I do not mean to vilify those with financial aptitude. I know many Christians whose skill with money is exceeded by their generosity. It's wonderful that they are so good at making money, and even more that their industry often develops employment for many. We can all applaud this. But if we are fortunate enough to be a recipient of this wonderful gift, then our obligation to give its fruits away is absolute — just as with any other gift of God. Is the preacher's sermon given for her own benefit, or the teacher's teaching for his gain? No! Such gifts are given for the body of the church. When money managers take from the funds that they oversee for their own personal gain, we rightly call it embezzlement. So why are we so indulgent toward the omnipresent misuse of God's resources, which fund the luxurious lifestyles of so many Christians gifted to be stewards over them?

We have been led out of the appropriate biblical attitude on this particular matter by an unbiblical absolutist sense of private property. If we earn something, our sense goes, we have rights to it. Such an attitude makes us lenient toward the idea that Christians who make money, however they give, are entitled to use a significant portion of their earnings for their own benefit and luxury. Yet, among the list of spiritual gifts in Romans 12, the rich are encompassed simply as "givers," and Paul exhorts them to excel in generosity. We who are good at making money ought to be unwilling to live at standards radically different from our brothers and sisters in Christ.

The problem is that Christians, like the rest of our culture, are addicted to wealth and comfort. And this will be our undoing as a peculiar people. Our prosperity radically isolates us from any meaningful solidarity with Christian brothers and sisters around the world who live in grinding poverty. (This matter is very much related to the above concern about interdependence.) Well-intentioned Christian relief efforts — almsgiving, actually — are not enough. The scriptural witness howls against our failure to live out our spiritual unity with the global church. From the Old Testament prophets to the Good Samaritan, from the parable of the sheep and goats to the story of the rich man and Lazarus, we are convicted over and over again. It is a wonder that the sleek "Bible-believing" churches that dot our landscape can even stand under the weight of the book that they weekly teach.

My point here is *not* to rehash the justifiable but predictable outcry against our failure to live out the fullest social implications of the gospel. That conclusion, while true, has proven easy enough to ignore. We're not perfect, just forgiven, right? And isn't the soul more important than the body? Yet it is the very soul of our church that is at stake. Choosing comfort in the face of the plight of Christian brethren is tantamount to spiritual self-mutilation. We fail to enter fully into the body of Christ because one hand is fixed on our wallets. And it seems that we would rather take our credit cards with us into hell than enter heaven with our pockets turned inside out.

Our addiction to comfort plays out through the allocation of re-sources dedicated to maintaining our church status quo — rolling lawns and endowments and fancy programs and anything at all ex-cept for missions that embody the gospel in word and deed. We have convinced ourselves that all these things are necessary for the func-tioning of the church and that they are a righteous use of our talents to maintain the institutions we have built. But perhaps we simply prefer our Christ air-conditioned.

As the preacher Will Campbell is wont to say, what we're often interested in knowing is how we can follow Christ in a radical way while *hanging on to everything we've already got.* Like the rich young man from the Gospels, we're willing to sacrifice anything to enter the kingdom of God, as long as it's not something we really like. But we have become so entangled in consumerism that we will need to be willing to put everything on the table in our attempt to weed it out. And this includes the contents of our pocketbooks.

Historical

I spent a significant portion of my twenties working directly for two remarkable octogenarians, so I have a particular empathy for the el-derly. I do not think that it is this personal affection, however, which drives the claim that the church must be far more historical and multigenerational than it currently is.

The attributes of being historical and multigenerational go together as a response to the crisis of the church's current ahistoricity. By this, I mean that the church, like the consumerist culture that pervades it, has a very limited vision of itself in time. Such limitation is natural to consumer culture, because the consumer's *being,* as a consumer, does not transcend death. One can only be a consumer while one is alive. Moreover, because the entirety of the consumer's existence is defined by the act of consumption, there is nothing in consumerist society that gives any reason to consider a world that does not contain the consumer himself. In other words, if we give any thought to future generations, we do so in spite of the prevailing consumerism. The concerns of the ideal consumer begin and end with his own life.

The church seems to have fallen prey to this trend, with all sorts of alarmist proclamations about the need to do this or that *immediately.* The most hyperbolic outcries proclaim the death of the American church in a generation unless drastic measures are taken. And the conviction that we must be living in the end time — popular in some Christian circles — is simply another aspect of an overall disposition toward viewing one's own existence as historically exceptional.

To refuse consumerism's dictates in this respect, the church needs to remember both its eternal ordination and its historical situation. For the former, this is simply the recognition that Jesus Christ himself has ordained the church's existence, and God has secured its future. If the church were ever to pass away, then onlookers might rightly conclude that the story it had told was all wrong. Fortunately, the church's continued existence does not depend on us. This doesn't mean we shouldn't be good stewards. But it does mean that we should back off from acting as if the patriarch is dead and we are the inheritors of the family business. No, the head of the church is very much alive.

For the latter — our historical situation — the church should acknowledge the fact that every age seems uniquely tumultuous to those who live in it. The history of interpretation of the book of Revelation is especially instructive in this regard, as it is full of those who believed its drama could only correspond to the chaos of their own times and places.[3] Yes, we live in a period of unique challenges. Everyone who has ever lived, however, can claim the same thing. Whether we occupy an epochal turning point at the twilight of modernity, or a set of years that will appear historically unremarkable, we need to live as just another generation of the body of Christ.

Doing this runs counter to all our tendencies toward American exceptionalism. But we have gotten ourselves into trouble by imagining that we are somehow uniquely special. Our speculation has allowed us to imagine that we are more than we are, and to forget the diversity of all those who have known and claimed Christ through the millennia. A historical sensibility would do a great deal to restore a humility that the American church sorely lacks.

If we are to live out this historical sensibility, it must at least take the form of churches that are consciously multigenerational. Think about how we describe churches with aging congregations: dead, dying, unexciting. Why is it that the church, like the prevailing culture, seems primarily interested in those individuals in their prime earning (and spending) years? We're as fixated on youth ministry as advertisers are with the youth market. It makes us feel vibrant, alive.

There's nothing wrong with the discipleship of the young, of course. But our undue focus on youth and young families means that the church does little to challenge the cultural sensibility that one's value as a human is linked to one's capacity to produce and consume. Our cultural interest in diversity stops short of age. But if we cannot even recognize the value of the elderly among us, how can we possibly claim communion with the cloud of witnesses that are the holy of God in all ages? And, denied that communion, how can we imagine that our discipleship is anything but crippled?

Our church behavior serves to divorce us from the historic people of God. We appear so blatantly interested in only what God will do for this generation, rather than what God has done and will do for all generations. We need a complete turnabout — one that will make us increasingly conscious that the redemptive work of Jesus Christ is not constrained to the puny boundaries of our own lives, but instead stretches to include all things. And this includes the world that preceded us, and the one that we will leave behind.

Perhaps this could take the form of a longer catechetical process of instruction for new converts or church members. In an age in which institutions attempt to strip away any obstacles to increase customer movement and access, it is counterintuitive to make the process of joining the church more difficult. But we ought to be more counterintuitive, given that our intuition is shaped by consumer habits. If every new church member had a better understanding of his or her place in the historical family of God, I do not doubt that we would see this rootedness manifested in the strength of the church's faithfulness.

Courageous

The age we live in has robbed us of courage. Consider two of the responses to modernity examined in these pages. Both the contemporary Christian culture war and consumerism are reactions to a world cut loose from any stable mooring. At the heart of both the culture warrior and the consumerist is an individual grasping at some handhold in a world that seems terrifyingly devoid of any grip.

The fundamentalism of today's Christian culture warriors seeks to roll back the horizons of human imagination. This nostalgic worldview wants to pretend that the stability of yesteryear — itself an illusion — can be recovered. It wants to re-create a world that didn't face scary choices, like all the identity options on offer today. But such a world is gone forever, no matter how loudly one reasserts one's doctrine.

Consumerism, by contrast, offers an ever-increasing spectrum of choices, promising a corresponding variety of identities. Where fundamentalism attempts to collapse all personal identities into one (under the known fundamental truth), the logical end of a consumerist society is one in which the only common ground that any one individual has with another is his or her shared act of consumption.

But neither of these responses gives any relief from fear. The former pretends that it shouldn't exist, and the latter never slows down enough to start trembling. If there is to be any integrity to the church's witness that the gospel is good news for this age, too, it will have to address this fear and teach Christians how to be brave.

The necessary bravery is a peculiar phenomenon, cutting a middle path between fundamentalism on the one side and secular consumerism on the other. The first step of this bravery is the honest recognition of our contemporary condition. We have to admit that the situation of our lives is one in which a potentially infinite number of truths compete for people's loyalty. This cannot be undone. But the second step is to wager the entirety of one's life on the all-encompassing claim that Jesus Christ is Lord.

I say *wager* because this understanding of discipleship, unlike the fundamentalist's, acknowledges the possibility of losing. It is, of course, possible that I am wrong in my convictions and that the commitment of my life to them — my wager — will fail. It is possible that the claims of Christianity are a sham, and that I am simply one participant in a well-intentioned delusion shared by billions. For my part, I am certain that this is not the case. But I must admit that from the perspective of many different others, I have certainly bet on the wrong horse. The bravery required to face this fact is the special attribute of the gambler.

Acknowledging the wager of faith, however, does not allow the disciple-gambler to slip into relativism — unlike the consumerist. To admit that I may be wrong in the end is not thereby to say that any and all understandings of ultimate truth are equally accurate portrayals of reality. I believe that Jesus Christ is Lord, which is to say I believe certain truths about God and the world that I also believe to be true for those who disagree with me. I believe that these truths have always been true and will always be so. I believe that these truths would be true whether or not I believe them — or, indeed, whether or not I had ever existed. So, though I recognize that our world offers a plurality of life choices, the fact of my wager precludes me from trying any of them on for size. The wager of Christian discipleship is one that requires one's entire life as a stake.

I cannot envision any way forward for American Christian discipleship other than understanding it as the courage of this wager. The consumerist way is no option at all, because consumerism demands that Christ be one among many options rather than Lord over all. And if we are content to take him as Brand Jesus, we do not have Jesus at all, and our discipleship is worthless.

On the contrary, though fundamentalism is at least conceivably an option, it is unsustainable and thus demonstrably untrue, given that God's promises endure. When we pretend, as fundamentalism does, that it is literally unimaginable that we might be wrong, the very existence of people who disagree with us proves that yes, in fact, the possibility of our being wrong can readily be imagined. But, by pretending that there is no choice, we have rejected the very possibility of making any *authentic* commitment to live as disciples of our Teacher and Lord, Jesus Christ. Leaving aside the theological problems with this, on a pragmatic level, we simply appear to non-Christians as ostriches with our heads in the sand, leaving our evangelistic witness crippled.

Whether we like it or not, truth must be translated in our day. We must find it to be plausible and understandable. I can have all the theological certainty in the world and it won't mean a thing to non-Christians. They will rightfully ask, "Why should I believe — why should I *live* as if — this is true?" In the face of such objection, there is no appeal to a shared, objective truth. Our society no longer believes that we share such a thing. This is not because such objective truth does not exist. It does. But objectivity cannot be *understood* as such in a society made up of individuals who understand their truth subjectively. The very language of "objective truth" is foreign gibberish to our ears, and our hearers are deaf to the cool calculus of modern apologetics. Objective truth is no longer imagined as an impartial mediator standing between you and me. Now there is only you and I and what each of our claimed truths looks like in our lives.

The only adequate translator of truth, therefore, is the bravery of discipleship. Words are insufficient. If my life does not resemble what I claim as the truth, no amount of prophecy-fulfillment Bible study is going to convince you that Christ is Lord. We can appeal to nothing but the church's living like Christ. A great many slanderers of Christ and his church are indeed small-minded, and perhaps deliberately ignorant. But there would be a great deal fewer such people if the church actually lived up to its calling. The future of our evangelism hinges on the integrity of our discipleship. The only plausible claim we have to Christ's Lordship is the life of his followers, which is the continuing presentation to a fallen world of the imminent kingdom of God. *In the wholly consumerist age that is dawning, Christian certainty will not exist in any meaningful way unless it takes the form of courage to lead the life that our Savior commands us to live.*

This is not simply the courage to name oneself a Christian and adopt one or the other expected religio-political stances; no, such action does not require courage at all, being both predictable and easy to do in these United States. Furthermore, it too quickly slides toward either fundamentalism or consumerist belief.

Instead, courage will look like authentic discipleship has looked in every age. In concrete form, such discipleship is the lived-out witness of peace to violence, love to hate, hope to despair, truth to power, healing to sickness, and resurrection to death. The disciple is brave enough to live this way because she wagers everything on her hope that Christ is the Lord and the kingdom of God has drawn near. And the wager is brave because it is unsupportable in a world that stones prophets and crucified God. Such is the courage needed to stand without falling in an already fallen world.

Chapter 23

An Invitation

I suffer from a failure of imagination.

I can't imagine what it would be like to live an unbranded life. A life relatively unconcerned with what I consumed. A life in which the things that I bought were simply the physical goods of life, rather than the building blocks of my identity.

I can't imagine what seems like it ought to be a simple step: What if Christians stopped shopping for fun? If we refused to buy name-brand goods (this is actually impossible), knowing the unavoidable hold they exert over us?

Could Christians self-impose private limits to our purchases? What if we evaluated our possessions according to whether they facilitated or hindered our fullest engagement with the gospel? If we had less to lose, would we give more? Would we have much left? How lean might our lives get?[1]

But, try as I might, I can't conceive of any way out of this marketplace.

I can't really imagine it because *I can't imagine something that isn't for sale.*

I suspect you might be in a similar bind.

We cannot continue to hear the story of our renewed humanity in Christ if our ears are full of advertising jingles. We cannot see ourselves as human beings, created in the *imago Dei*, if our bodies and minds and souls are simply consumer space, walking advertising crammed with as much brand placement as a NASCAR track. We need ears to hear and eyes to see.

And this is where we need the church to broaden our imaginations.

We need the church to teach us spiritual disciplines and practices that aid in the radical nonconformity to this world and that orient our hearts to transformation through renewal. In a world marked more and more by the exercise of personal consumer preferences, we need to be cultivated as congregations who genuinely don't care about buying our way into a world that we've made after our own image. Whose sense of discipleship ethics extends beyond the narrow sphere of our own personal agency. Whose concern for the kingdom leads us to know — or at least consider — where our food and clothing has come from, and how they have traveled along the way. Who are growing in our indifference to material comfort. Who esteem others, even and especially our enemies, more than ourselves. Whose simplicity in consumption has led us to contentment and the ever-increasing knowledge of the radical provision of God.

None of the above is new, of course. But our situation does not require new ideas. It requires the will to be that which is of old.

Speaking realistically, I have little hope that the alarm of this book will be taken seriously by many churches, Christian organizations, or even individuals. To recognize the full scope of our problem is to acknowledge the need for changes that are simply too hard to make. As Naomi Klein laments, "We are living, as Susan Sontag said, in the 'Age of Shopping' and any movement that is primarily rooted in making people feel guilty about going to the mall is a backlash waiting to happen."[2]

Furthermore, unless we as a church truly come to believe — and proclaim with our actions — that the witness of Christianity is not based around the cultural dominance of our religio-social ethics, our faith will never live up to its mission. Only a church (I use the term in its broadest sense, encompassing denominations and associations) that renounces cultural domination as its goal will be able to undertake the effort necessary to engage in such a radical witness.

The evangelist John records Jesus' saying that his disciples would be recognizable by their mutual love. Matthew writes the even more remarkable imperative that we love our enemies. And the church father, Tertullian, wrote in disarmingly contemporary language that "there is no buying and selling of any sort in the things of God. . . . It is mainly the deeds of a love so noble that lead many to put a brand upon us.

See, they say, how [the Christians] love one another" (*Apology* 39). Is this brand visible in our actions, without the external cues of Brand Jesus? *If we cannot be recognized as Christians by what comes out of our hearts rather than by what we wear on our bodies, ought we to be recognized as Christians at all?*

There *are* glimmers of hope. In the neighboring cities of Philadelphia and Camden, two very different communities are testifying to the one hope of all Christians. Philly has birthed The Simple Way, one example of the urban neo-monasticism that has developed over the last decade. This community, arising (not without friction) out of its founders' solidly evangelical upbringing, may represent a new direction in which some of the church is heading. In their own quiet, unpretentious, perhaps even unselfconscious — and yes, simple — way, their life together demonstrates a nonconformity to the pattern of our age. And just across the Delaware River, a youth ministry called Urban Promise stands as a testimony to God's faithfulness even to the urban blight of Camden, New Jersey. It is a ministry established in the desert of consumerism — because nobody has money to buy, in Camden — and for nearly two decades, it has cultivated a sense of God-given humanity among the forgotten urban poor.

Some might be surprised to find the claim here that the same Spirit of God is at work in the arid wealth of California's Orange County. After all, Saddleback Church, with tens of thousands attending every Sunday and an annual budget of $30 million, seems far removed from The Simple Way and Urban Promise.[3] Yet this megachurch refuses to conform to the too-easy condescension of its critics. After twenty-five years of astronomical numerical growth — a quarter century that roughly corresponds to the ascension of evangelical political and economic interests in America — Saddleback decided that it would be known for its fruits, rather than the Brand Jesus identity adopted by so many American churches. And so it has quite consciously dedicated its staggering amount of influence and financial wealth to the service of the destitute and dispossessed. The church does so not because the world can be perfected, but because God in Christ has revealed a better way than is on offer at the malls that surround the church. And Saddleback wants to share it with the world.

None of these examples offers a utopian model that every church should emulate. Each has its problems, and certainly none is removed from the specter of Mammon. But their failures are the inevitable stumblings of mortal institutions, not fatal flaws. And so, while they are remarkably different from one another, each testifies to the one Spirit who is their common guide, the one Christ who is their common Lord, and the one Father whom they worship.

The one God is not done with this world yet. These are only three examples of faithfulness with integrity. There are undoubtedly many more. We see how diverse that faithfulness can appear. Whether it commands the power of numbers or not, it has the power of God that is unique to the faithful remnant in this and every age.

What if the church's message were true to the gospel that God has given us? What if there was never a pitch to take on Brand Jesus by inviting Christ into your life? What if the church wasn't making our Lord into some disposable commodity to improve your lifestyle: "Here's what we've got and here's why it's better than the stuff at all those other stores." What if, instead, the church was issuing the invitations on God's behalf, inviting people to come and abide in the body of Christ?

You're out for a Saturday shop — whether the Roman bazaar or the Mall of America makes little difference — and you pop into what you take to be a new retail outlet. Imagine that the people who seem to be employed there appear genuinely interested in your welfare, but also appear utterly uninterested in getting you to buy anything. You're curious and perhaps a bit offended, since, as a prospective customer, you're used to a bit more fawning treatment. So, you point to one item or another and ask, "How much does that cost? Because I think I saw an item that would work just as well in a kiosk down the way, and it was very affordable." Secretly, you are looking forward to a bargaining session. Now, imagine your astonishment at the reply: "It's free, actually. And I'm afraid you must be mistaken. We actually don't have any competitors."

"Well, how about that?" you say, pointing at another item.

"Free, as well."

"And that? And that? And that?"

"Yes, yes, and yes. You are welcome to it all."

You're mulling this over. What kind of lousy store is this? Or: What kind of *terrific* store is this? Or: Am I on one of those hidden camera shows? Or: Is this even a store at all?

"You look hungry and thirsty and tired," says one of the people hanging about. You had thought she was an employee, but now you're not so sure. "And it's hot out there," she continues. "Wouldn't you like to rest?"

Well, yes, you think, that actually sounds rather nice. Shopping is, after all, pretty tiring. "But — don't I need to buy a latte or something to sit inside?"

"No, no!" comes the laughing response. "Just rest, and we'll bring you some food and a drink."

These people are fools, you think.

But you sit anyway, and you eat and drink when it comes. And it is good. Really good. And the prospect of going out into the hot marketplace is getting less and less attractive.

"Do I have to listen to some pitch for a timeshare?" you burst out.

"No," with another laugh. "Rest."

This food is great, you think. Where am I?

"Welcome to the church, stranger. This isn't a store. We're the servants of the one who owns the land on which this whole marketplace is built, and this is his son's house. You are welcome here.

"We know you can leave any time you want. And you could go ahead and keep shopping — that's your decision. But you're not really up to it, you know. The stuff you'll buy, it won't do what you want it to. Not for long enough.

"It's because you're not really a shopper at heart. You think you are. But you're not. You're just like everyone else out there, who found money in their pocket and thought it was theirs to spend.

"What we're about here isn't what all those stores are about. You can rest, because there's nothing to buy — the whole place was bought up a long time ago.

"I know why you thought we were a store. It's because we've got a door in the marketplace. But we're nothing like that. This is a home. A waystation. A place of rest for pilgrims on the road.

"And, friend — can I call you friend? We have room for you."

Afterword

Ecclesiastes, which could hardly be more different from Romans, tells us both that there is "nothing new under the sun," and that "for everything there is a season." The moral of the story? There's nothing new, but people will always think that there is.

Consumerism and Christianity seem to be on the country's mind — sometimes, and increasingly so, in the same thought. Here are snapshots of some events since the final manuscript for this book came together in the late autumn of 2006:

- The Democrats swept the midterm elections and reclaimed both houses of Congress. Much was made of the closing God gap, or the broadening of moral values, or the disillusioned Religious Right, or any other pithy phrase one could use to describe the situation. As usual, nothing was being said about the relationship between consumerism and politics. From where I stand, it appears that the Religious Right has been revealed as an inadequate brand. It collapsed under the weight of its constituents' expectations. There is hope for this republic, yet — substance still matters. Regardless of where we go, I suspect that we will not see a commensurate alignment between religious and political interests again in my lifetime. The age of religio-political fundamentalism is passing for good. In its place only consumerism, that god of a million faces, will remain.

- Attention to consumer trends in religion seems to be on the rise. The December 18 issue of the *New Yorker* features an article about the big business of Bible marketing. In other (digital) pages, the editors at *Leadership,* a Christian quarterly, continue to blog about the relative merits and drawbacks of marketing, branding, and other business tactics increasingly employed by the church. On the publishing front, a book from a popular author, arguing that the church should learn lessons from a mega-brand, is currently available for preorder from online retailers.

- The *Washington Post* reports that DaimlerChrysler, eager to reach African American customers after a scandal about allegedly racist financing policies, is offering test drives of its new vehicles at black megachurches. Each test driver gets a ticket to a Patti LaBelle gospel concert (the tour is also sponsored by Chrysler) and Chrysler makes a five-dollar donation to a cancer charity. When asked about this church-corporation partnership, the head of Chrysler's brand marketing remarked that churches helped Chrysler reach "opinion leaders who are involved, upscale, new-car-buying types of people."[1]

- Joel Osteen, pastor of Lakewood Church, best-selling author of *Your Best Life Now*, and a proponent of what might be termed "prosperity gospel lite," is named by Barbara Walters as one of 2006's "10 Most Fascinating People." He is the only pastor ever so designated since Walters started the show in 1992. Walters, citing the growth of "evangelicalism," said that in the producers' search for an evangelical representative, they asked, " 'Who is the most charismatic, interesting pastor?' Well, Joel Osteen."[2]

- In case there is any doubt about the glorification of the individual so endemic to consumerism, at the end of 2006, *Time* magazine named "You" as the person of the year. This, exactly three decades after the same magazine named 1976 the "Year of the Evangelical."

Let those with ears to hear, listen.

There is a time for all of this. And there is nothing new under this old sun. For our part, let us just keep faith. The rest, which is everything, belongs to God.

Notes

Introduction

1. I list four authors here who may be of interest. The first is Douglas Coupland, whose 1991 novel *Generation X* offers a superb narrative accounting of a world falling under the dominance of consumerism. Completely divorced from any sense of inherited, ancestral stories, the novel's three protagonists band together to make stories of their own lives. Their tool in doing so is cultural debris that they employ to create their own sense of meaning. I have no idea if Coupland would agree with my assessment of consumerism's historical causes, and his novel predates Marlboro Friday in 1993, which I identify as the point of no return for brand dominance in American culture (see Part I). But for any reader intrigued by Part 1 of this book, who wants a description of the cultural rootlessness that has led to the triumph of consumerism, *Generation X* — as well as Coupland's other novels, especially *Life after God* — will be invaluable.

Second, in Andy Crouch's July 2001 column for *Christianity Today*, he writes a narrative mockup of "the First Great Mammon Awakening." Stumbling across it only days after finishing my manuscript, I was shocked to find what seemed to be a digest version of many sections in this book. It's humbling and helpful to remember that I'm far from the first writer to tackle issues of consumerism and faith. A search of Andy Crouch's work will explore many of the church/culture issues tackled in these pages, and would be well worth the concerned reader's time.

Third, any reader will profit from undertaking Alan Wolfe's excellent survey, *The Transformation of American Religion.* I wish I could have included it in this book, but — like many other worthy works — there simply wasn't the space or specific occasion. Nevertheless, Wolfe's book is so good that I at least wanted to promote it here to anyone desiring further resources.

Fourth, keep an eye out for a forthcoming book version of "Disciples and Citizens," the Right Reverend Graham Cray's 2005 London Lectures in Contemporary Christianity. In listening to the (borrowed) audio tapes, I found his treatment of contemporary society — especially consumerism — to be among the best I have encountered. His discussion is far too rich to summarize here, but I would urge it as a source for those who would like a cultural critique that maintains pastoral concern and scholarly rigor to an equally exceptional standard. I wish that the four lectures had been converted and published in time for me to use them.

Chapter 1: Point-of Purchase Devotion

1. Cited in statistics from Packaged Facts, "The Fashion of the Christ," by William Symonds, David Kiley, Tom Lowry, and Kirsten Dorsch, *BusinessWeek online*, May 23, 2005.

Chapter 2: Buy to Be, Be to Buy

1. James Twitchell, *Lead Us into Temptation* (New York: Columbia University Press, 1999), 196.
2. Ibid., 282.
3. Naomi Klein, *No Logo* (Toronto: Vintage Canada, 2000), 12.
4. Ibid., 16.
5. Ibid., 21.
6. Twitchell, *Lead Us into Temptation*, 271.
7. Ibid., 75.

Chapter 8: Mammon Worship Hits the Mall

1. I am indebted to Michael Peppard, Ph.D. candidate in New Testament at Yale University, for this comparison between consumer spending cycles and the sacrificial calendar of ancient Rome.

Chapter 9: Hypersexuality

1. This is convincingly argued by Dale Martin, "Heterosexism and the Interpretation of Romans 1:18–32," *Biblical Interpretation* 3 (October 1995): 332–55.
2. Giles Morris. "Man or Mouse? Or: How I Learned to Stop Wasting My Life and Give Up Internet Porn," *Esquire* (UK), October 2005, 112.

Chapter 10: Every Kind of Wickedness

1. Karl Barth, *Epistle to the Romans*, trans. E. Hoskyns (Oxford: Oxford University Press, 1968), 53.
2. Matt Richtel and Michel Marriott, "Ring Tones, Cameras, Now This: Sex Is Latest Cellphone Feature," *New York Times*, September 17, 2005.
3. Kurt Eichenwald, "Through His Webcam, a Boy Joins a Sordid Online World," *New York Times*, December 19, 2005.
4. Jose Antonio Vargas, "Virtual Reality Prepares Soldiers for Real War," *Washington Post*, February 14, 2006.
5. Ibid.

6. Ibid.

7. Ibid.

8. Ruben Castaneda and Allison Klein, "'Flash-Point' Killings: Murder Most Casual," *Washington Post,* March 17, 2006.

9. Ibid.

10. Ibid.

Chapter 11: Our Better Judgment

1. James Twitchell, *Lead Us into Temptation* (New York: Columbia University Press, 1999), 2.

2. Ibid., 273.

3. Ibid., 286.

4. Ibid., 20.

Chapter 12: Sins of the Body

1. John R. W. Stott, *Romans: God's Good News for the World* (Downers Grove, IL: InterVarsity Press, 1995), 86.

2. Naomi Klein, *No Logo* (Toronto: Vintage Canada, 2000), 297.

3. Ibid., 302.

4. Ibid., 301.

5. Ibid., xviii, 420.

Chapter 13: You That Boast

1. Ronald Sider, *Scandal of the Evangelical Conscience* (Grand Rapids, MI: Baker Books, 2005), 28.

2. Ibid., 12.

3. "Born Again Christians," www.barna.org (accessed September 21, 2006). Barna distinguishes between "born-again" and "evangelical" Christians based on the latter group's assent to a more restrictive set of doctrinal statements. While this division is functionally useful here, it is also fair to say that the two terms are virtually synonymous in popular usage, and the average Christian — let alone American — could not provide anything like the nuanced artificial definition that Barna uses. We will use the two in roughly interchangeable ways unless specifically indicated.

4. Joseph Fitzmyer, *Romans,* Anchor Bible Commentaries (New York: Doubleday, 1993), 320.

5. Douglas Atkin, *The Culting of Brands* (New York: Portfolio, 2004), 16.

6. Ibid., 112.

Chapter 14: Consumer Theology in the American Church

1. This helpful "Team A vs. Team B" image comes from a sermon by Bruxy Cavey, teaching pastor at The Meeting House in Ontario, Canada.

Chapter 15: The Righteous Shall Live By...

1. Peter Rollins, *How (Not) to Speak of God* (London: SPCK, 2006), 2–3.
2. Charles Spurgeon, "Sermon 742: A Sermon to Open Neglecters and Nominal Followers of Religion," in *Spurgeon's Sermons,* vol. 13, Christian Classics Ethereal Library, www.ccel.org (accessed September 27, 2006).

Chapter 16: Evangelical Brand Ascendancy

1. "Save the E-Word," *Christianity Today,* October 2006, 39.
2. For the remarkable story behind the Bob Jones case, see Randall Balmer's firsthand account in chapter 1 of *Thy Kingdom Come* (Grand Rapids, MI: Basic Books, 2006).
3. Rick Bragg, "Brooksville Journal: Vision of Community Guided by Hand of God," *New York Times,* December 30, 1998.

Chapter 17: We Preach Ourselves

1. "CBA Timeline: 1950–2000," *www.cbaonline.org/General/CBA_History.jsp* (accessed October 4, 2006).
2. Helen Hendershot, *Shaking the World for Jesus* (Chicago: University of Chicago Press, 2004), 17.
3. Ibid., 17–18.
4. *www.kerusso.com* (accessed October 4, 2006).
5. Naomi Klein, *No Logo* (Toronto: Vintage Canada, 2000), 278.
6. Ibid., 285–86.
7. Hendershot, *Shaking the World for Jesus*, 19.
8. "Have You Heard the Word?" *Actionsportsjournal.com* interview, February 1, 2006, actionsportsjournal.com/home/?p=836 (accessed September 30, 2006).
9. "Aurelio Barreto's Testimony: Founder and CEO of C28 Stores," *www.c28 .com/founder.asp* (accessed October 4, 2006).
10. "C28 Mission, Values, and Often Asked Questions," *www.c28.com/message .asp* (accessed October 4, 2006).
11. "Hot Trends and Topics at CBA Advance," *Religion Bookline,* February 1, 2006, *www.publishersweekly.com/article/CA6303702.html.*

Chapter 18: Called to Be a Demographic

1. John Styll, president of the Gospel Music Association, quoted in Packaged Facts, "The Fashion of the Christ," by William Symonds, David Kiley, Tom Lowry, and Kirsten Dorsch, *BusinessWeek online*, May 23, 2005.

2. *www.boxofficemojo.com/alltime* (accessed October 3, 2006).

3. Bill Symonds, "The Media Hears the Sermon," *BusinessWeek online*, December 14, 2005.

4. Ibid.

5. Ibid.

6. Sharon Waxman, "The Passion of the Marketers," *New York Times*, July 18, 2005.

7. Stuart Elliot, "G.M. Gets Criticism for Backing Tour of Christian Music Performers," *New York Times*, October 24, 2002.

8. Waxman, "The Passion of the Marketers."

9. Elliot, "G.M. Gets Criticism for Backing Tour of Christian Music Performers."

10. Symonds, "The Media Hears the Sermon."

11. Waxman, "The Passion of the Marketers."

12. Mary Schmitt Boyer, "Marketing the Games with the Gospel," *Cleveland Plain Dealer Reporter*, September 17, 2006.

13. Ibid.

14. Ibid.

15. Bill Muller, "Success of Christian Films Lends Clout to Religious Media," *Arizona Republic*, December 9, 2005.

16. Dick Staub, "The Dick Staub Interview: Chuck Palahniuk," online at *www.christianitytoday.com/ct/2002/octoberweb-only/10-7-21.0.html*.

Chapter 19: Consuming Politics

1. Laurie Goodstein, William Yardley, and Marjorie Connelly, "President Benefits from Efforts to Build a Coalition of Religious Voters," *New York Times*, November 5, 2004.

2. Mark Lilla, "Getting Religion," *New York Times*, September 18, 2005.

Chapter 20: Therefore I Urge You

1. James D. G. Dunn, *Romans 9–16*, vol. 38 of *Word Biblical Commentary* (Nashville: Thomas Nelson, 1988), 709.

2. Ibid., italics mine.

3. Ibid., 714.

4. James Twitchell, *Lead Us into Temptation* (New York: Columbia University Press, 1999), 8, 6.

Chapter 21: Fasting and Prayer in the Age of Mammon

1. In Naomi Klein, *No Logo* (Toronto: Vintage Canada, 2000), 295.
2. James Twitchell, *Lead Us into Temptation* (New York: Columbia University Press, 1999), 175n6.
3. John Leland, "Rebels with a Cross," *New York Times*, March 2, 2006.
4. John Leland, "Ideas & Trends: Alt-Worship; Christian Cool and the New Generation Gap," *New York Times*, May 16, 2004.

Chapter 22: How Dare We?

1. Madison Trammel, "Axis Denied," *Christianity Today*, October 2006, 25.
2. For this point, I am indebted to Vincent Miller's *Consuming Religion* (New York: Continuum, 2003), which offers a thorough analysis of how the ideal of the single-family home is at the heart of consumer culture. It is well worth a read.
3. Bernard McGinn, "Revelation," in *The Literary Guide to the Bible*, ed. R. Alter and F. Kermode (Cambridge, MA: Harvard University Press [Belknap], 1987), 523.

Chapter 23: An Invitation

1. I am indebted to Bruxy Cavey for this insight.
2. Naomi Klein, *No Logo* (Toronto: Vintage Canada, 2000), 429.
3. Gwendolyn Driscoll, "God's Business," *Orange County Register*, November 12, 2006.

Afterword

1. G. Jeffrey MacDonald, "Car and Churchgoer," *Washington Post*, December 16, 2006.
2. Mike McDaniel, "Television: Walters Comes to Osteen's House," *Houston Chronicle*, December 11, 2006.